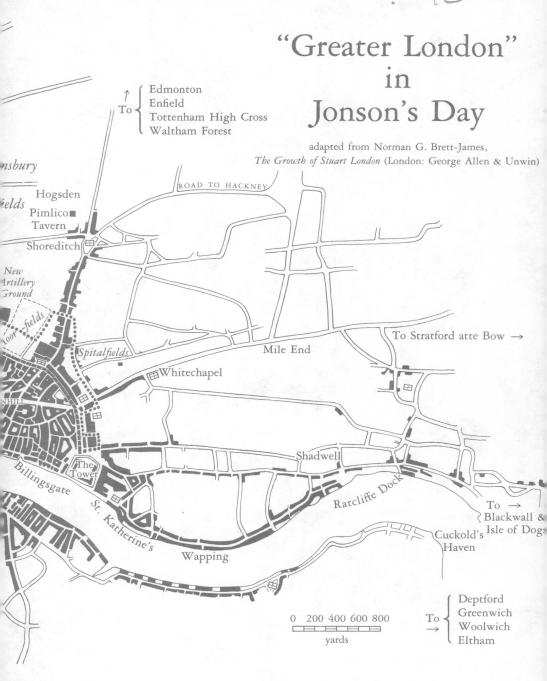

"Greater London" in Jonson's Day

adapted from Norman G. Brett-James,
The Growth of Stuart London (London: George Allen & Unwin)

To → Edmonton
Enfield
Tottenham High Cross
Waltham Forest

ROAD TO HACKNEY

nsbury

Hogsden
Pimlico ■
Tavern
Shoreditch

ields

*New
Artillery
Ground*

oor-fields

Spitalfields

HILL

Mile End

To Stratford atte Bow →

Whitechapel

Shadwell

The
Tower

Billingsgate

St. Katherine's

Ratcliffe Dock

Wapping

Cuckold's
Haven

To →
Blackwall &
Isle of Dogs

0 200 400 600 800

yards

To → Deptford
Greenwich
Woolwich
Eltham

BEN JONSON'S LONDON

Ben Jonson's London

A Jacobean Placename Dictionary

FRAN C. CHALFANT

THE UNIVERSITY OF GEORGIA PRESS
ATHENS

Library of Congress Catalog Card Number: 75–32125
International Standard Book Number: 0–8203–0392–5

The University of Georgia Press, Athens 30602

Set in 11 on 12 point Mergenthaler Garamond type
Printed in the United States of America

Contents

Preface

The purpose of this book is to add to the appreciation of Jonson's artistry by collecting and commenting upon all of the London placenames mentioned in his plays, masques, and poems. It aims to combine the virtues of a gazetteer, concordance, and analytical study. The locations of all entries are provided, both in relation to Jonson's London and to the city familiar to the present-day reader. Whenever possible, a placename's historical background and appearance in the literature of Jonson's time are discussed. Citations are provided for every occurrence of a London placename in Jonson's works. Finally, whenever appropriate, the function of the placename in its particular context is discussed.

All streets, rivers, important buildings, villages, and miscellaneous topographical features within twenty-five miles of St. Paul's Cathedral are included. This results in the treatment of nearly every placename mentioned in the "London in Jonson's Day" section of the Herford and Simpson index (plus some which they omitted). The only exceptions in this book are the names of counties (Middlesex, Surrey, Kent, and Essex) within the above area and references to "London" or "the City." Also not included are places whose sole significance is biographical. However, the biographically related placenames that are also mentioned in the poet's works are pointed out and discussed when they are relevant to a better understanding of Jonson's writing. When alternate spellings of a placename exist, e.g., "Brainford" and "Brentford," the older form is used in the alphabetization of entries.

Nearly all the literary and historical sources cited by Herford and Simpson, Sugden, and Wheatley and Cunningham used herein have been verified in either the current standard editions or, in a few cases, an accessible recent text. These are listed in the bibliography. Unless stated otherwise, distances mentioned near the start of each entry represent the approximate road mileage from St. Paul's.

Abbreviations

Alch	*The Alchemist*
BF	*Bartholomew Fair*
CHM	*Christmas His Masque*
CR	*Cynthia's Revels*
DA	*The Devil Is an Ass*
EB	*An Entertainment at the Blackfriars*
EH	*Eastward Ho*
EMI	*Every Man in His Humour* Unless designated Q, all references are to Folio text, which H&S believe was prepared during 1612.
EMO	*Every Man out of His Humour*
Epic	*Epicoene*
Epig	*Epigrams*
FI	*The Fortunate Isles, and Their Union*
For	*The Forest*
GM	*The Gypsies Metamorphosed*
H&S	Herford, C. S., and Percy and Evelyn Simpson, eds. *Ben Jonson*. 11 vols. Oxford: Clarendon Press, 1925–52. All quotations from Jonson's works will be from this edition.
K	Kent, William. *Encyclopaedia of London*. 3rd ed., rev. London: Dent, 1970. First published 1937.
Kingsford	This editor's notes to Stow's *Survey of London,* see below.
LR	*Love Restored*
MA	*The Masque of Augurs*
MB	*The Masque of Beauty*
MBl	*The Masque of Blackness*
ML	*The Magnetic Lady*
MO	*The Masque of Owls*
MQ	*The Masque of Queens*
NFNW	*News from the New World Discovered in the Moon*
NI	*The New Inn*
NT	*Neptune's Triumph for the Return of Albion*
Poet	*Poetaster*

S	Sugden, Edward. *A Topographical Dictionary to the Works of Shakespeare and His Fellow Dramatists.* Manchester: University Press, 1925. The text, however, was completed in 1918.
SN	*The Staple of News*
Stow	Stow, John. *A Survey of London* (1603), ed. C. L. Kingsford. 2 vols. Oxford: Clarendon Press, 1908. This is the text used for all independent citations of Stow. H&S also primarily rely on it. On the few occasions when these editors refer to the 1598 edition, I have so indicated.
TT	*A Tale of a Tub*
TV	*Time Vindicated to Himself and to His Honours*
Und	*The Underwood*
UV	*Ungathered Verse*
Volp	*Volpone*
W&C	Wheatley, Henry, and Peter Cunningham. *London Past and Present.* 3 vols. London: John Murray, 1891.

ACKNOWLEDGMENTS

To Ernest W. Talbert, Alumni Distinguished Professor of English Emeritus, University of North Carolina at Chapel Hill, goes first thanks for the initial idea and support for this project. I am also most grateful to Professors Dennis Donovan and Peter G. Phialas, also of Chapel Hill, for their further professional help and guidance. Especial thanks go to the staff of the Guildhall Library, London, for several summers of expert assistance, advice, and immeasurable patience. I give grateful acknowledgment as well to help from Professor James W. Mathews, Head, Department of English, West Georgia College, and also to the college for a research grant which covered some study and illustration expenses.

My thanks to the Folger Shakespeare Library, Greater London Council Print Room, Guildhall Library Department of Prints and Maps, and George Allen and Unwin Ltd. for permission to reproduce material from their collections and publications. Credit also goes to Mr. Ralph Hyde, Curator of Prints and Maps, Guildhall Library, for much assistance and good advice during my search for and selection of maps and illustrations.

Finally, for their counsel, encouragement, and necessary prodding, hearty thanks to Mrs. E. M. Lofthouse, Mrs. E. Cernocky, Mrs. M. Willmott, and most bountifully to my husband Don, who gave up many evenings and several glorious English summers to act as courier, research aide, photographer, proofreader, and typist.

F.C.C.

The Significance
of Jonson's
London References

As Shakespeare has remained the "Swan of Avon," so Jonson's name has been inextricably linked with London and its sister-city of Westminster, which was the scene of his early years and death. During his lifetime Jonson left London for only relatively limited periods.[1] With few exceptions, Jonson's dramas—especially his most successful ones—have quite specific London settings, together with a wealth of local topographical references usually restricted to a small area.[2] Jonson's London references deserve study because they are handled with the same conscious artistry that typifies his use of mythology and iconography. This is apparent in three main aspects of Jonson's work. First, London references display Jonson's skillful use of classical dramatic principles, especially unity of place. Next, references to London are employed in a variety of ways to intensify the author's satiric emphases. Finally, mention of certain London locales enriches the encomiastic or nonsatiric facets of a characterization or work. The latter portion of this essay will show that the resultant overall picture of Jonson's London is comprehensive in its geographic range and portrayal of the major social and economic movements of early seventeenth-century London, yet selective in its repeated use of certain locales, as governed by his above-mentioned artistic principles.

A major classical feature of Jonson's London comedies is unity of place. With the exception of parts of *Every Man in His Humour*, the setting of the main action in these plays is always quite specific. References in the dialogue inform the audience that the scene is never merely "London" or "The City," as it so often is in other "City comedies" of this period. As the

1. On Jonson's early connections with Westminster, Herford and Simpson, *Ben Jonson* (Oxford: Clarendon Press, 1952), 11:571, cite Mark Eccles, *Review of English Studies* 12 (1936), 262. There is no documentary evidence of Jonson's birthplace; his ties with Westminster began when his widowed mother married a bricklayer who lived in Hartshorn Lane. The tradition that Jonson was once a soldier in Flanders has been discussed by Abraham Feldman, "Playwrights and Pike-Trailers," *Notes and Queries* 198 (1953):184–87. Jonson's other periods away from London include a visit to the Continent with Raleigh's son in his charge, which commenced in late summer of 1612 and ended before June 29, 1613 (date of the burning of the Globe, which Jonson witnessed). Jonson's walk to Scotland, discussed by H&S, 1:77, 82, lasted from summer, 1618, to early 1619.

2. The following plays are considered "London dramas" for this discussion: *Every Man out of His Humour, Eastward Ho, Epicoene, The Alchemist, Every Man in His Humour* (Folio), *Bartholomew Fair, The Devil Is an Ass, The Staple of News, The New Inn, The Magnetic Lady,* and *A Tale of a Tub.* Although its setting is Venice, *Volpone* contains several references to areas in London; some are cited later in this essay.

following summary reveals, the action of the plot is usually confined to a relatively limited area which has the play's principal setting as its focal point. In most instances these settings correlate quite effectively with the characters and themes of their respective dramas.

If *A Tale of a Tub* is considered one of Jonson's last plays, and the Folio version of *Every Man in His Humour* a product of 1612, then his first play with a particularized London background is *Every Man out of His Humour*. Its wide range of locales—including St. Paul's, Whitehall, the Mitre Tavern, one of the City prisons, and the countryside near London—results from its looseness of plot and its concern with the diverse character types found in these areas. In contrast, the scope of *Eastward Ho* is more limited. Its chief setting is the "City," the once-walled central portion of London. The shop of Touchstone the goldsmith is in Cheapside, the main business street of Tudor-Stuart London, and the roistering scenes featuring the "Virginia voyagers" take place at a well-known City tavern, the Blue Anchor at Billingsgate. After their trip is thwarted by a storm, these hapless adventurers are washed up at Wapping, Cuckold's Haven, and St. Katherine's—all riverside districts less than four miles east of the City. The final scenes in *Eastward Ho* return to the City, where in one of the Counters (debtors' prisons), the wastrel apprentice Quicksilver repents of his careless ways.

Epicoene demonstrates the topographical tendencies of Jonson's most memorable comedies. Although there are references to places as far apart as the Tower, the outlying northern village of Ware, Eltham Palace, and the Bear Tavern at the south end of London Bridge, the play's action is confined to several residences near the newly fashionable district in the Strand, the street which joined the cities of London and Westminster. Its characters are the social types (well-born youths, pretentious social climbers, and eccentrics) then inhabiting this region.[3] *The Alchemist* has the most restricted London setting of all major Jonsonian dramas. The entire play takes place within the Blackfriars home of Lovewit, a City businessman. There are several reasons why Blackfriars is an appropriate setting for the alchemical escapades of Face and Subtle. After the Dissolution, this area was cleared of nearly all its ecclesiastical buildings and partly given over to the residences of well-off yet ambitious folk like Sir Epicure Mammon and Kastril, who would have found their acquisitive impulses fulfilled by the promises of

---

3. *Epicoene*, ed. L. A. Beaurline (Lincoln: University of Nebraska Press, 1966), p. xvii. A slightly different setting has been suggested by Ralph Cohen, "London and the Techniques of Setting in Ben Jonson's Comedies," dissertation, Duke University, 1973, pp. 212–14. Cohen believes that though the values and interests stressed by *Epicoene's* characters are in keeping with the ideals of the Strand locale, Morose's house is located well to the east: in the City, near the river, and southeast of Bow Church.

alchemy. Also, many Puritan artisans resided in Blackfriars; such a setting for this play's "business," patronized in part by Puritans, may have been another of Jonson's jokes at their expense. Finally, Blackfriars retained its immunity from City jurisdiction; thus it would have been a logical district for rogues such as Face and Subtle to practice their skills.

Every Man in His Humour displays a limited City setting which enriches characterization and satire. By changing the Quarto's generalized Italian setting for a very specific English one, Jonson was able to utilize his intimate knowledge of London's geography and inhabitants. He was often able to employ details relating to topography or familiar institutions to emphasize aspects of temperament or to make a satiric point. The chief setting of this play is a good example of this practice. Nearly all of *Every Man In* takes place within a few blocks, roughly between the Old (Royal) Exchange and the Guildhall. In Jonson's time, as today, this area was the commercial and governmental heart of London. This is appropriate to the nature of two of the play's chief characters—the shrewd, materialistic merchant Kitely and the wise and witty Justice Clement.[4] Kitely's residence is in the Old Jewry (1.2.57); Justice Clement lives in nearby Coleman Street (3.2.52).[5] The only scenes located out of this area occur at Knowell's home in the northern suburb of Hogsden (1.1–3), and in the adjoining open ground of Moorfields (2.4–5).

The scenic unity of *Bartholomew Fair* is nearly as tight as in *The Alchemist*. All but the first act takes place in Smithfield, site of this most famous holiday celebration. Even the few scenes which are not set at Smithfield occur but a few hundred yards away. These take place at the home of John Littlewit, a clerk at the ecclesiastical Court of Arches, which sat at the church of St. Mary-le-Bow in Cheapside. According to the induction (ll. 5–6), Littlewit resides "about the *Hospitall*." This is most likely Christ's Hospital, a school on the premises of the former Grayfriars Monastery in Newgate Street. (See the Newgate Market entry for evidence on the location of Littlewit's house.)

The history of Smithfield harmonizes very well with the play's multitude of activities: rival wooing, cheating, public amusements, the administration (or miscarriage) of justice, debates and arguments, and personal travails. In several instances important historical events associated with

4. Lawrence Levin, "Clement Justice in *Every Man in His Humour*," *Studies in English Literature* 12 (1972):291–307, shows Justice Clement to be the play's "normative agent" who displays Jonson's "attitudes toward law, justice, and social order." The justice is not a typical Elizabethan dull-witted officer; he is rather "a new type of magistrate who is a shrewd humanist" (p. 291).

5. All quotations from Jonson's works are from C. S. Herford and Percy and Evelyn Simpson, eds. *Ben Jonson*. 11 vols. Oxford: Clarendon Press, 1925–52. References are to act, scene, and line.

Smithfield were similar to the happenings depicted in the play. At Smithfield, according to Stow (1:245), tourneys and jousts were presented before the leading figures of the realm. These were more vigorous counterparts of the verbal sparring portrayed in the "vapours" episode (4.4). Smithfield was also the place for public executions in Middlesex before the gallows were moved to Tyburn in the reign of Henry IV. Also, in the Middle Ages trials by combat were held in this locale. In *Bartholomew Fair* the administration of justice is portrayed in the attempts of Justice Overdo to purge the fair of "enormities." During the Marian period Smithfield became the infamous scene of many Protestant martyrdoms. The martyr motif is suggested by Jonson when he allows the justice to be humiliated and punished while ostensibly engaged in improving social conditions.[6] In a more cheerful vein, it is Stow again (1:93) who notes that in 1391 the local parish clerks staged plays "at the Skinners well besides Smithfield" and that closer to his own time (1:74) scholars would often debate there "upon a bank boorded about under a tree." This suggests two events near the close of *Bartholomew Fair*—the puppet play and the dispute between Rabbi Busy and Leatherhead over the sinfulness of such entertainments. Finally, Smithfield was long the scene of a market for horses, cattle, and sheep, being especially notorious for the unscrupulous tricks practiced by the horse dealers. Jonson's Dan Jordan Knockem, designated as a *"Horse-courser, and ranger o' Turnbull,"* a disreputable London street, is an unforgettable practitioner of this dubious trade.

In *The Devil Is an Ass* the setting is once again narrowly restricted. The stage business is almost totally confined to the neighborhood near the home of the selfish demonophile Fitzdottrel. His residence is located in the fashionable area west of the City and close to some chambers in Lincoln's Inn (2.2.52–54). These rooms are advantageously used by Wittipol for his amorous exploits (2.6). Several scenes take place at the pretentious Lady Tailbush's house. She must also live in this area because in a scene at Fitzdottrel's house her residence is described as "here, hard by. I' the lane" (3.5.11) and "hard by . . . over the way" (ll.66–67). This unity is broken

---

6. Justice Overdo's liberation from the stocks comes about when the madman Trouble-all fights with the watchmen, making them forget that the stocks are unlocked. This suggests an ironic "echo" of Smithfield history: Lord Mayor Sir William Walworth's rescue of Richard II when the latter was threatened by Wat Tyler's rebels in 1381. For a discussion of this event's prominence in Tudor entertainment, see David M. Bergeron, "Jack Straw in Drama and Pageant," *Guildhall Miscellany* 2, no. 10 (1968):459–63. The appropriateness of the Smithfield setting is noted by Joel Kaplan, "Dramatic and Moral Energy in *Bartholomew Fair*," *Renaissance Drama*, n.s. 3 (1970):137–56, "*Bartholomew Fair* consists of a succession of verbal and physical explosions in which the energy of Smithfield imposes itself upon the fair visitors, aggravating their absurdities and provoking clashes that increase in frequency as the play gathers momentum" (p. 141).

(5.6; 5.7) when Pug's spectacular "release" from Newgate Prison is depicted. The focal point of *The Staple of News* is in the same general part of London as that of *The Devil Is an Ass*. Although the location of the Staple's headquarters is not explicitly mentioned, several references lead one to assume that its "business" was carried on somewhere in the eastern portion of Fleet Street (roughly a quarter mile south of Lincoln's Inn). Several scenes occur at the Old Devil Tavern, a famous Fleet Street establishment. Also, in act 2, scene 5, which takes place at the home of Penniboy Senior, Ram Alley (a notorious thoroughfare off Fleet Street) is termed "hard by" (l. 112).

The setting of *The New Inn* is one of the "typically Jonsonian" characteristics of a play which in its courtly and philosophical aspects is a departure from Jonson's usual dramatic interests. This play's single setting is a hostelry in Barnet, a town some twelve miles north of the City. Mentioned several times during the action, the setting gives the play some of the topographical specificity typical of Jonson's London dramas. Today a part of metropolitan London, Barnet was well known to seventeenth-century Londoners as a place for assignations and holiday excursions. It was also a major stop for long-distance travelers. All these purposes are embodied by this play's characters, who also come from a wide variety of social and economic backgrounds. An inn setting thus becomes a very logical choice, as it was one of the few places where such human diversity might be encountered. The City setting of *The Magnetic Lady* reflects its social spectrum, which is much narrower than that of *The New Inn*. The plot chiefly deals with the acquisition of the heiress Placentia. Thematically, the play reveals the destructive effects of greed and narrow-mindedness. Nearly all of the characters are professional people—doctors, lawyers, and ministers—who betray their learning and integrity through their actions. Thus a City setting would seem quite appropriate for such characters and activities, and Jonson adheres to this expectation. Lady Loadstone's house, the scene for all the action, is located in the heart of London. This may be determined from the fact that the parish church in this play stands "behind the old Exchange" (4.6.10–11, 22–23). The Old (Royal) Exchange stood in Cornhill, which was then—and still is—a major commercial thoroughfare in the City.

Although most scholars have tended to consider *A Tale of a Tub* as primarily an early play with a few later changes, a strong case may be made for viewing its "late" features as being more significant than hitherto pointed out.[7] Besides the 1633 date of *A Tale's* first performance and the

7. The majority view that *A Tale* is primarily an early play is exemplified by H&S, 1:279–301, and 9:268–75; C. R. Baskervill, *English Elements in Jonson's Early Comedy* (Austin: University of Texas Press, 1911), pp. 77–80; R. E. Knoll, *Ben Jonson's Plays: An Introduction* (Lincoln: University of Nebraska Press, 1964), pp. 17–22; and Larry S.

anti—Inigo Jones insertions, there are several other points which deserve consideration. Most important is its setting—the semirural area northwest of the most fashionable part of London. By 1633 this locale was a recreative area popular with status-conscious residents of the Strand, staid City merchants and their wives, gallants, and law students. In addition, several prominent Londoners had residences in this district. There is also another circumstance which would have made the play appealing to a 1633 audience. It was precisely at this time that a vogue arose for "topographical comedies," usually artificial, sophisticated plays which gained some authenticity by means of a "real-life" setting which often served as the title of the work, e.g., Nabbes's *Covent Garden* and *Tottenham Court*, Brome's *Covent Garden Weeded* and *The Sparagus Garden*, and Shirley's *Hyde Park*.[8] Even though *A Tale*'s action ranges over a wide part of the semirural region northwest of the City, Jonson is always careful to keep the reader informed of the precise setting of virtually every scene. The home neighborhoods of all the characters are specified, and where the main characters are concerned, these areas are quite appropriate to their occupations and interests. The lighthearted Squire Tub lives at Tottenham Court, a manor house which was situated across the road from a popular resort with the same name. Constable Turfe, father of Tub's intended bride, lives at Kentish Town, which was then the largest village in this area and a logical place for the home of an important public official. In addition, the arch-intriguer, Canon Hugh, is explicitly designated as the "Vicar of Pancrace." Numerous contemporary references indicate that the term "Pancridge parson" (synonymous with "Pancrace") referred to a cleric with lax standards, especially in matrimonial matters. Also, local records show that the incumbents of this post indulged in some questionable professional tactics and that the area near the church was a haven for rogues and vagabonds. (See the St. Pancras entry for evidence supporting the above assertions.)

Another characteristic of classical comedy is its preponderance of middle- and lower-class characters. Jonson's London comedies, while not excluding the higher ranks, tend to emphasize people well below these strata but with intents of moving upward in society. A survey of his plays reveals that their action usually takes place in districts favored by those hoping to improve

Champion, *Ben Jonson's "Dotages"* Lexington: University of Kentucky Press, 1967), p. 133. Although J. A. Bryant discusses *A Tale* in the final chapter of *The Compassionate Satirist* (Athens: University of Georgia Press, 1973), he believes that Jonson "was most likely to have written *A Tale of a Tub* in the decade that saw compilation of his great Folio of 1616, but certainty about that matter is impossible" (p. 175).

8. Theodore Miles, "Place-Realism in a Group of Caroline Plays," *RES* 18 (1942): 428–40; also Richard H. Perkinson, "Topographical Comedy in the Seventeenth Century," *ELH* 3 (1936):270–90.

their social standing. Jonson's concentration on the social strata below the aristocracy allows him to "follow the ancients" and also to protect himself from charges of libel. Time and again Jonson uses a particularized London setting to remind us that although he may be mocking practices especially rampant among current court figures, the characters in his plays are not meant to represent them. Records from the court of King James I provide ample testimony of the activities of projectors, alchemists, and social climbers. Jonson's artistry lies in his ability to satirize such contemporary situations, usually without offense to specific, usually prominent, individuals.[9] In *The Alchemist* the somewhat racy Blackfriars locale is emphasized, thus giving the audience little grounds for associating the play's plot with royally supervised alchemical projects. Likewise the Smithfield background in *Bartholomew Fair* creates such a sense of pungent realism that one is bound to accept Jonson's assertion that the *"Seller* of *Mouse-trappes"* (induction, l. 145) does not represent any particular *"conceal'd States-man."* The semirural setting of *The New Inn* at a Barnet hostelry is a much-needed distancing detail in a play which is concerned with the validity of the current code of "precieuse" ethics at the court of Queen Henrietta Maria. Finally, the fact that the outrageously blatant avarice and selfishness in *The Magnetic Lady* occurs in a residence near the populous heart of London aids the reader in accepting the view expressed during the second chorus in this play, that "A *Play*, though it apparell, and present vices in generall, flies from all particularities in persons" (ll. 13–14).

As outlined earlier, another major feature of Jonson's London settings is that they illustrate his satiric skill. Jonson chooses references to streets, districts, and buildings in London which vividly expose the flaws in attitude and behavior with which he is concerned. Topographical references help to undercut a character's pretensions, motives, and illusions. These references work in several ways. Some allude to places with disreputable or otherwise unfavorable associations which establish a discrepancy between a character's illusions about himself and his true nature. Others, through details which emphasize distance, reveal his dishonesty. A third group uses details which stress size to illustrate the grossness of a particular personal trait. Finally, there are a few references which reveal a character's distorted

9. An exception to this tendency is *Eastward Ho*, where topographical details appear to have contributed to the material which displeased the king and ended in a brief prison stay for Jonson. As C. G. Petter has pointed out in a recent edition of this play (New Mermaids, London: Benn, 1973), p. xxiii, King James's court was probably headquartered at Greenwich when this play was first acted. Hence the cry of the Thames watermen which is the play's title and which is adopted as a motto by the prodigal apprentice Quicksilver could also apply to those pursuing favor at court. Also, when the roguish Sir Petronel Flash is cast up on the Isle of Dogs, directly across from Greenwich, he is greeted by an anonymous gentleman with a Scots accent.

sense of values as he either makes too much out of minor topographical details or exaggerates his own importance by equating petty aspects of his life with major London sights. As the following examples reveal, Jonson mastered most of these techniques relatively early in his career.

In *Every Man out of His Humor* Jonson satirizes certain characters by means of topographical references emphasizing size and distance. Sogliardo's extreme niggardliness is illustrated by the exaggeration in his comment that before he will sell his crop, "Ech corne I send shall be as big as *Paules*" (1.3.101). In two instances the mention of towns which are many miles apart discredits the plausibility of Shift's boasts about the art of tobacco-taking. In a bill posted at St. Paul's, Shift advertised that he could teach a person to inhale *"here at* London, *and evaporate at* Uxbridge, *or farder, if it please him"* (3.3.58–59). Uxbridge was sixteen miles from London. In the same vein, Shift later avers that his student will soon be able to "take his horse, drinke his three cups of *Canarie*, and expose one at *Hounslow*, a second at *Stanes*, and a third at *Bagshot*" (3.6.147–49). In this statement the distances involved (over thirty miles) cast further doubt upon the speaker's veracity.

In *Eastward Ho* Jonson employs topographical details which illustrate the discrepancy between the heroic pretensions held by his satiric targets and their petty accomplishments. These references pertain to the failure of their "Virginia voyage." In this sorry exploit the adventurers are humiliatingly ruined even before they begin the voyage itself. En route by river to the mooring place of their ocean vessel at Blackwall, their expedition ends up storm-tossed and foundered. The voyagers then stumble ashore on the Isle of Dogs and other riverside areas nearby, less than five miles from the City.[10] This group's delusions of nautical grandeur are illustrated by another geographical detail: their conscious identification with Blackwall and Deptford (riverside areas associated with English naval heroes). As mentioned before, Sir Petronel and his crew had planned to depart from Blackwall, the sailing point for many noted explorations. The pseudoheroes

10. C. G. Petter (see n. 9) points out, p. xxxi, how the places where these adventurers are rescued are appropriate to their "humours." The jealous husband Security comes ashore at Cuckold's Haven, his errant wife near the onetime nunnery of St. Katherine's, and the wild apprentice Quicksilver at Wapping (the execution site for river thieves and pirates). As noted earlier, the upstart knight Sir Petronel Flash lands suspiciously close to the royal palace at Greenwich. Brian Gibbons, *Jacobean City Comedy* (Cambridge: Harvard University Press, 1968), although useful in discussing the social and economic context of such plays, is not much concerned with the significance of London topographical references. Gibbons passes over the profusion of these details in *Eastward Ho* with the comment, "The play's setting in the city of London is accurately achieved with many playing references to street and district names to attract local interest; for similar reasons, lawyers and usurers' jargon is accurately reproduced" (p. 23).

had also hoped to celebrate their impending voyage with a supper on board Sir Francis Drake's ship, then on view at Deptford as a national monument.

The few London placenames in the otherwise Italianate *Volpone* are skillfully employed to satirize the pompous and vain English tourist Sir Politik Would-be. He displays his warped sense of values when he refers to the recent whelping of the lions in the Tower of London as an event of national magnitude (2.1.35–38). His magnificently administered humiliation in act 5 is made more memorable by the Merchants' comment that Sir Pol's attempt to hide in a tortoise shell is "a rare motion, to be seene in *Fleet-street*" or "in the faire" (5.4.77–78). Both Fleet Street and Bartholomew Fair were familiar places for the exhibition of wonders or freaks.

Epicoene is the first drama in which Jonson extensively used the adverse connotations and reputations of certain London regions for satiric purposes. In this play London placenames frequently reflect the vulgar pretensions to gentility assumed by the Ladies Collegiates and their selfish admirers Sir Amorous La Foole and Sir John Daw. Sometimes the undercutting remarks are made by Clerimont and his fellow "true-wits"; in other instances the foolish ones cut their own throats. An excellent example of the latter instance involves Lady Haughty, a domineering shrew who repeatedly attempts to assert her right to lofty social status. At one point her progress is soundly scuttled when, in order to make a point about her refined tastes in fashion, she lets slip a chance reference to a town noted as an assignation spot. Its mention casts considerable doubt on her sexual mores: "A fourth time, as I was taking coach to goe to *Ware*, to meet a friend, it dash'd me a new sute all over . . . with a brewers horse" (3.2.72–75). The market and coaching town of Ware, about twenty-four miles north of London, was an extremely popular center for illicit meetings and sprees throughout the Tudor-Stuart period. (See the Ware entry for full details.) Another set of pertinent placenames concerns collectively the Ladies Collegiates, who are quite fond of visiting three London landmarks often frequented by curiosity seekers, parvenus, and parasites. These places—the New Exchange in the Strand, Bedlam, and the China Houses (shops for the sale of Eastern wares)—were either recently established, or, as was Bedlam, popular because of current interest in irrational behavior.[11] The unflattering qualities associated with these places—an acquisitive urge, materialism, and mental eccentricity—are part of the women's temperaments. The Ladies'

11. A large part of the Strand's popularity came from the establishment of the New Exchange in this street in 1609. This institution, also known as "Britain's Burse," was more of a showplace for novelties and luxuries than its staid predecessor, the Royal Exchange in the City. The "China Houses" were shops where Eastern wares, notably porcelains, were sold. The prominence of Bedlam as a tourist attraction is evident from passages in several Tudor-Stuart plays. For full details see these respective entries.

obsession with the bizarre and the abnormal is but one of the many examples of deviation from the norm portrayed in this comedy that explores standards of "nature, normality, and decorum."[12] Topographical details also reflect unfavorably upon the ideals of La Foole when he overzealously boasts of his residence in the newly fashionable Strand and of his continual visits to the New Exchange. Placenames are also used in *Epicoene* to reveal Morose's self-indulgent aversion to noise. His tendency to exaggerate his sufferings is apparent when he claims to prefer the loudest and most discordant sounds available—"the tower-wharfe . . . *London*-bridge, *Paris*-garden, *Belins*-gate, when the noises are at their height" (4.4.14–16)—to the chatter of his "wife." Later, a London audience probably laughed at his presumptuousness in equating his private idiosyncracy with a well-known tourist attraction when he declared, "The perpetuall motion is here, and not at *Eltham*" (5.3.63). Eltham Palace, southeast of London, was the site of a current scientific wonder which purported to demonstrate the principles of cosmic movement.

In *The Alchemist* references to London districts and institutions are employed with striking success to deflate Sir Epicure Mammon's efforts to mask his alchemical goals as philanthropic exercises. After this scheming voluptuary indulges himself over the restorative powers of his elixir, Surly remarks, "The decay'd *Vestall's* of *Pickt-hatch* would thanke you, / That keepe the fire a-live, there" (2.1.62–63). Pict Hatch was a notorious haven for prostitutes. Earlier, Mammon's civic plan for distributing his gains was mocked by Subtle as he envisioned Mammon "walking *more-fields* for lepers; / And offring citizens-wives pomander-bracelets, / As his preservative, made of the *elixir*" (1.4.20–22). In Jonson's time the once swampy acres of Moorfields north of the City wall were a popular middle-class recreational area, as well as a favorite place for leprous beggars to conduct their "business." Finally, when Mammon promises to give away his share of the gains, he is put down by Surly's sarcastic analogy, "As he that built the water-worke, do's with water?" (2.1.76). This rejoinder refers to Sir Bevis Bulmer, an entrepreneur who was among the first to provide a private water system (at no small cost) to eminent individuals.

As in *Epicoene*, Jonson in the Folio version of *Every Man in His Humour* satirizes characters by associating them with London districts having unfavorable connotations. When Stephen avows that he disdains soldiering, Wellbred responds with the "innocent" observation, "As I remember your name is entred in the artillerie garden?" (3.5.149–50). The association of Stephen with the often clumsy militia who trained at the Artillery Garden

12. E. B. Partridge, *"Epicoene,"* in *Ben Jonson: Twentieth-Century Views*, ed. Jonas Barish (Englewood Cliffs, N.J.: Prentice-Hall, 1963), pp. 128–31.

destroys his pretensions to urbane gentility. Later Captain Bobadil, anxious to impress his hearers with his military refinement and sophistication, unwittingly identifies himself with some of the most disreputable areas in London, as he tells of how swordsmen have accosted him "in divers skirts i' the towne, as *Turne-bull, White-chappell, Shore-ditch*" (4.7.44–45). These three districts were all beyond the limits of City jurisdiction but within easy access of adventuresome Londoners. Loose women, gambling, opportunities for thievery, and (in the case of Shoreditch) theaters were the chief attractions of these suburbs.

Although Bartholomew Fair contains the largest number of London placenames in any Jonsonian drama (see the discussion near the close of this essay), only a few may be classified as satiric. The majority either provide realistic details about a character's background or clarify one character's impressions about another. On the whole, the foolish actions of Cokes, Rabbi Busy, and Justice Overdo require no assistance from topographical allusions. The major satirical use of topographical references occurs when Jonson gently laughs at the devotees of classical romantic narrative by burlesquing this genre in the puppet show near the close of the play. In this presentation, the story of Hero and Leander is set in a decidedly unromantic part of London. Bankside, Puddle Wharf, and the Thames replace Sestos, Abydos, and the Hellespont. Leander then becomes enamored of Hero after seeing her disembark at Trig Stairs, and the lovers have a tryst at the Swan Tavern in Old Fish Street.

In *The Devil Is an Ass* vulnerable characters are identified with places and institutions not so much disreputable as provincial. Such associations destroy the pretensions of both Pug and Fitzdottrel to worldly sophistication. In the first scene the devil Iniquity mocks the efforts of his infernal subordinate Pug: "Some good Ribibe [old woman], about *Kentish* Towne, / Or *Hogsden*, you would hang now, for a witch" (1.1.16–17). These topographical references to unpretentious suburban villages show that Iniquity believes Pug's talents to be incapable of triumph over a city victim. When Wittipol wishes to express his low estimate of Fitzdottrel's abilities, he urges that Fitzdottrel be made *"Duke o' Shore-ditch* with a project" (4.7.64–65). "Duke of Shoreditch" was a mock title jestingly awarded to winners of City archery contests.

On one occasion in *The Staple of News* Jonson pokes fun at his neighbors in Westminster. During the third intermeane the gossips offer their views about where better news than that gathered by the play's "reporters" may be found. According to these ladies, Westminster contained the largest number of newsworthy places: the Almonries, the Bowling Alley, Chanon Row, Gardiner's Lane, King Street, the Mill, the Abbey Sanctuaries, Tuttle Street, and the two Woolstaples. At the time of this play's presentation in 1625, Westminster was not only a center for court, religious, and legal business, as the catalogue given above shows, but was also probably Jonson's own place of residence. It is possible that the playwright was familiar with some escapades associated with these landmarks in the Westminster area. For example, according to Gossip Mirth, Gossip Tatle knows *"what fine slips grew in* Gardiners-lane" (ll. 24–25). Beyond the obvious punning appropriateness in regard to "Gardiners' lane," "slips" may also refer to illegitimate children.[13]

Jonson's technique with London placenames in *The New Inn* and *The Magnetic Lady* is quite similar to his practice in *Every Man out of His Humour*. Topographical references suggesting large distances are employed to satirize certain characters. As before, these details expose both their gross desires and their dishonest boasts. In *The New Inn* the tailor Nick Stuffe and his wife Pinnacia unashamedly discuss their very unprofessional conduct, wherein they dress in clothing intended for their clients and parade through the outlying towns near London, "to *Rumford, Croyden,* / *Hounslow,* or *Barnet,* the next bawdy road" (4.3.71–72). The distance of this circular journey (over sixty miles) vividly illustrates the selfishness of this couple by showing the extent to which they exploit the property of others. In *The Magnetic Lady* the devious Dr. Rut declares that before he "cured" Sir Moth Interest of sleepwalking the latter would "walke to Saint *John's* wood, / And *Waltham* Forrest" (5.8.13–14). This play's setting is near the old Royal Exchange; thus the circuit described is over twenty-five miles, making Rut another character whose word is not to be trusted.

In *A Tale of a Tub* one character unwittingly satirizes another through a topographical reference. In this case the bumbling, provincial Council of Finsbury is trying to praise the deeds of its leader, Constable Turfe. Exulting over a recent victory, Turfe avows, "I will ride / Above Prince *Arthur*," and he is seconded by one of the council, "Or our *Shore-ditch* Duke" (3.6.4–5). As mentioned in connection with *The Devil Is an Ass*, this was no hereditary or meritorious honor but rather a mock title mirthfully bestowed upon the winners of City archery contests. Of course, to the Finsbury Council this would have been a worthy title as well, but it is doubtful that a Jonsonian audience would have thought so.

Some of Jonson's masques and poems also satirically employ London references. In these works his targets include himself and his rival Inigo

13. One cannot determine the precise date when Jonson left the city, but he was a Westminster resident when questioned by the attorney general in 1628 (H&S, 1:98). Earlier, he was described as "Ben Jonson of Gresham College" when he appeared in a 1623 Chancery suit on behalf of Lady Raleigh (H&S, 11:582). The dual meaning of "slips" was pointed out by E. H. Sugden, *A Topographical Dictionary to the Works of Shakespeare and His Fellow Dramatists* (Manchester: University of Manchester Press, 1925), p. 214.

Jones, as well as his literary creations. In *Epigram* 3, Jonson laughed at his own poetry, declaring that if it were not acceptable, it should be sent to Bucklersbury, a grocers' and apothecaries' district where unwanted poetry could be used for wrapping parcels. Jonson's use of the Bucklersbury reference to criticize himself probably made it easier for him to accept the comments of later detractors who made similar allusions to this street and the quality of his work.[14]

Inigo Jones, the best known of Jonson's professional adversaries, terminated a long, somewhat stormy period of successful collaboration by displacing Jonson as chief deviser of masques at Charles I's court. Ill and aging, Jonson fought back by poetically impaling Jones as a petty social climber whose artistry consisted of uninspired stage mechanics and crude optical tricks. London references were used several times to intensify this impression. In *Ungathered Verse* 35, "To Inigo Marquess Would be: A Corollary," Jonson compared Jones's creation of the "artificiall sea" in *The Masque of Blackness* to "Dowgate Torrent falling into Thames" (l. 16). Because Dowgate Torrent usually contained polluted floodwaters, the image suggested by Jonson was most unflattering. In *Epigram* 129, "To Mime," Jonson attacked Jones by portraying him as an inveterate court campfollower: "There's no journey set, or thought upon, / To *Braynford, Hackney, Bow,* but thou mak'st one" (ll. 3–4). These towns, notably Brainford, were popular centers for conviviality and amorous intrigues. Full details are given in their respective entries.

Finally, one of Jonson's most successful uses of topography to emphasize a work's satiric meaning is in *The Masque of Augurs*, where the antimasquers, chiefly a bearkeeper, some alewives, and a sham "projector" (impresario) of masques all hail from the district of St. Katherine's, just east of the Tower. Jonson's typical antimasques stress undesirable attitudes and characteristics which are dispelled in the main masque. *The Masque of Augurs* follows this pattern. In this courtly entertainment the bad reputation which the St. Katherine's region has acquired influences the audience's attitude toward the antimasquers. As a dockside area St. Katherine's had the usual complement of roisterers, prostitutes, and thieves. It also was a haven for a large number of Flemish refugees who were often stereotyped as drunken and ignorant.[15] Vangoose, the "projector" of masques, conforms

14. The Bucklersbury reference was later adopted by the vituperative Alexander Gill (see the Star Chamber entry), who expressed his displeasure with Jonson's *The Magnetic Lady* by commenting "From Bucklers Burye lett itt not be barde, / But thincke nott of Ducke lane or Paules Churchyarde." From Bodleian (Oxford) MS. Ashmolean 38, p. 15; cited by H&S, 11:348.

15. Sugden, p. 290, provides dramatic references; Stow, *Survey of London*, ed. C. L. Kingsford (Oxford: Clarendon Press, 1908), 1:124, discusses the crowded conditions in St.

to this image. He is unaware of the proper form and content of an antimasque and speaks in ridiculous "stage Dutch." Adding to Jonson's low estimate of this region is his inclusion of some vulgar alewives from the breweries which were a prominent part of the St. Katherine's district. These women delight in the antics of a bearkeeper who leads the "ladies" in a round of doggerel song and dance in praise of the area.[16]

It has been shown how Jonson thoughtfully chose London topographical references to intensify his satire.[17] But there remain a considerable number of such references used for praise or characterization without satiric intent. Again, this playwright's thorough knowledge of his city enabled him to make some quite appropriate comments. In several of his encomiastic poems Jonson also employed details stressing distance or number. *Underwood* 75, an epithalamium for Jerome Weston and Frances Stuart, states that the coaches of those attending the wedding were lined up "all the way, / From *Greenwich*, hither to *Row-hampton* gate" (ll. 11–12). As the distance from Greenwich to the Westons' chapel at Roehampton was at least ten miles, this is indeed quite a compliment to the nuptial pair. *Forest* 6, "To the Same [Celia]," uses a local allusion as the basis for complimentary hyperbole. He promises that the volume of his love equals the number of "sands in *Chelsey* fields, / Or the drops in silver *Thames*" (ll. 14–15). "Sands in *Chelsey* fields" refers to the riverside south of Whitehall. In Jonson's time this shore was composed of a mixture of sand and tiny pebbles known as chesel, a term which some authorities believe was the etymological basis of "Chelsea."[18]

Sometimes Jonson only briefly mentions a topographical detail to praise. In *The Gypsies Metamorphosed* the Second Gypsy lists the royal palaces and gardens at Greenwich and St. James's Park as among the "finer walled

---

Katherine's; David Bevington, *Tudor Drama and Politics* (Cambridge: Harvard University Press, 1968), p. 134, is helpful in explaining reasons for anti-Flemish prejudice during this period.

16. As many dramatic references testify, Jonson held bearbaiting in very low esteem. Some of his most powerful denunciations mention this "sport" and its Bankside arena, the area popularly known as Paris Garden. A fine example of this is Jonson's manifesto to ignorant audiences in *Poetaster* (To the Reader, ll. 44–46); for a similar view see ll. 1357–58 in *The Gypsies Metamorphosed*. See the Bear Gardens and Paris Garden entries for other examples.

17. Other topographical references which Jonson successfully used for satirical purposes are discussed in the following entries: Cheapside (in *Eastward Ho*); St. Sepulchre (*Epicoene*); Newgate, Tottenham High Cross, Tyburn (*The Devil Is an Ass*); and Inns of Court (*A Tale of a Tub*).

18. This traditional etymology for Chelsea dates back to John Norden, *Speculum Britanniae* (London: Norden, 1593), p. 17; William Kent, *Encyclopaedia of London*, 3rd ed., rev. (London: Dent, 1970), p. 72, gives several alternatives.

places" (ll. 94–95). This technique is also used in *Underwood* 2, part 6, where he refers to current court entertainments, "You were more the eye, and talke, / Of the Court, today, then all / Else that glister'd in *White-hall*" (ll. 14–16).

On another occasion an association with a particular London area is maintained throughout a work. In the *Entertainment at Highgate*, written to honor a royal visit to the home of Lord Cornwallis five miles north of St. Paul's, this area's favorable associations are stressed. Highgate's lofty elevation and salubrious climate enabled Jonson to compare it effectively to Mount Cyllene, the Arcadian home of Mercury, who acts as the host of Jonson's production, leading the guests on a tour of the grounds and in a jovial drinking bout, which is also attended by Mercury's son Pan. This accent on conviviality is appropriate to both the London region and its classical counterpart. Highgate was a market town and coach stop known for the number of taverns on its main street, and Cyllene was also the home of Pan, one of the most jocund and festive of the Greek gods.

While discussing Jonson's use of London references in his encomiastic poems, one should not overlook his achievements in a genre closely associated with London and with praise: the civic pageant. His record of such work (part of a royal entry, one lord mayor's show) is understandably brief, considering his consistent employment as writer of court entertainments for over twenty years.[19] Yet, judging from the one major example of Jonson's work in this field, he approached his assignment with the same diligence and skill that he soon brought to Whitehall, making his contribution rank with the best products of Jacobean London pageantry.[20]

---

19. The Yeomanry Account of the Haberdashers' Company (cited by H&S, 11:586) indicates that Jonson was paid £12 for his share in devising the 1604 lord mayor's show, for which there is no extant text. Jonson also wrote some speeches addressed to King James at an important banquet given in 1607 by the Merchant Taylors' Company (see the Merchant Taylors' Hall entry). Late in life, Jonson was associated with the City in yet another way. In 1628 he was appointed City chronologer upon the death of the incumbent, Thomas Middleton (H&S, 1:240–41). Perhaps Jonson regarded this as an attempt to buy his favor, or perhaps poor health was too great a drain on his creativity, for in 1631 the City stopped his annual "fee or wages" of one hundred nobles until "some fruits of his labours" could be brought forth. Three years later, King Charles intervened on Jonson's behalf to have his "pension" reinstated and the arrears paid. H&S, 1:101, comment that the change in terminology shows that the city now regarded the office as a sinecure rather than a productive appointment.

20. This subject is exhaustively covered in David M. Bergeron, *English Civic Pageantry* (Columbia: University of South Carolina Press, 1971). Bergeron asserts that in the Fenchurch show Jonson "succeeds in fusing action, speech, visual spectacle, and theme" (p. 77). In the Temple Bar pageant he is credited with inventing "viable dramatic characters" (p. 86), and his brief moral exhortation in the Strand is a "fit conclusion to a lavish entertainment" (p. 87).

King James's official coronation progress through London (delayed a year because of the plague) took place in 1604; the City spared no expense in obtaining the best poets and artificers for the occasion. London's tribute to the monarch consisted of seven lavishly decorated triumphal arches erected at strategic City locales. Symbolic tableaux, music, and welcoming speeches awaited the guest of honor at each site. Jonson devised the brief pageants presented at two of the major locations (Fenchurch Street and Temple Bar), plus a short address delivered in the Strand (H&S, 7:83–109). Thomas Dekker composed the shows at three other arches; the remaining two were planned by the Italian and Dutch merchants of London. Finally, a single speech in one of Dekker's scenes was written by Thomas Middleton. The architect Stephen Harrison joined with the dramatists in designing the arches; he published his drawings in a handsome folio pamphlet *The Arches of Triumph* (1604).[21]

Jonson's first pageant, also the first in the entire progress, was presented in Fenchurch Street on an arch bearing an intricately carved model of the City. The baroque-styled arch also contained several niches for the actors costumed in rich emblematic detail and two chambers for musicians. Jonson's intent was to display "the very site, fabricke, strength, policie, dignitie, and affections of the Citie" (ll. 245–47). The figure of Monarchia Britannica occupied the most exalted position on the arch, with Theosophia (divine wisdom) seated beneath her. On another part of the arch was London's guardian spirit, Genius Urbis, attended by two figures representing London's wise counsel and her warlike power.[22] Especially striking was the personification of an integral feature of London, the Thames. His costume included "a skin-coate made like flesh, naked and blue," bracelets of sedge and willow, and other details "alluding to VIRGILS description of *Tyber*" (ll. 102–7). Genius Urbis and the Thames were the only speakers in this pageant. The former gave a lengthy, eloquent welcome appropriate to a high civic official, while the Thames testified to the happiness of London's less articulate masses, "Not my fishes heere, / Though they be dumbe, but doe express the cheere / Of these bright streames" (ll. 315–17).

---

21. For discussion of the discrepancies between the Harrison drawings and the texts written by Jonson and Dekker, see D. M. Bergeron, "Harrison, Jonson, and Dekker: The Magnificent Entertainment for King James (1604)," *Journal of the Warburg and Courtauld Institutes* 31 (1968):445–48. Harrison's illustrations have been reprinted in Bergeron's *English Civic Pageantry*.

22. The "rich, reverend, and antique" costume worn by Genius Urbis included a purple mantle and buskins with a crowning wreath of plane tree leaves. In one hand he held a goblet, in the other "a branch full of little twigs, to signifie increase and indulgence" (ll. 70–74). C. F. Wheeler, *Classical Mythology in the Plays, Masques, and Poems of Ben Jonson* (Princeton, N.J.: Princeton University Press, 1938), points out that this figure "recalls the statue of the *genius populi Romani* who was personified in the Forum as a bearded man holding the cornucopiae" (pp. 102–3).

Jonson's other main show in the 1604 progress was presented at Temple Bar. Here the arch represented a Temple of Janus, whose four faces (representing the seasons) were not enough "to behold the greatnesse and glorie of that day" (ll. 407–8). The chief figure in this tableau was "IRENE, or *Peace*." The dialogue consisted of a debate in which the Flamen Martialis was persuaded by the apparently ubiquitous Genius Urbis to abandon his outdated "superstitious fumes" in favor of the Genius's stewardship of the flame of peace. This pageant's emphasis on transition and order harmonized well with its setting: Temple Bar is for ceremonial purposes the most important of the City boundaries. Just as the Genius Urbis banished the Flamen Martialis from the precincts of the temple, so too could the City refuse entry to those who would disturb her stability.

There are also several occasions when Jonson uses London references to enrich a characterization without notable satiric or encomiastic effects. In *Every Man in His Humour* Kitely's worried comment that if his man Cash proved untrustworthy, "I were gone, / Lost i' my fame forever, talke for th'Exchange" (3.3.61–62), adds realism to the bourgeois temperament of this "rich merchant i' the old *Jewrie*" (1.2.57). For a man with Kitely's desire for commercial success, his reputation among his fellow businessmen at the Royal Exchange would be of prime importance. Another character from *Every Man In*, the wily servant Brainworm, confesses that he obtained his ragged-soldier disguise from a *"Hounds-ditch"* man (3.5.31). This detail adds to the vividness of Brainworm's assumed role, for Houndsditch was notorious as the haunt of fences and rag dealers. In *Eastward Ho* another characterization is heightened by a London allusion. The goldsmith Touchstone suggests the possible fate of the profligate apprentice Quicksilver, "Mee thinkes I see thee already walking in Moore fields without a Cloake, with halfe a Hatte, without a band, a Doublet with three Buttons, without a girdle, a hose with one point and no Garter, with a cudgell under thine arme, borrowing and begging three pence" (1.1.137–41).[23]

One of the most entertaining portions of *The Devil Is an Ass* is the "infernal grand tour" of London outlined by the devil Iniquity to his subordinate Pug. In this speech Jonson chooses details of London topography especially appropriate to the nature of these would-be travelers. Iniquity's promise to "fetch thee a leape / From the top of *Pauls*-steeple, to the Standard in *Cheepe*" (1.1.55–56) would require supernatural ability for two reasons. Such a jump would be about a quarter of a mile long; it would also require some quick reconstruction, for the steeple of St. Paul's had been destroyed by lightning in 1561, well before the play's presentation in 1616. The entertainment proposed by Iniquity is similarly consistent with

23. For Moorfields as a haunt of beggars and ruined men, see Sugden, p. 353; also H&S, 10:67, citing Stow, *Survey of London*, 2:145–47.

a devil's festive spirit: "Nay, boy, I wil bring thee to the Bawds, and the Roysters, / At *Belins-gate*, feasting with claret-wine, and oysters" (ll. 68–69) and "We will survay the *Suburbs*, and make forth our sallyes, / Downe *Petticoate-lane*, and up the *Smock-allies*" (ll. 59–60). The "smock-allies" were disreputable byways appropriately situated close to Petticoat Lane, itself a questionable locale.[24] An even more notorious array of places is catalogued by Iniquity when he promises to go "To *Shoreditch, Whitechappell,* and so to Saint *Kathernes,* / To drinke with the *Dutch* there, and take forth their patternes" (ll. 61–62). Shoreditch and Whitechapel, as explained earlier, were rowdy and licentious suburbs northeast of the City wall, and St. Katherine's, also previously discussed, was a dockside area east of the Tower popularly associated with drunken disorder because of the many Flemish immigrants residing there.

There are also some instances where a placename clarifies a comparison or example, again without positive or negative emphasis. In *News from the New World Discovered in the Moon* Jonson uses a topographical allusion to explain social conditions upon the moon. In this masque the Second Herald tells an earthling that the moon offers "above all the *Hide-parkes* in Christendome, farre more hiding and private" (ll. 250–51). In 1621 when this masque was presented, Hyde Park was gaining prominence as a fashionable meeting place.[25] In *The Alchemist* the disreputable quality of the customers frequenting Subtle and Face's headquarters in Blackfriars is suggested by the fact that among them is "your giantesse, / The bawd of *Lambeth*" (1.4.2–3). Lambeth, then a marshy area across the Thames from Whitehall, was notorious for the whores, thieves, and vagabonds it harbored.

This introductory essay has attempted to reveal some of the successful ways in which Jonson employed London topographical references. It is far from a complete representation of his purposes and techniques. Not only are there other examples in the "nonsatiric" category just discussed,[26] but two additional functions of topographical references deserve attention: entertainment by means of wordplay and the provision of verisimilitude from references to actual places even in the least significant conversations.

24. F. H. W. Sheppard, ed., *Spitalfields and Mile End New Town*, Survey of London, 27 (London: London County Council, 1957), p. 226).

25. Sugden, p. 259, provides evidence supporting this early date for Hyde Park's emergence upon the social scene. The Hyde Park entry contains three more Jonsonian references to this newly fashionable resort. Most of Jonson's work was written before the appearance of such other leafy meeting places as Covent Garden, the Sparagus Garden, Ranelagh, and Vauxhall.

26. See the Counters entry for a fine comparison of these institutions to the conscience; also the Bridewell entry for a topographically related comparison from *Epigram* 133, "On the Famous Voyage." A vivid illustration of the piratical nature of many London sharpers is given in the Bermudas, Strand, and Streights entries.

In several of his works Jonson uses topographical references as the basis for parodies, puns, and other forms of wordplay. These verbal acrobatics are more than appealing tidbits for the audience's amusement; they are also excellent examples of the fusion of Jonson's inventive ingenuity with his encyclopedic knowledge of London. In *The New Inn* Jonson indulges in a bit of Chaucerian parody when a character's command of classical languages is described as "a little taynted, fly-blowne *Latin*, / After the Schoole. Of *Stratford* o' the Bow. / For *Lillies Latine*, is to him unknow" (2.4.22–24).[27] Apparently the linguistic situation in this area hadn't improved much since the days of the fastidious Prioress in the *Canterbury Tales*. The wordplay in one of Captain Otter's comments from *Epicoene* has no literary basis; it merely takes advantage of certain London street names for vituperative purposes. The henpecked Otter delivers a long-overdue insult to his shrewish wife when he declares that her eyebrows were made in the Strand, her teeth were procured in Blackfriars, and her hair was fashioned in Silver Street (4.2.92–94). This is certainly an original way of stating that her eyebrows were coarse, her teeth black from decay, and her hair a steely gray.

Christmas His Masque is crammed with wordplay involving topographical references. This lighthearted holiday entertainment depicts a procession of Londoners paying tribute to Father Christmas. Much of the humor comes from the introduction of merrymakers whose names are comically or wittily related to their places of residence. The participants include "Clem Waspe *of Honey-lane*" (l.225), "*young* Little-worth" of "*Penny-rich-street*" (ll.232–33), and "*John Butter* o' Milke-street," who is allowed to "slip in for a Torch-bearer, so [long as] he melt not too fast" (ll. 87–90). There is also "Child Rowlan, *and a straight young man*," even though he hails from "*Crooked-lane-a*" (ll. 236–37). A welcome guest is Cupid, who of course dwells in Love Lane (l. 119); his mother Venus resides in Pudding Lane, a thoroughfare a short distance west of Love Lane. Cupid and Venus are not the only figures from classical mythology in this masque. According to the presenter, Father Christmas, another reveler is "*my Sonne Hercules, tane, out of Distaff-lane, / but an active man, and a Porter.*" (ll. 212–13). Jonson's topographical selectivity is explained when one remembers Hercules' temporary sojourn in woman's attire, armed with a distaff rather than a club.[28]

Finally, there are a number of topographical references which neither accomplish any of the preceding objectives nor exemplify Jonson's virtuos ity with language. These places are often mentioned as part of the exposi-

27. "Lilly's Latine" refers to the scholarship of William Lilly, master of St. Paul's School, who compiled the standard Latin text used in Tudor–Stuart times.

28. The following entries, all from *Christmas His Masque*, are other amusing examples of various types of wordplay: Doo-Little Lane, Fish Streets (Old and New), Friday Street, Philpot Lane, Pope's Head Alley, and Threadneedle Street.

tory information provided about a character. Although they do not de-
lineate character in the manner of the placenames discussed earlier in this
essay, they do have an important role in contributing to the realism of
Jonson's portrayals. The significance of these details lies in the fact that they
are the names of actual streets, districts, inns, open spaces, and taverns.
Even the supernumerary characters become more human, more credible,
when they can be associated with the tangible. The same holds true for the
many eccentric, obsessed, or "humours" figures who are found throughout
Jonson's dramatic world.

The Alchemist contains several examples of this technique. The characters
involved are Dapper and Drugger, two of the "clients" duped by Face and
his assistants. Their visits to the rogues' Blackfriars headquarters are the
opening episodes in a plot which increases in momentum, complexity, and
hilarity with the introduction of each willing victim. There was no need for
Jonson to expend a great deal of effort on their characterizations; what
mattered was that they won the audience's interest in part through the
illusion of verisimilitude. The plausibility of Dapper's situation is increased
when it is revealed how he became acquainted with Face and his crew—a
chance meeting with Face at the Dagger Tavern in Holborn (1.1.191).
There were several Dagger Taverns in London during this period. The
Alchemist itself contains references to two of them. Jonson's specificity adds
to the realism of this bit of exposition. Holborn, an important London
thoroughfare, would have been a likely place for the law clerk Dapper to
seek recreation because of its proximity to some of the Inns of Court and
legal offices. (See the Dagger and Holbourne entries for full details.)

In this same play the audience is also reminded of obscure corners of
London, as when the aspiring tobacconist Drugger boasts that his only
hangover was cured by "a good old woman" who dwelled in Seacoal Lane
(3.4.118–19), a very modest thoroughfare near the Fleet Ditch. It was
chiefly occupied by cookshops, ship provisioners, and other unpretentious
businesses. Seacoal Lane was a logical place for Drugger to find his practical
physician, but one needed to be familiar with London to know of its
existence. This reference also becomes completely plausible when it is
revealed soon after that Drugger is a native of the City. Face mentions that
this client once became sick with grief "for being sess'd at eighteene pence, /
For the water-worke" (ll. 123–24). This refers to the charges levied on City
residents to help finance the cost of the "New River," a project which
provided London with fresh water from springs in Hertfordshire. Finally,
toward the close of the play when Dapper receives some of the "orders" of the
Queen of Faery, several other references to London taverns and eating places

add to the credibility of her commands. Full details are provided in the Dagger, Woolsack, and Heaven & Hell entries.[29]

Geographically speaking, Jonson's works mention virtually every part of early seventeenth-century London and its environs: in the far west Windsor, Hampton Court, and Brentford; in the near west Hyde Park, Paddington, and St. Giles in the Fields; just southwest of Westminster Chelsea, Tothill Street, and Tothill Fields; in the northwest Kentish Town, Hampstead, Marylebone, and the other districts which are the setting of *A Tale of a Tub*; due north the coaching villages of Barnet, Highgate, and Ware; northeast Waltham Forest, Tottenham High Cross, and Hackney; and eastward Stratford atte Bow, Whitechapel, Shadwell, and Wapping. To the south Jonson mentions Bankside, Paris Garden, Lambeth, Croydon, and (to the southeast) St. Thomas a Watering, Deptford, Greenwich, and Eltham Palace. Within the City and Westminster are references not only to major thoroughfares but also to such byways as Scalding Alley, Seacoal Lane, Penny-rich Street, and Smock Alley.

Unlike the geographically comprehensive but sociologically bland picture of London depicted by Stow, London as presented by Jonson is vivid, racy, and lively.[30] We learn of respectable resorts and recreative areas such as Tottenham Court, Finsbury Fields, the Bowling Alley in Westminster, and Mile End, as well as those frequented by a more raffish and disreputable crowd such as Ram Alley, the Bermudas, and the Streights. There are a number of references to the "red-light district" of Jonson's London: Turnbull Street, Pict Hatch, the Bankside Stews. The northwest movement of London's most significant expansion is accurately reflected by the many references to places north and west of the Strand, notably in *Epicoene, The Devil Is an Ass,* and *A Tale of a Tub*. Yet Jonson did not neglect the City, presenting its merchants, craftsmen, and officials in *Eastward Ho, Every Man in His Humour,* and *The Magnetic Lady*, and some of its lower ranks in *Bartholomew Fair* and *The Alchemist*.

Topographically and socially, there are a few parts of London and aspects of life therein not mentioned by Jonson. Three rapidly expanding neighborhoods just north of the City wall (near the former religious foundations

29. Other examples of topographical details which provide verisimilitude are included in the following entries: Bear Tavern, Three Cranes in the Vintry (in *Epicoene*); Bermudas, Bucklersbury, Cow Lane, Harrow on the Hill, Newgate Market, Pannier Alley, Streights, and Uxbridge (*Bartholomew Fair*); London Wall (*Every Man In*); and King's Head Tavern (*The Magnetic Lady*).

30. C. L. Kingsford, in his edition of Stow's *Survey*, pp. xxxix–xli, discusses the strengths and weaknesses in Stow's description of London at the opening of the seventeenth century.

at Clerkenwell, the Charterhouse, and St. John's Priory) are not directly cited in any of Jonson's works.[31] South of the river, Jonson does not refer to the hamlet of Newington Butts, about a mile south of London Bridge, which had a theater in the late sixteenth century. Neither does he mention two features of this area to which Shakespeare, however, did allude: the Elephant and Castle Inn and St. George's Field.[32] As mentioned earlier, Jonson's London dramas tend to stress the mobile strata of society; therefore he makes few references (and these are found mainly in his encomiastic and occasional poems) to the London homes of the comfortably rich nobility. Also, as one would expect, when Jonson refers to the lowest levels of society, the lives of beggars, inept petty rogues, and laborers are not his chief concerns. Rather, such folk usually are exploited as foils, victims, and object lessons by the wits, gulls, and social climbers who dominate the plays.

The thoughtful employment of local topographical references is certainly a significant aspect of Jonson's creativity, even if numerical strength alone is considered. Jonson's London dramas average about twenty-nine different references apiece to places within London and its environs. *Bartholomew Fair* and *The Devil Is an Ass* have approximately forty-six and forty-four different references respectively. *The Magnetic Lady* and *The New Inn* bring up the rear with fifteen and twelve. The Italianate *Volpone* contains nine references to areas in London, and the nonlocalized *Poetaster* and *Cynthia's Revels* four and two respectively.[33]

31.. Chapter 8 in Norman G. Brett-James, *The Growth of Stuart London* (London: George Allen & Unwin, 1935), is devoted to population growth in this locale during the first half of the seventeenth century. The influx of upper and middle-class residents helped to reduce crime in what was once quite a disreputable area, and by the Restoration many "distinguished people . . . especially City magnates" (p. 218) lived there. Although Jonson does not mention this area in regard to its changing social composition, his references to the prostitutes of Turnbull Street and Pict-Hatch show his awareness of the "traditional" associations of one part of the locale directly north of the old municipal wall.

32. In *Twelfth Night* Antonio tells Sebastian that good lodgings are to be had "in the south suburbs, at the Elephant" (3.4.39), and later Sebastian complains about not meeting Antonio there (4.3.5). In *2 Henry IV* St. George's Field is where, in their younger days, Falstaff and Shallow spent one night in a windmill (3.2.207).

33. These totals include references to specific locales within larger areas, e.g., the Cloisters, Cloth Quarter, Pie Corner, and Court of Pie-Powders (all within or close to Smithfield in *Bartholomew Fair*) or the Middle Aisle, Lollards' Tower, Duke Humphrey's Tomb, and Paul's Churchyard (parts of St. Paul's in *The Staple of News*). The play with the greatest overall number of London references is *A Tale of a Tub* with one hundred twenty-seven, including twenty-two mentions of "Pancras" or "Pancridge" (St. Pancras). Repetition of relatively few locales accounts for the high total. Totten[ham] Court has nineteen; Finsbury, Kentish Town, and Kilburn all twelve; and Paddington (including its Red Lion Inn) nine references. The play names twenty-three different places around London, somewhat below the average of twenty-nine.

Much also may be learned—or corroborated—by a survey of Jonson's most frequently mentioned references. The places which appear most often in different contexts include the Exchanges (both Royal and New), Cheapside, St. Paul's, Moorfields, the Tower of London, the Strand, the Inns of Court, Blackfriars, Smithfield, Bankside, the Thames, the Counters, Newgate Prison, and Tyburn. This group clearly reflects Jonson's creative interests. As a sincere satirist, he was concerned with exposing greed, hypocrisy, and undue pride. He consistently depicted persons either hoping for social advancement through accepted methods or those preferring to enrich themselves by means of usually illegal ingenuity, wit, or trickery. Those areas most referred to—containing important business institutions, places for social display, locales which encouraged the presence of rogues, habitats of witty youths, and entertainment areas where some made sport and others were made sport of—accurately illustrate the milieu of Jonson's London dramas and a number of his poems, masques, and entertainments.

The Dictionary

A

ALDGATE. One of the seven main gates in the old City wall, located between the Tower of London and Bishopsgate.

According to S (p. 10), Aldgate was pulled down in 1606. Re-erected in 1609, it featured figures of Peace and Charity on the east front, copied from Roman coins discovered during excavations on this site. H&S (10:7) furnish a description from Munday and Dyson's edition of Stow's *Survey* (1633, p. 122): "To grace each side of the Gate, are set two feminine personages, the one Southward, appearing to be Peace, with a silver Dove upon her one hand, and a guilded wreath or garland on the other. On the North side standeth Charity, with a child at her breast, and another led in her hand: Implying (as I conceive) that where Peace, and love or Charity, do prosper, and are truly embraced, that Citie shall be for ever blessed." Also on the east facade of Aldgate was placed a statue of King James I "in gilt armour, with a golden lion, and a chained unicorn, both couchant at his feet."[1]

Truewit, *Epic*, in arguing that gentlemen ought not to approach their ladies until they have finished primping, makes a City comparison: "How long did the canvas hang afore *Ald-gate*? were the people suffer'd to see the cities *Love*, and *Charitie*, while they were rude stone, before they were painted, and burnish'd?" (1.1.122–25). This passage may be a subtle thrust at the Ladies Collegiates, who soon reveal themselves as quite the opposite of "the cities *Love*, and *Charitie*."

ALMONRY, GREAT, AND LITTLE. Almshouses erected just west of Westminster Abbey by Henry VII and his mother, Lady Margaret Beaufort.

S (p. 13) informs us that the Great Almonry lay on an east-west axis and had an entrance from the Dean's Yard of the Abbey. The Little Almonry stood at the east end of its sister institution and ran southward; here Caxton set up the first printing press in England. Stow (2:123) states that the Little Almonry "is now turned into lodgings for the singing men of the colledge."

Gossip Tatle, *SN*, deprecates the news offered by the Staple and says that some of the better information to which she has access is "*all the newes of* Tutle-*street* [q.v.], *and both the* Alm'ries" (third intermeane, ll. 20–21). As Kingsford has pointed out (2:374), this portion of the play provides an

---

1. Thomas Allen, *The History and Antiquities of the Cities of London, Westminster, and Southwark*, 2nd ed., 4 vols. (London: Virtue, 1839), 3:87.

intimate topographical glimpse of the neighborhood where Jonson resided during his later years. It is logical to assume that a contemporary audience, aware of current gossip about this area, would find Jonson's highly specific references quite amusing.

ANNIS CLEARE, SPRING OF. A spring just north of the City in Hoxton, near the present intersection of Old Street and Paul Street.

H&S (10:196) cite Stow (1598, p. 14), who discusses the "speciall wels, in the Suburbes sweete, wholesome, and cleare, amongst which *Holywel, Clarkes wel,* & *Clementes wel*, are most famous and frequented by Schollers, and youths of the City. . . . Somewhat North from *Holywell* is one other, well curbed square with stone, and is called *Dame Annis the cleare*." H&S here also refer the reader to R. Johnson, *The Pleasant Walkes of Moore-fields* (1607, sig. B2ᵛ), who states that this spring was named after a rich alderman's widow who drowned herself after her second husband, "a riotous Courtier," spent all her wealth and deserted her.

In *BF* Captain Whit tries to promote Ursula's menu of roast pig by promising Dame Purecraft and Win, "Tou shalt ha' de cleane side o' de table-clot and di glass vash'd with phatersh of Dame *Annesh Cleare*" (3.2.64–66). Both women, especially the widowed Dame Purecraft, would do well to heed the monitory associations of this reference, as Captain Whit's intentions are anything but honorable.

ARCHES, COURT OF. The ecclesiastic appeals court for the province of Canterbury.

This court's name, declares S (p. 27), results from its sitting in the church of St. Mary de Arquebus, later known as Bow Church (q.v.) in Cheapside. Stow (1:253–54) briefly explains this etymology in his discussion of Bow Church. This court, as W&C (1:508) have noted, was the highest judicial body attached to this important province.

The Stage-keeper in the induction to *BF* states that Littlewit "playes one o' the *Arches*, that dwels about the *Hospitall*" (ll. 5–6). This makes Littlewit similar to Justice Overdo, a person in a responsible position who is satirized because of his shortcomings in perceptiveness. The "Hospitall" referred to could be either St. Bartholomew's (q.v.) or Christ's Hospital, a school located between Bow Church and Bartholomew Fair at Smithfield. (See the Newgate Market entry for evidence suggesting the latter location as Littlewit's home neighborhood.)

ARTILLERY YARD. The exercise ground of the Honourable Artillery Company, then located in Teasel Close (now Artillery Lane), east of Bishopsgate Street Without.

This site was used also by the City Trainband (a home guard originally raised against the Spanish invasion) and by the Tower of London gunners. As S (pp. 3 1–3 2) has shown, dramatists often poked fun at its frequenters. In *The White Devil* the "dead" Flamineo arises, mocking his would-be assassins, "How cunning you were to discharge! Do you practice at the Artillery-yard?" (5.6.1 60–6 1). Shirley's *The Witty Fair One* has a reference to "a spruce captain . . . that never saw service beyond Finsbury [q.v.], or the Artillery-garden" (5.1). H&S (9:378) supply details about the Honourable Artillery Company, which was first incorporated in 1507 and reorganized in 1610–11. In 1641 the company moved farther north, leasing the grounds in City Road which it occupies today. H&S (10:56) also point out a discussion of the company's 1610 revival in Edmund Howes's continuation of Stow's *Annales* (1631, p. 995). Finally, they comment (1 1:8 1–82) that Jonson's poem, *Und* 44, cited below, is "in the spirit of Horace's attacks on national degeneracy" and that "Jonson's main criticism is levelled at the aristocracy who had given up the use of arms. So national defense was left to amateur bodies like the Artillery Company." H&S follow with evidence for dating this poem 1625 or 1626.

Jonson thus addresses the Artillery Yard in *Und* 44, "Well, I say, thrive, thrive brave Artillerie yard, / Thou Seed-plot of the warre, that hast not spar'd / Powder, or paper, to bring up the youth / Of *London*, in the Militarie truth" (ll. 23–26). In *Alch* Face compares Subtle's pockmarked complexion to "poulder-cornes [grains of powder], shot, at th'*artillerie-yard*" (1.1.31). In *EMI* when Stephen protests that he is not a soldier, Wellbred replies, "As I remember your name is entred in the artillerie garden?" (3.5.149–50). In the epilogue to *CHM* Father Christmas sings, *"Nor doe you thinke their legges is all / the commendation of my Sons, / For at the Artillery-Garden they shall / as well (forsooth) use their Guns"* (ll. 275–78). This masque chiefly consists of a procession of Londoners singing and dancing in praise of the holiday season. The dates of the last two references (1610–16) show how Jonson's allusions capitalized on public awareness of the Artillery Company's activities after its early seventeenth-century resurgence.

B

BANKSIDE. The district bordering the south bank of the Thames from Southwark Cathedral westward to the present Blackfriars Bridge.

Because it was outside City jurisdiction, Bankside possessed many disreputable haunts, which to Londoners of strict conscience included theaters.[1] In 1616 an east–west survey of this region would have included the bishop of Winchester's palace and outbuildings, the Clink Prison, the Globe and Hope theaters (q.v.), the Stews (q.v.) or Bordello, and the manor of Paris Garden (q.v.) containing the decaying Swan Theater. S (p. 44) provides dramatic evidence attesting to the flourishing of fortune tellers and other quacks on the Bankside. In Heywood's *The Wise Woman of Hogsden* "Mother *Phillips* of the *Banke-side*, for the weaknesse of the backe" is recommended, as is also "Mistris *Mary* on the *Banke-side* . . . for recting a Figure" (2.1). H&S (9:475) point out that this region's name results from its originally being a row of dwellings on a bank or dike fronting a swamp and also (11:79) that Paris Garden Stairs was the favorite landing spot for boatmen ferrying merrymakers over to Bankside.

Bankside's position relative to the river has changed little—in contrast to the large body of reclaimed land on the Thames's north bank.[2] The bishops of Winchester were granted extensive Bankside lands early in the twelfth century. Most of this property was alienated fairly soon after, but the bishopric retained possession of a plot at the river end of the Bear Gardens (q.v.) and of a triangular piece of land at the west end of the Clink. Winchester House, the London residence of these bishops, was a place of much importance until the mid-sixteenth century, after which references to it are scarce. In 1632 it was turned into a prison with Jonson's friend Sir Kenelm Digby as one of its inmates. The nearby Clink Prison was a notoriously unpleasant place. In 1642 it was described as lying under part of Winchester House and probably was below high-water level. North of

1. Like most of Southwark, the Bankside theater district was under the jurisdiction of the Surrey county justices. David Johnson, *Southwark and the City* (London: Oxford University Press, 1969), pp. 224–26, states that these magistrates were notoriously lax in enforcing municipal or parliamentary laws; only an ordinance passed by the Privy Council could spur the Surrey justices to action. The council was "the only body able to exercise a general supervision and it intervened whenever problems [the plague, masterless men, Sabbath play productions] became too big for one local authority to deal with" (p. 225).

2. All information in this paragraph is from Sir Howard Roberts and Walter H. Godfrey, eds., *Bankside*, Survey of London, 22 (London: London County Council, 1950), pp. 45–58.

the Clink lay the river and to the west the common sewer. The prison's approximate position today would be just south of Clink Street and west of Stoney Street. Here were incarcerated victims of religious persecutions under Mary and Elizabeth. Near the start of the seventeenth century it was termed by Stow (2:55–56) as a prison "for such as should brabble, frey, or breake the Peace on the saide banke, or in the Brothell houses." In 1720 Stow's continuator, John Strype, declared the Clink "of late years of little or no account."

Jonson utilizes many of the above associations of the Bankside locale in his works. In *EMO* a character comments about Puntarvolo's poisoned dog, "Mary, how, or by whom, that's left for some cunning woman here o' the *Banke-side* to resolve" (5.5.19–21). In *Epic* Mistris Otter threatens to banish her husband over to Bankside in custody of the chief bearkeeper (3.1.28–30). The "Articles of Agreement" discussed in the induction to *BF* refer to one of the contracted parties as "the *Spectators* or *Hearers*, at the *Hope* on the Bankeside" (ll. 64–65). Damon and Pythias, the chief characters in the hilarious puppet show at the close of *BF*, are introduced as "two faithfull friends o' the Bankeside" (5.3.9–10). This play-within-a-play parodies the Hero and Leander and the Damon and Pythias stories by having these classical figures act out a debased version of a love and friendship legend in the streets and taverns of Jonson's London. Hero is "a wench o' the *Banke-side*" (5.3.124; 5.4.153), and the Bankside district also serves as the modern counterpart of Sestos (5.4.121). *Epig* 133, "On the Famous Voyage," includes an expository detail referring to the frequent floods along Bankside: "It was the day, what time the powerfull *Moone* / Makes the poore *Banck-side* creature wet it' shoone" (ll. 29–30). In *Und* 43, "An Execration upon Vulcan," the poet declares, "Well fare the wise-men yet, on the *Banckside*, / My friends, the *Watermen*" (ll. 123–24). In this poem the Globe Theater is praised as "the Glory of the *Banke*" (l. 132), and venereal disease is labeled "the *Winchestrian* Goose / Bred on the *Banck*" (ll. 142–43).

BARNET. A village on the Great North Road about twelve miles north of London.

Barnet's importance as a coaching stop is reflected in drama of this period. Many of the dramatic references furnished by S (p. 48) suggest that travelers came to this village for amorous purposes. In Massinger's *The City Madam* Luke describes "the raptures of being hurried in a coach to Brainford [q.v.], Staines [q.v.], or Barnet" (2.1.107–8). Dalavill in Thomas Heywood's *The English Traveller* refers to Barnet as "a place of great resort" (3.1). H&S (10:299–300) provide a quotation from *Sir Giles Goosecap* (1.3) with similar connotations.

All of the action of *NI* takes place at a hostelry in Barnet, a location which Jonson reiterates several times in the play (persons, l. 4; argument, l. 30; and 1.2.39). Later it is also revealed that Barnet is one of the towns where the tailor Stuffe and his wife display themselves wearing clothes ordered by their customers (4.3.70–72).

BARTHOLOMEW FAIR. England's most famous fair, held until 1855 on every August 24 west of the City in the open space known as Smithfield.

The fair was originally instituted as a cloth fair and in medieval times was England's chief cloth mart. Dramatists found the fair's activities useful for making colorful comparisons and illustrations, as S (pp. 48–49) has amply shown. In *2 Henry IV* Doll Tearsheet calls Falstaff "Thou little tidy Bartholomew Boar pig" (2.4.250), while in Heywood's *Challenge for Beauty* the Clown says that Hellena is so fair "that all *Bartholmew*-fayre could not match her againe" (2.1). Finally, in Dekker and Middleton's *The Roaring Girl*, a usurer is described as ready to flay off his father's skin "and sell it to cover drummes for children at Bartholmew faire" (3.3.151–52).

The fair spread over a relatively large area, ranging from near Christ Church and Newgate in the south to the suburbs of the City in the northwest.[3] Jonson reminds his audience of this wide range through several references in *BF*. Gingerbread and trinkets were sold in the cloisters of Christ Church, and H&S (10:182) cite some contemporary descriptions of this practice. More centrally located was the Cloth Quarter, a line of booths running along the north wall of the church of St. Bartholomew the Great. As H&S (10:173–74) have noted, there is a present-day reminder of this custom in the street named Cloth Fair, which runs east from Smithfield. Offenses committed during the fair were adjudicated at the special Court of Pie-powders. This term, as H&S (10:185–86) point out, is a corruption of the French *pied pouldreux*, or "dusty feet." According to Edward Hatton, *A New View of London* (1708, 2:214), this court met to try offenses "committed contrary to the Proclamation at the Great Gate going into Cloth Fair." One of the statutes asserted "that no person sell any Bread, but if it keep the assize, and that it be good and wholesome for Man's Body, upon pain that will befall thereof."

Jonson's first reference to the fair comes in *EMO*, where Carlo tells Puntarvolo to stuff his dead dog with straw "as you see these dead monsters

---

3. The anonymous pamphlet, *Bartholomew Faire, or Variety of Fancies* (1641) states that the fair is "of so vast an extent, that it is contained in no less than four several parishes, namely, Christ Church, Great and Little Saint Bartholomews, and Saint Sepulchres." Parts of this pamphlet are reprinted in Henry Morley, *Memoirs of Bartholomew Fair* (London: Chatto and Windus, 1880), pp. 144–47; quote on p. 145.

at *Bartholmew* faire" (5.6.44). The action depicted in *BF* reflects the wide
range of events associated with the fair. We hear of "the buying of gingerbread i' the *Cloyster*" early in the play (1.4.37). The succulent *"Bartholmew*-pigge" is the object of both Win's gustatory longing and Rabbi Busy's
Puritan frenzy (1.6.43, 54–55), one of his many assaults on *Bartholmew*-
abhominations" (4.1.93). The Stage-keeper tells the audience that had
Dicky Tarlton lived to act in *BF*, they would have seen him "coozened i' the
Cloath-quarter, so finely" (induction, 1. 40). As H&S (10:173) have
noted, one of Tarlton's *Jests* dealt with just such a predicament. The
Stage-keeper also pokes fun at the playwright's skill, saying that "hee has
not convers'd with the *Bartholmew*-birds, as they say" (ll. 12–13). Although Leatherhead purports to sell the feathered variety (2.5.6), there
appears to be more profit in the tricks of such two-legged *"Bartholmew*-
birds" as Knockem and Whit (4.5.13–19). The fair jargon is criticized by
the straightlaced Waspe, who warns Cokes to "keepe your debauch, and
your fine *Bartholmew*-termes to yourselfe" (3.5.211–12). Ursula, the seller
of roast pig, is reminded to use her *"Bartholmew*-wit" to answer a jest
(2.5.102–3), while after Cokes buys a load of trivial merchandise, Grace
gives thanks for his *"Bartholmew*-wit" (3.4.166–67). Justice Overdo has
had the honor of sitting as a judge at the Court of Pie-powders (2.1.42–
43). Leatherhead twice threatens Joan Trash with arraignment at this court
for selling "stale bread, rotten egges, musty ginger, and dead honey"
(2.2.9–10, 22; 3.4.100–102). Ursula, of the "pig-quarter" (3.2.13),
has also appeared before it (2.2.72–74). Trouble-all, once an officer at this
court, was ejected from it by Overdo (4.1.54–55); later Knockem calls
Trouble-all "mad child o' the *Pye-pouldres*" (4.6.2). Ironically, because of
Overdo's desire to put down vice at the fair personally, the court cannot
meet (4.6.67–71).

BEAR GARDENS. Bankside (q.v.) resorts whose location may be ascertained by the map of Elizabethan London attributed to Ralph Agas and
by today's street named Bear Gardens Alley.

The popularity and respectability of bear and bull baiting are reflected in
official mandates such as the Privy Council order of 1591 prohibiting
Thursday performances of plays because they interfered with the bear
baitings. This was followed soon by a lord mayor's injunction blaming
actors for "reciting their plays to the great hurt and destruction of the game
of bear-baiting." S (pp. 51–52), who gives the above information, also
notes that in Richard Brathwaite's *Barnabee's Journal* (p. 71), the Bear
Gardens rank as one of the seven best sights of London. H&S (9:582) direct
the reader to the "Agas" map and comment that the bears were fed with offal
sent from Newgate and Eastcheap markets. Dramatists of Jonson's time

found the Bear Gardens a rich source of direct and allusive references. In
Beaumont and Fletcher's *The Scornful Lady*, a character is advised, "Tye
your She Otter up . . . / She stinkes worse then a beare-bayting"
(4.1.326–27).

It has been determined that the Bear Gardens were in the Liberty of the
Clink and not in Paris Garden Manor (q.v.), where literary allusions have
often placed them.[4] Modern historians suggest that these two places
became linked through "transference" in colloquial usage. There was a
gaming and drinking resort at Paris Garden to the west of the landing spot
by this name, and as the bear gardens to the east became more popular, the
manor's name came to designate them as well. A detailed account of
sporting activities at the Bear Gardens in 1599 is furnished by the German
traveler Paul Hentzner.[5] Philip Henslowe was a major property owner in
this region, and in 1604 he obtained the office of master of the bears and
bulls. Two years later he contracted with Peter Street to renovate the
existing rings for £65. In 1613 these were demolished, and the Hope arena
(q.v.) was erected to replace them.

Jonson, in "To the Reader," *Poet*, declares about bad audiences "I can
affoord them leave, to erre so still: / And, like the barking students of
Beares-Colledge, / To swallow up the garbadge of the time" (ll. 44–46). As
H&S (9:582) have noted, the "barking students" were the dogs set on the
bulls or bears. We are told that Captain Tom Otter in *Epic* "has beene a
great man at the beare-garden in his time: and from that subtle sport, has
tane the witty denomination of his chiefe carousing cups" (2.6.60–62).
After being told of some animal metamorphoses from the classics, Otter
exults, "I will have these stories painted i' the beare-garden, *ex Ovidii
metamorphosi*" (3.3.130–32). In response to the captain's defense of his
bull, bear, and horse as *"in rerum natura,"* Mrs. Otter vows to *"na-ture* 'hem
over to *Paris* garden, and *na-ture* you thether too, if you pronounce 'hem
againe" (3.1.16–18). In *Epig* 133, "On the Famous Voyage," the poet
declares, "The meate-boate of Beares colledge, *Paris Garden*, / Stunke not so
ill" (ll. 117–18). In *Und* 43 "An Execration upon Vulcan," the burning of
the Globe Theater (q.v.) was an ominous "threatning to the beares; / And
that accursed ground, the *Parish-Garden*" (ll. 146–47). These last three
quotations are examples of the habit of "transference" discussed above.
Similar to the invective which the poet hurled at imperceptive audiences in
Poet, cited earlier, is the Boy's declaration to Probee and Damplay in the
second chorus of *ML*, "You are fitter *Spectators* for the *Beares*, then us, or the
Puppets" (ll. 71–72).

4. Roberts and Godfrey, *Bankside*, p. 66.
5. William B. Rye, ed., *England as Seen by Foreigners in the Days of Queen Elizabeth and
James the First* (London: J. R. Smith, 1865), pp. 215–16.

BEAR TAVERN. Properly the Bear at the Bridgefoot, a tavern located in Southwark just below Old London Bridge.

As S (p. 51) has noted, it is mentioned as a meeting spot in Shirley's *The Lady of Pleasure* (4.2), Field's *A Woman Is a Weather-cock* (3.4.35–36), and Brome's *A Mad Couple Well Matched* (2.1). Because of the narrowness of Old London Bridge, coaches from Dover and the south discharged their passengers on the Surrey side of the Thames. Twenty-three inns and taverns served the many travelers in this area.[6] When London Bridge was widened in the mid-eighteenth century, this tavern was demolished after a 450-year history. In Queen Elizabeth's time it was known as the White Bear and had its own landing stairs.[7] Among Jonson's contemporaries, Suckling was a frequenter of the Bear, where on one visit he wrote the prose piece, "The Wine Drinkers to the Water Drinkers." This tavern was noted for its dinners; some elaborate ones were served to the vestrymen of St. Olave's Church while Edward Alleyn was a parish officer there.[8] Pepys mentions over half a dozen occasions when he either visited the Bear or landed nearby.

In *Epic* Morose rants about how Dauphine's knighthood will bring him only heavy debt and insecurity: "When one of the foure-score hath brought it knighthood ten shillings, it knighthood shall go to the Cranes [q.v.], or the Beare at the *Bridge*-foot, and be drunk in feare" (2.5.112–15).

BELSIZE. A settlement directly southeast of Hampstead, about four and one-quarter miles northwest of St. Paul's.

During the Tudor-Stuart period the lands of Belsize Manor were held by Westminster Abbey, but the house was leased to secular tenants. Chief among these was William Waad, clerk of the Privy Council and special ambassador to Spain. A friend of the Cecils, Waad was knighted by James I and appointed lieutenant of the Tower. It is reported that Robert Carr, while plotting the Overbury murder, found the "integrity and uprightness of Sir William Waade too much inconvenient" and in 1613 had him removed from this post.[9]

Quite different is the bumbling member of the "Council of Finsbury"

6. Harold P. Clunn, *The Face of London*, rev. ed. (London: Spring Books, 1970), pp. 352–53.

7. Kenneth Rogers, *Signs and Taverns round about Old London Bridge, Including Gracechurch Street, Fenchurch Street, and Leadenhall Street*. (London: Homeland Association, 1937), p. 11.

8. Leopold Wagner, *London Inns and Taverns* (London: George Allen & Unwin, 1924), pp. 127–28.

9. Quoted by Anna Maxwell, *Hampstead: Its Historic Houses, Its Literary and Artistic Associations* (London: Clarke, 1912), p. 86. See Rosemary Manning, "Belsize," in Ian Norrie, ed., *The Heathside Book of Hampstead and Highgate*, (London: High Hill Books, 1962), pp. 63–64, for a full account of Waad's career.

(q.v.) who hails from Belsize in *TT*. He is one To-pan, a *"Tinker*, or *Mettal-man"* (persons, l.15; 1.1.38). During the play both he and Squire Tub remind the audience of his associations with this outlying locale (scene interloping, l. 25; 5.2.15).

BERMUDAS. The popular name for a warren of courts and lanes once found north of the west end of the Strand (q.v.), specifically near the bottom of St. Martin's Lane.

Both S (p. 58) and H&S (10:195) comment that this area was the haunt of whores, bullies, and vagrants. H&S write, "The old name of the Bermudas, 'The Isle of Devils,' from their being supposed to be the haunts of witches who kept sailors away by storms, no doubt suggested the transference of name to the London district." These editors also state that in 1829 this entire area was cleared for the creation of Trafalgar Square. A recent study of the Strand explains that the squalid "Bermudas" were formed by the making of narrow thoroughfares from inn-yards in order to facilitate travel between the Strand, Drury Lane, and the church of St. Martin in the Fields.[10]

In *BF* Justice Overdo declares, "Looke into any Angle o' the towne (the Streights [q.v.], or the *Bermuda's*) where the quarrelling lesson is read, and how doe they entertaine the time, but with bottle-ale, and tabacco?" (2.6.76–79). Everill, Meercraft's accomplice in *DA*, is usually found in this locale (2.1.142–44). Later in this play, Meercraft mentions how he once lost money on a loan: "There's an old debt of forty, I ga' my word / For one is runne away, to the *Bermudas*" (3.3.148–49). The poet in *Und* 13, "Epistle to Sir Edward Sackville," calls attention to the dangers posed by some London sharpers, "All as their prize, turne Pyrats here at Land, / Ha' their *Bermudas*, and their streights i' th' *Strand*" (ll. 81–82).

BET'LEM (BEDLAM) HOSPITAL. An institution for the insane, formerly part of the priory of St. Mary of Bethlehem, which came under City control in 1546 and in Jonson's time stood in Bishopsgate Without, near the present Liverpool Street Station.

To collect funds for Bedlam's maintenance, some of the patients were sent out begging with metal identification tags on their arms. S (pp. 53–54), notes this practice, as well as the fact that in Richard Brathwaite's *Barnabee's Journal* (p. 71), the "Bedlam poor" are mentioned as one of the seven main sights of London. In act 5, scene 2 of Dekker and Middleton's *1 Honest Whore*, set in Milan, a visit is paid to *"Bethlem Monasterie*," where various types of madmen are paraded forth. H&S (10:34–35) state that

10. Sir George Gater and E. P. Wheeler, eds., *The Strand*, Survey of London, 18 (London: London County Council, 1937), p. 124.

Bedlam was a popular promenade until 1770, deriving an annual revenue of £400 from visitors' admission fees. W&C (1:172) point out a passage in Dekker and Webster's *Northward Ho* where two gallants decide to spend the time while their horses are being saddled by going over to Bedlam to "see what Greekes are within" (4.3.30). A contemporary observer, Donald Lupton, wrote of Bedlam, "It seemes strange that any one shold recover here, the cryings, screechings, roarings, brawlings, shaking of chaines, swearings, frettings, chaffings, are so many, so hideous, so great, that they are able to drive a man that hath his wits, rather out of them."[11] Shakespeare's audience thus knew just what to expect from the disguised Edgar's behavior as a Bedlamite in *King Lear*.

In the Prologue to *Volp* the author vows to abstain from "such a deale of monstrous, and forc'd action: / As might make *Bet'lem* a faction" (ll. 25–26). In *Epic* the comparison of Morose's "wife" to "some innocent out of the hospitall" (3.4.39–40) is probably a Bedlam reference. Bedlam as a tourist sight figures several times in Jonson's plays. Lady Haughty in *Epic* tries to persuade Morose's "wife" to "goe with us, to *Bedlem*, to the *China* houses [q.v.], and to the *Exchange* [q.v.]" (4.3.24–25). According to Subtle in *Alch*, Dame Pliant will soon be able to have a splendid coach "to hurry her through *London*, to th'*Exchange*, / *Bet'lem*, the *China*-houses" (4.4.47–48). This trio of popular City resorts (China houses displayed wares from the newly-opened Oriental markets) is typically Jonsonian in the association of these places with the acquisitive urge, the stress upon the aberrational, and the interest in the exotic which are often present in his works. Also in *Alch* Face tells Mammon he may yet have the philosophers' stone "for some good penance . . . / A hundred pound to the boxe at *Bet'lem*" (4.5.85–86). Lovewit, unable to figure things out upon his return in this same play declares, "The world's turn'd *Bet'lem*" (5.3.54). In *BF* Littlewit discloses that Dame Purecraft "has been at *Bedlem* twice since, every day" to look for eligible suitors after she was thus counseled by a fortune-teller (1.2.54–55). Also in *BF* Waspe attributes Justice Overdo's sharpness to "being at *Bet'lem* yesterday" (1.5.25). Finally, Joan Trash cries, "A poxe of his *Bedlem* purity" (3.6.135) after Rabbi Busy overturns her gingerbread stall. In *DA* Pug mocks the frustrations of Ambler, whose clothes he has stolen, by commenting, "Your best song's *Thom. o' Bet'lem*" (5.2.35). This song was apparently new at the time of this play's composition. H&S (10:251) point out that the earliest known version is in a 1615 songbook in the British Museum (Add. MS. 24665). Shunfield, *SN*, taunts Picklock, "Have at you, then, Lawyer. / They say, there was one of

---

11. Donald Lupton, *London and the Countrey Carbonadoed and Quartred into Severall Characters* (London: N. Okes, 1632), pp. 75–76.

your coate in *Bet'lem*, lately" (4.1.11–12). In *ML* Doctor Rut advises Lady Loadstone, "Tye your Gossip up, / Or send her unto *Bet'lem*" (5.5.36–37).

BILLINGSGATE. An important landing place on the north bank of the Thames situated just east of London Bridge.

Billingsgate was the usual landing spot for travelers from the lower stretches of the Thames or from abroad and was well stocked with taverns. As S (p. 61) has shown, the noise from the fish market at Billingsgate was proverbial and often mentioned by dramatists of Jonson's day. H&S (10:36) quote Stow's description of Billingsgate (1:206), "a large Water-gate, Port or Harbrough for shippes and boates, commonly arriving there with fish, both fresh and salt, shell fishes, salt, Orenges, Onions . . . Rie, and graine of divers sorts for service of the Citie, and the parts of this Realme adjoyning." The market at Billingsgate and its convenient below-bridge location helped it become busier than Queenhithe (q.v.) as a shipping area by the Elizabethan era, as W&C (1:181) have pointed out.

Two features of this locale deserve special notice, for they are mentioned by Jonson: the Blue Anchor Tavern and the "Boss." The Blue Anchor once stood at 26 St. Mary at Hill, a site leveled for urban redevelopment in 1969. H&S (9:660) state that the tavern figured in Samuel Rowlands' *Diogines Lanthorne* (1607, sig. A4). The "Boss" has two possible meanings. H&S (10:655) cite Stow (1:208) on the presence in Jonson's era of a boss (projecting pipe of spring water) on the north side of Thames Street near Billingsgate. H&S also state (p. 656) that this term may also refer to a fat woman, and they cite a work printed by Wynken de Worde entitled *A Treatise of a Galaunt, with the Maryage of the Fayre Pusell the Bosse of Byllyngesgate unto London Stone*. These editors also remind us that in 1603 Henslowe paid for a play, *The Boss of Billingsgate,* of which no more is known.

Billingsgate is one of the London pleasure spots catalogued by Iniquity to Pug in *DA*, "Nay, boy, I wil bring thee to the Bawds, and the Roysters, / At *Belins-gate,* feasting with claret-wine, and oysters" (1.1.68–69). It also figures in a list of noisy places given in *Epic* (4.4.15–16). In *EH* Touchstone recounts that the would-be adventurer Sir Petronel Flash "tooke in fresh flesh [a usurer's wife] at *Belingsgate,* for his owne diet" (4.2.244). The Blue Anchor Tavern is the site of Sir Petronel's pre-voyage feast in this play (3.1.51; 3.2.204), and all of the third scene in act 3 takes place there. Curses are called down upon Billingsgate later (3.4.2–4) when the usurer Security finds out that his wife has run away after joining her lover at the Blue Anchor (4.1.80–82). According to the honest apprentice Goulding, Sir Petronel drank a good deal of wine at this tavern (where some of his followers were later arrested) before leaving for his ship moored farther down the Thames (4.2.85–86, 94). The ambiguous "Boss" is mentioned in *TV* when Eyes brags to Time about Chronomastix, "You'l see / That he ha's favourers, *Fame*, and great ones too. / That unctuous Bounty, is the Bosse of *Belinsgate*" (ll. 139–41).

BLACKFRIARS. The former precincts of the Dominican Order in London, located southwest of St. Paul's, north of present-day Queen Victoria Street and east of Water Lane.

Although its church was pulled down during the Dissolution, many other monastic buildings were converted into upper-class residences. The right of sanctuary retained at Blackfriars was certainly an asset to some of the inhabitants, who by Jacobean times displayed a wide variety of social, religious, and moral backgrounds. Some of the dramatic characters associated with this locale, as noted by S (p. 63) are the Essex gentleman Easy in Middleton's *Michaelmas Term* (4.3.30) and the rich widow pursued by Ancient Young in William Rowley's *A Match at Midnight* (1.1). A substantial number of Puritans resided in this area, and they, along with their common trade in feathers and plumes, or "feathermaking," were popular satiric targets. In the induction to Marston's *Malcontent*, the actor Sly hides his feather in his pocket because stage mockery of these artisans had become so prevalent that "Blackfriars [theater] hath almost [de]spoiled Blackfriars for feathers" (ll. 40–41). H&S (10:59) also comment on the popularity of this occupational taunt, citing the opening lines from Randolph's *The Muses Looking-Glasse* (1630), where two vendors at a London theatre are described as "Bird *a Featherman, and* Mrs Flowerdew *wife to an Haberdasher of small wares; the one having brought feathers to the Play-house, the other Pins and Looking-glasses; two of the sanctified fraternity of* Black-friers." These editors point out (10:232) that because Blackfriars was outside the jurisdiction of any City guild, it became in Jacobean times a painters' quarter, boasting as its residents Van Dyck, Cornelius Janssen, and the miniaturist Isaac Oliver. Among the socially eminent persons then living in Blackfriars, according to W&C (1:197), were Robert and Frances Carr, the earl and countess of Somerset; Jonson's friend Esmé Stuart, Lord Aubigny; and Lord Herbert of Cherbury.

Jonson makes use of most of the above associations, being especially sportive with gibes at Puritan activities in Blackfriars. Lovewit's house, the scene of the frenzied chicanery in *Alch*, is located in this area (1.1.17). In this play Doll Common insults Face by calling him "A whore-sonne . . . / Whom not a puritane, in black-*friers*, will trust / So much, as for a feather" (1.1.127–29). Later, Mammon tries to flatter Doll by saying "I'am pleas'd, the glorie of her sexe should know, / This nooke, here, of the *Friers*, is no climate / For her, to live obscurely in" (4.1.130–32). One of the puppets in *BF* rebukes Rabbi Busy by citing *"feather-makers i' the* Fryers, *that are o' your faction of faith"* (5.5.85–86) as examples of pride and vanity. In *LR* Robin Goodfellow tries to enter the court disguised as a "feather-maker of *black-fryers* . . . but they all made as light of mee, as of my feathers; and wonder'd how I could be a *Puritane*, being of so vaine a vocation" (ll. 98–102). Wordplay rather than satire is the basis of the local allusion in *Epic*, where Captain Otter gets in a long overdue rejoinder to his wife's nagging, as he declares that "all her teeth were made i' the Blacke-*Friers:* both her eye-brows i' the *Strand* [q.v.], and her haire in *Silver-street* [q.v.]" (4.2.92–94). As H&S (10:33) have noted, this comment puns on the literal denotations of these placenames. Besides stating that his spouse's teeth are of a coaly hue, Otter also informs us that her eyebrows are coarse and her hair gray and metallic in texture. In *DA* one of the urban pleasures suggested to Wittipol and Mrs. Fitzdottrel by her doltish husband is visiting the Blackfriars painters' studios (1.6.216–17). In *NI* the boastful Sir Glorious Tiptoe disparages modern fencing techniques, including Fly's reference to one *"Hieronymo* . . . / That plaid with Abbot *Antony*, i' the Friars, / And *Blinkin-sops* the bold" (2.5.82–84). H&S (10:311) note that this alludes to an Italian fencing teacher mentioned in George Silver's *Paradoxes of Defence* (1599, pp. 64, 72). The Blackfriars residence of Jonson's close friend Sir William Cavendish was the setting for an entertainment (H&S, 7:769–78) written by the poet for the christening of Cavendish's second son in May 1620. The entertainment, which portrays the behavior of local gossips attending the christening, closes with a semicomic beseechment "that still theire come gossips, the best in the land, / to make the Black Fryars compare with the Strande" (ll. 285–86).

The Blackfriars locale was also Jonson's home during some of his most productive years. The recusancy citation filed against him in 1606 (H&S, 1:220–23) places him in the parish of St. Anne, Blackfriars. Mark Eccles's research (H&S, 11:575) has discovered a child, "Beniamin Johnson sonne to Beniamin," baptized at St. Anne's, Blackfriars, on February 20, 1608, and buried there on November 18, 1611. As stated earlier, the mansion of Jonson's close friend Esmé Stuart, Lord Aubigny, stood in Blackfriars, and the poet's stay, dates as yet undetermined, with this gentleman further strengthened his ties with this part of London.[12] There are also two Exchequer receipts (H&S, 1:232–33) for payments to messengers summoning Jonson from Blackfriars to Whitehall in 1617. Finally, Jonson's residency in this area is made certain by the "Dedicatory Epistle" to *Volp*, which is dated "From my house in the Black-friars this 11 of February 1607."

12. H&S, 1:31n., favor the period between 1602–3 and 1607, noting, p. 56, that Aubigny married in the final year of this stretch. They also discuss with reservations, 11:576–77, Mark Eccles's idea that the dates of the protracted visit were 1613–18.

BLACKFRIARS THEATER. An important indoor theater of the period and the site of the performances of several Jonsonian plays.

Two playing areas and several acting companies figured in the history of this theater. A playhouse was adapted from several private chambers in 1576–77 by Richard Farrant to accommodate the Chapel Boys and Oxford's Boys between 1577 and 1584, at which time the area was reconverted into lodgings. The "Second Blackfriars" was built out of the Upper Frater Hall by James Burbage in 1596 and housed the Chapel Royal Boys and the Children of the Queen's Revels from 1600 to 1608. The King's Men commenced regular performances at this theater in the winter of 1609–10, continuing until 1642.[13]

According to their Quarto title pages, *The Case Is Altered, CR,* and *Poet* were acted at the Blackfriars near the turn of the seventeenth century by the children's companies; the same type of evidence also shows that the troublesome *EH* was also staged at this theater in 1605. A recent editor of *Alch*, F. H. Mares, believes that this play was first put on by the King's Men at the Blackfriars in 1610.[14] This site would have been very close to the play's own setting, a practice followed with *Epic* (see Whitefriars), *BF* (Hope), *TT* (Cockpit), *SN* and *DA* (both Blackfriars). In the last example, this theater was not far from *DA*'s setting near Lincoln's Inn (q.v.) and catered to a sophisticated, if not too select, audience. Thus Fitzdottrel's self-indulgent vow in this play to "goe to the *Black-fryers Play-house,* / Sit i' the view, salute all my acquaintance" (1.6.31–32) has special pertinence. This theater was also the scene for the premiere presentation of *NI* and was referred to in the prologue as the *"old house"* (l. 2). In October 1632, *ML* had a brief and troublesome run. The play was scathingly denounced by Jonson's enemy Alexander Gill (see the Bucklersbury entry) and apparently had only three performances. Even so, the play attracted enough attention to get the actors bound over before the Court of High Commission in Lambeth to answer charges of "uttring some prophane speeches in abuse of Scripture and wholly thinges, which they found penned, for them to act and playe."[15]

13. Richard Hosley, "A Reconstruction of the Second Blackfriars," in David Galloway, ed., *The Elizabethan Theatre—1* (Waterloo, Ontario: Macmillan of Canada, 1969), pp. 74–75. Virtually no dimension is left upspecified in this persuasive study. Gerald E. Bentley, *The Jacobean and Caroline Stage,* vol. 6, *Theatres* (Oxford: Clarendon Press, 1968), pp. 41–42, cites some manuscript notes found in a copy of Stow's *Annales* (1631) which state that this theater was pulled down in 1655.

14. *The Alchemist,* ed. F. H. Mares, The Revels Plays (Cambridge: Harvard University Press, 1967), p. lxv.

15. Cited by Bentley, *The Jacobean and Caroline Stage,* 6:26, from a 1632 letter from John Pory to Viscount Scudamore, transcribed by J. P. Feil in *Shakespeare Survey* 11 (1958):109.

BLACKWALL. Then a London suburb four miles east of St. Paul's on the north bank of the Thames at its junction with the River Lea.

Blackwall was a busy shipping center in Elizabethan times, well before it became one of England's major port facilities. In describing the economic expansion of Jonson's era, Norman G. Brett-James (*The Growth of Stuart London*, London: George Allen and Unwin, 1935, p. 188) declares, "Stepney [the environs of the City east of the Tower], with its harbors of Blackwall and Ratcliffe, became, with Deptford, the cradle of the Royal Navy." It was at Blackwall in 1614, notes Brett-James (p. 196), that the East India Company began building its dockyard. A famous early exploit associated with Blackwall was the voyage of the *Susan Constant*, the *Goodspeed*, and the *Discovery* from this area late in 1606, which resulted in the founding of the American colony at Jamestown.[16]

In *EH* the ship of the self-styled "Virginia voyager" Sir Petronel Flash is scheduled to depart from Blackwall (3.3.143–44), which lends a mock-heroic note to the play's action. The storm which almost drowns the adventurers occurs while they are on their way to board their ocean vessel after a bacchanalian celebration at the Blue Anchor Tavern at Billingsgate (q.v.). This is made clear in a comment by one of the group after having been washed ashore on the Isle of Dogs (q.v.): "Let us go to our ship at *Blackwall* and shift us" (4.1.190–91). Both the Isle of Dogs (q.v.) and Wapping (q.v.), where more of the voyagers are picked up, are west of Blackwall, between it and Billingsgate. Jonson's estimate of these sorry "sea dogs" is thus implicitly conveyed to the audience by having the pretentious expedition founder even before it could reach its starting point.

BOSOMES (BLOSSOMS) INN. A famous City hostelry which stood on the west side of Laurence Lane running north from Cheapside (q.v.).

It is a familiar fact of London history that this inn provided twenty beds and stabling for sixty horses when Charles V and his party visited London in 1522. *Maroccus Extaticus*, a late Tudor tract on Bankes and his famous horse Marocco, stated on the title page that it was "written by John Dando, the Wier-Drawer of Hadley, and Harrie Runt, Head Ostler of Besomes [*sic*] Inne," a detail noted by S (p. 69), who also locates the exact site of this inn at 23 Laurence Lane. H&S (10:564) quote Stow's description (1:270–71): "Among many fayre houses [in Laurence Lane], there is one large Inne for receipt of travelers, called Blossoms Inne, but corruptly Bosoms Inne, and

16. Hector Bolitho and Derek Peel, *Without the City Wall: An Adventure in London Street-Names, North of the River* (London: John Murray, 1952), p. 96. The authors also point out that American settlers carried over their London associations by designating the general area on the south bank of the James River "Surry" (without the "e") and a parish therein "Southwark."

hath to signe Saint *Laurence* the Deacon, in a Border of blossoms or flowers."
These editors also mention that Kingsford (2:332) states that its name
originated from the family name of Blosme. This inn continued in business
until the mid-nineteenth century.[17] Its site is occupied today by a modern
office building called Blossoms Inn House.

One of the merrymakers in *CHM* is "Tom *of Bosoms Inne*," who "*presenteth*
Mis-rule*" (ll. 196—97). In Jonson's time Laurence Lane was the chief
approach to the Guildhall from Cheapside. Thus the idea of a disorderly
figure hailing from a place so close to such a symbol of civic propriety as the
Guildhall is an ironic touch quite within our expectations of Jonson's
artistry.

BOW CHURCH. Officially St. Mary-le-bow or St. Mary de Arcubus, an
important City church recently restored in an adaptation of Wren's style,
which stands on the south side of Cheapside (q.v.). This church's name
derives from its being once built on stone arches or "bows."

Dramatic references to Bow Church, provided by S (p. 71), usually deal
with either its associations with the City or the loudness of its bells. In
Shirley's *Contention for Honour and Riches*, Gettings swears by a host of
London landmarks including "Cheapside-cross, and loud Bow-bell" (scene
3). In Middleton's *Anything for a Quiet Life*, a man says of his wife,
"Bow-bell is a still organ to her" (1.1.142). The same idea is expressed in
Rowley's *A Shoemaker a Gentleman* by another harassed husband who complains, "Sfoot, will Bow-bell never leave ringing?" (4.1.205). H&S
(9:652) furnish only brief comments on this institution, citing the *Itinerary*
of Fynes Moryson (1617, part 3, p. 53: "Londiners, and all within the
sound of Bow-bell, are in reproch called Cocknies." Stow declares (1:254)
that Bow Church "hath beene made more famous than any other Parish
Church of the whole Cittie, or suburbs" and recounts many noteworthy
events which occurred on its premises.

In *Epic* the "delicate steeple" of Bow Church is termed by Truewit as a
choice place from which Morose may jump (2.2.23—24). Gertrude, the
dissatisfied daughter of a goldsmith in *EH*, asks her suitor to "carry mee out
of the sent of *New-castle Coale*, and the hearing of *Boe-bell*" (1.2.123—24).
Just before this, Gertrude had put down her sister's sound moral advice as
bourgeois trivia by labeling her "*Boe-bell*" (l. 30). In her repentance the
chastened Gertrude tells how she had scorned her family and "would make a
mouth at the Citty, as I ridde through it; and stop mine eares at *Bow-bell*"
(5.5.167—69).

17. Wagner, *London Inns and Taverns*, p. 55. C. L. Kingsford, "Historical Notes on
Mediaeval London Houses," *London Topographical Record* 10 (1916):72, states that it
"existed as an inn at least as late as 1855."

BOWLING ALLEY. A recreative spot which, judging from the context of its Jonsonian references, was located in Westminster.

S (p. 72) furnishes six Shakespearean references to bowling, plus information on its early history in London. James I authorized licenses to be issued for twenty-four alleys in the City and Westminster, four in Southwark, one in St. Katherine's, one in Shoreditch, and two in Lambeth. Critics such as Stephen Gosson (*School of Abuse*, 1579, p. 35) argued that "common bowling allyes are privy mothes, that eate uppe the credite of many idle citizens," and even the moderate Earle in *Micro-cosmographie* (p. 41) declared that a bowling alley "is the place where there are three things throwne away beside Bowls, to wit, time, money, and curses." H&S (10:281) state that Bowling Street, leading from the Dean's Yard to Tufton Street near the Abbey, occupies the site of Jonson's reference below. According to current maps, however, Tufton Street has been extended northward, covering the course of Bowling Street. Helping to locate this area in Jonson's time is a 1565 entry in the overseer's books of the parish of St. Margaret, Westminster, cited by W&C (1:232). Here is listed "the Myll next to Bowling Alley." This is very likely the "Mill" which is mentioned in the same context as Jonson's reference to the "bowling alley" below. For further details, see the Mill entry.

During the third intermeane in *SN*, Gossip Mirth includes "*what matches were made in the* bowling-Alley" (l. 26) as a juicy morsel of news. The above location of a bowling alley in Westminster is pertinent because it is in keeping with the other sources of newsworthy information in this scene, which are all, as Kingsford has noted (2:374), close together in Westminster. Furthermore, they are all in that part of Westminster with which one may associate Jonson's residence during his later years. All of the places catalogued by Mirth are quite near his rooms in the dwelling between St. Margaret's Church and Henry VII's Chapel, as described by H&S (11:576) from Abbey records.

BRAINFORD (BRENTFORD). A village at the junction of the Brent and Thames rivers ten miles west of St. Paul's.

In Tudor-Stuart drama, as S (p. 73) has shown, Brentford is often mentioned as a place for assignations. In Massinger's *The City Madam* Luke pictures to Goldwire "the raptures of being hurried in a coach to Brainford, Staines [q.v.], or Barnet [q.v.]" (2.1.107–8) with a complaisant companion. In Dekker and Middleton's *The Roaring Girl* a gallant tells a City wife that her husband that morning went "in a boate with a tilt [cover] over it, to the three pidgions at *Brainford*, and his puncke [harlot] with him" (4.2.24–25). According to James Wright (*Historia Histrionica*, 1699, p. 10), John Lowin (1576–1653), an actor and manager with the Chamberlain's / King's Men, spent his last years as innkeeper of the Three Pigeons.

Jonson keeps up this town's questionable reputation in *Alch* when Subtle tells Doll they can give Face the slip by going upriver to Brainford (5.4.76–77), later promising her, "Wee'll tickle it at the *pigeons,* / When we have all" (ll. 89–90). The poet's target in *Epig* 129, "To Mime," apes others in their trips to "*Braynford, Hackney* [q.v.], *Bow* [see Stratford atte Bow]" (l. 4). If Jonson had Inigo Jones in mind here, as H&S (11:28) have suggested, these allusions to his suburban excursions are certainly not complimentary.

BREAD STREET. A City thoroughfare which in Jonson's day ran south from Cheapside to Old Fish Street; today it ends at Queen Victoria Street.

Stow declares (1:344) that Bread Street was "so called of bread in olde time there sold," and (p. 346) that it "is now wholy inhabited by rich Marchants, and divers faire Innes bee there, for good receipt of Carriers, and other travellers to the city." Milton was born in 1608 near the north end of Bread Street, where his father was a scrivener at the sign of the Spread Eagle. Several important taverns, notably the Mermaid (q.v.), patronized by Jonson stood here. Until fairly recently, however, scholars such as S (p. 74) and H&S (10:178) were mistaken in their designation of the portion of Bread Street where this rendezvous stood. The meticulous research of Kenneth Rogers has fixed the site of the Mermaid associated with Jonson's circle in the lower part of Bread Street, between its eastern side and Friday Street, the next street to the west.[18]

The heroes of *Epig* 133, "On the Famous Voyage," made merry "at *Bread-streets* Mermaid" (l. 37) before setting out on their "epic" adventure of rowing up the Fleet Ditch (q.v.). The site fixed by Rogers lay much closer to the river than the previously supposed site and thus would be most appropriate to the events occurring in this poem. In 1616 Thomas Coryat addressed part of his *Greeting from the Court of the Great Mogul* to the "Sireniacal Gentlemen, that meet the first Fridaie of every Moneth, at . . . the Mere-Maide in Bread-streete" (p. 37) and sent specific greetings to Jonson and to such mutual friends as Sir Robert Cotton, Inigo Jones, Sir Richard Martin, John Donne, and Hugh Holland (pp. 35, 44–46).

BRIDEWELL. A prison and workhouse for idle persons and women of ill repute located on the west side of the Fleet Ditch (q.v.) near where it discharged into the Thames. Today the site is marked by Bridewell Place, a

18. See the Mermaid entry for a discussion of Rogers's findings in *The Mermaid and Mitre Taverns in Old London* (London: Homeland Association, 1928), pp. 9–14.

thoroughfare off the west side of New Bridge Street approaching Blackfriars Bridge.

Both S (p. 76) and H&S (9:671) point out that Bridewell was originally a palace occupied by Cardinal Wolsey and later by Henry VIII, who enlarged it and often held court there. In 1553 Edward VI gave Bridewell to the City. Its shortcomings as a reformatory are illustrated by such comments as Bungler's in Middleton's *Your Five Gallants:* "And as for Bridewell, that will but make him worse; 'a will learn more knavery there in one week than will furnish him and his heirs for a hundred year" (3.5.137–39). Along the same lines is a comment from Brome's *The Northern Lass*, "If she be Mistris of her Art, there is no deceit among Tradesmen . . . nor whore out of Bridewell" (3.3). Stow provides an ample discussion of this institution (2:43–45) with Kingsford (2:363–64) believing that Dekker's vivid description of Bridewell in *2 Honest Whore* is drawn from this historian. Bridewell became a source of serious concern to citizens because of the many vagrants who settled in London under pretext of seeking asylum there, according to W&C (1:241). During the seventeenth century, declares K (p. 48), religious fanatics began to be sent to Bridewell, and after a whipping post and ducking stool were installed in 1633, the weekly punishments there became popular attractions.

In *EMI* Cob avers in an exasperating moment, "Then, I am a vagabond, and fitter for *Bride-well*" (3.6.37). Goulding, the steadfast apprentice in *EH*, asks the constable why the errant Sir Petronel and his cohorts are not promptly carried to Bridewell "according to your order" (4.2.190–91). In *BF* Ursula taunts Punk-Alice with being lately whipped at Bridewell (4.5.78–79). The adventurers in *Epig* 133, "On the Famous Voyage," embark at Bridewell Dock (ll.41–42) in their "epic" voyage up the Fleet Ditch. As Jonson declares in this poem, Bridewell serves as an appropriate counterpart to Avernus, the volcanic lake near Naples long regarded as the entrance to the infernal regions.

BUCKLERSBURY. A city street running southeast from Cheapside (q.v.), near Poultry, to Walbrook.

Both S (p. 82) and H&S (10:183) refer to Stow's account in the 1598 edition of his *Survey* (p. 209): "This whole streete called Bucklesbury on both the sides throughout, is possessed of Grocers and Apothecaries towards the west end thereof." Dekker reinforced these associations in *The Wonderfull Yeare* (*Non-Dramatic Works*, 1:112), where during the plague every street looked "like Bucklersbury for poore *Methridatum* and *Dragon-water* were bort [brought] in every corner." In Dekker and Webster's *Westward Ho* a servant is ordered to "go into Bucklers-bury and fetch me two ounces of preserved *Melounes*" (1.2.39–40). Bucklersbury's medieval associations with grocers and apothecaries were strengthened by England's increased commerce during the Renaissance, which resulted in the import of new medicinal products and the formation of the Society of Apothecaries in 1618.[19] Because apothecaries also sold tobacco, Jonson's reference to Bucklersbury in *BF* below is appropriate.

In *Epig* 3, "To My Booke-seller," Jonson directs that his unpopular work be sent here (ll. 11.12). As H&S (11.2) have pointed out, it would be of practical value in Bucklersbury—for wrapping groceries. A similar barb is directed at Jonson by Alexander Gill in "Uppon Ben Jonsons Magnettick Ladye" (H&S, 11:346–48). In this poem Jonson's adversary remarks, "From Bucklers Burye lett ytt not be barde,/But thincke nott of Ducke lane or Paules Churchyarde" (ll. 49–50). The latter places were printers' quarters. In *BF* Waspe laments Cokes's escapades, declaring "I thought he would ha' runne madde o' the blacke boy in *Bucklers-bury*, that takes the scurvy, roguy *tobacco*, there" (1.4.116–18). With the increasing trade

Guildhall Library

The "Black Boy" was a common London apothecaries'
and tobacconists' sign.

19. S. R. Hunt, "Bucklersbury and the Merchant-Venturers," *Pharmaceutical Journal*, 24 December 1966, pp. 660–61.

with Africa and the Indies, the "blackamoor's head" grew familiar as a shop sign for dealers in goods from these regions. Seventeenth-century trade tokens depicting Negro heads still exist, and in 1897 there was yet a stone sign over a doorway at 13 Clare Street not far from Covent Garden, carved in relief displaying two Negroes' heads facing each other, separated by the date 1715 and the initials W^{s}M.[20]

BUDGE ROW. A City street in Jonson's time running from Watling Street south to Cannon Street. Today it is reduced to a pedestrian walkway connecting Queen Victoria Street with Cannon Street, alongside Bucklersbury House.

"Budge" is lambskin dressed with the fur outward; thus the street is named for the furriers who worked there. S (pp. 82–83) states that an act of 1365 directed that all pelterers "shall dwell in Walebrooke, Cornehulle, and Bogerow." H&S (10:178) cite Stow (1598, p. 200), whose few comments chiefly deal with the skinners doing business in this street.

In *BF* John Littlewit marvels at his wife's modesty; if she had her way, she would be satisfied with a hat of "rough countrey Beaver, with a copper-band, like the Conney-skinne woman of *Budge*-row" (1.1.21–22).

BURDELLO. The collection of brothels on Bankside, more commonly known as the "Stews." See the latter entry for full details.

In *EMI* some of the allusions in Wellbred's letter give rise to the elder Knowell's caustic comments on its origin: "From the *Burdello*, it might come as well" (1.2.92). In *MA* Vangoose declares that current masque writers have no originality, that they are as common as "*de bench in de* Burdello" (l. 104).

---

20. Philip Norman, *London Signs and Inscriptions* (London: Elliot Stock, 1893), pp. 24–25. The Guildhall collection of tradesmen's bills, cards, and letterheads has several interesting examples of the "Black Boy" sign.

C

CANBURY (CANONBURY). In Jonson's time a manor in Islington (q.v.), once belonging to the priory of St. Bartholomew in Smithfield.

The manor became crown property after the Dissolution and later was rented by such inportant figures as the wealthy Lord Mayor Sir John Spencer. His daughter's elopement in 1599 with William Compton, later first earl of Northampton, was the cause célèbre of the close of the sixteenth century. Other important tenants of Canonbury in the early seventeenth century included Lord Keeper Egerton (1605), Francis Bacon (1616), and Sir Thomas Coventry (1625), all cited by W&C (1.325). A portion of the Canonbury manorial range still exists. Canonbury Tower, dating from the late sixteenth century, rises sixty-six feet above Canonbury Square southeast of the Highbury and Islington railway and Underground stations.[1]

Lady Tub, near the close of her perambulations northwest of the City in *TT*, tells her maid, "We will crosse ore to *Canbury*, in the interim; / And so make home" (3.8.20–21). This would require a detour to the east, as the Tub estate at Tottenham Court (q.v.) was situated south and a little west of Kentish Town, where this speech was delivered. The trip would have been a tiring way to end the afternoon, although affording Lady Tub added opportunities for gossip and display. One should be aware of the inaccuracy of S's comment (p. 96) on this reference. His statement, "She would go east to Canonbury and then strike the Kingsland Road, which goes right up [north] to Tottenham" would be valid only if the Tub estate were located at Tottenham High Cross (q.v.), a village in north Middlesex which has often been confused with Tottenham Court.

CHALCOT. As depicted on maps of the late seventeenth century and thereafter, a name given to two estates or hamlets near Primrose Hill and several miles northwest of the City.[2]

Upper Chalcot, the more northerly of the pair, was once part of the estate of Chalcottes, owned by the Hospital of St. James in Westminster and later

1. Bolitho and Peel, *Without the City Wall*, pp. 4–5, state that several rooms in Canonbury Tower contain panelling installed by Sir John Spencer. The estate today is controlled by the Marquess of Northamptonshire Trust and is opened to the public on special occasions.

2. A small reproduction of Robert Morden's 1695 map of Middlesex in H. Ormsby, *London on the Thames* (London: Sifton, 1924), p. 139, shows this distinction, as does also a contemporaneous map bound into John J. Park, *The Topography and Natural History of Hampstead* (London: White, 1814).

by Eton College. Upper Chalcot's location corresponds with that of a house known as Chalcots which as late as 1880 stood on the south side of England's Lane along the southern slope of Haverstock Hill. Lower Chalcot, just east of Primrose Hill, is believed to have been the site of the manor house of Rugmere in the parish of St. Pancras and was known in the late seventeenth century as the White House. After the mid-eighteenth century, Lower Chalcot became a popular resort with tea gardens and was frequented by duelists. Its name by then had changed to Chalk Farm Tavern.[3] Sir Walter Besant, a reputable London historian, mentions that according to tradition Lower Chalcot was an occasional residence of Jonson's.[4] Unfortunately, Besant furnishes no evidence in support of this view, although the suggestion, considering Jonson's dramatic references to Chalcot below, is certainly intriguing.

Hailing from Chalcot is perhaps the most fascinating member of the comic "Council of Finsbury [q.v.]" in *TT*. This is Diogenes Scriben, whom Jonson terms *"the great* Writer" (persons, l.16; 1.1.39; 5.2.12). Like his colleagues, Scriben is blunt and unsophisticated. However, a close study of his comments, especially those regarding literature and learning, shows him to be well ahead of the others in erudition and insight. He desires accuracy even in minor details (1.2.13–15), upholds the study of law and poetry (ll.39–40), and gives a respectable etymology for the word "clown" (1.3.40–43). He acts several times as a spokesman for the Jonsonian point of view by refuting the enemies of verse (1.3.18–19) and by giving an accurate summary of Medlay's (Inigo Jones's) artistic philosophy

3. On the site and history of Upper Chalcot, see F. E. Baines, ed., *Records of the Manor, Parish, and Borough of Hampstead* (London: Clay, 1890), pp. 28, 139, 442. An 1880 journey to Hampstead wherein the two Chalcots are clearly differentiated and located is contained on pp. 511–12. Percy W. Lovell and William McB. Marcham, eds., *Old St. Pancras and Kentish Town*, Survey of London, 19 (London: London County Council, 1938), p. 2, fix Lower Chalcot as the site of the Rugmere manor house. The manor ceased to exist after Henry VIII used much of it to form Marylebone Park in 1538. On Lower Chalcot during the late seventeenth century and after, see Thomas G. Barratt, *The Annals of Hampstead*, 3 vols. (London: Black, 1912), 1:162; 2:52–55, 283–86.

4. Sir Walter Besant, *London North of the Thames* (London: Black, 1911), p. 394. Fifty yards south of the summit of Primrose Hill, the three erstwhile boroughs of Hampstead, St. Pancras, and St. Marylebone meet. This has made collecting information on this area difficult because local historians have at times been in conflict in their discussions of land holdings in the Lower Chalcot region. None of the tenants mentioned, however, appears to have had any connection with Jonson. The earliest rate book for Lower Chalcot is for 1805–10. A final possible link between the Chalcot area and Jonson's time is furnished by John Norden, *Speculum Britanniae . . . Middlesex* (London: Norden, 1593), p. 50, where a list of "Noble men and Gentlemen, for the most part, having residence within this shire" includes "Quynnye at Chalcot or Chalkhill."

(5.2.35–40). Thus, because of Scriben's intriguing similarities to Jonson himself, it is a disappointment that so little significant information concerning Chalcot during Jonson's time has been discovered.

CHANON ROW (CANNON ROW). A thoroughfare in Westminster which led from New Palace Yard to the Privy Garden. Today it begins on the north side of Westminster Bridge Street at a point opposite New Palace Yard and runs a short way northward.

Chanon Row took its name from being the residence of the dean and canons of St. Stephen's Chapel, as S (p. 97) has pointed out. H&S (10:281) add that Stow (2:102) mentions that "as now divers Noblemen and Gentlemen" live there, including the earls of Hertford, Lincoln, and Derby. This street had other famous residents during the sixteenth century. In 1544 Thomas Wriothesley, later earl of Southampton, had a home there. So did Anne, duchess of Somerset (widow of Lord Protector Edward Seymour), and also Sir Henry Sidney. The earl of Sussex died there in 1557.[5]

With such notable persons living in this street, it is not at all surprising that Gossip Tatle, *SN*, in her catalogue of news sources in Westminster, should include Chanon Row among them (third intermeane, l. 23).

CHEAPSIDE. The chief commercial street of old London, running east from St. Paul's to the thoroughfare known as Poultry.

S (pp. 111–14) provides a survey of its history and numerous dramatic associations. The widest street in the City, Cheapside had four structures erected in the middle of the roadway at various points along its course: the Little (or Pissing) Conduit, the Cross opposite Wood Street, the Standard, and the Great Conduit. The Standard, opposite the end of Milk Street, was a square pillar which also contained conduits, with statues round its sides and a figure of Fame on top. During City pageants, the conduits served as places for the delivery of orations. Both of the Counters (q.v.) were in streets just off Cheapside, as were also many dealers in textiles and the famous block of fine houses known as Goldsmiths' Row (q.v.). H&S (10:222) furnish historical background on the Standard, citing Stow (1:264–65) and on the Cross (10:387), where they note that during James I's official entry into London, the City recorder read a welcoming address and presented a gold cup to the royal family there. H&S (9:496) also provide Stow's lively discussion (1:266) of how the Cross was broken and replaced in the late sixteenth century. Because of its centrality and business impor-

5. Kingsford, "Historical Notes," p. 83.

tance, Cheapside was the appropriate place for public exposure of those who broke civic regulations. As W&C (1:373–74) point out, the Standard was often the site of punishments and the burning of seditious books. W&C also refer the reader to Nichols (*Progresses*, 1:49–52, 60) for a description of the lavish ceremonies at the Little Conduit during the coronation procession of Queen Elizabeth. In contrast, several trenchant observations on City morality are provided by Donald Lupton, who in 1632 said about Cheapside: "There are a great company of honest men in this place, if all bee gold that glisters. . . . Their monies and coines are used as prisoners at Sea, kept under hatches. . . . Puritans doe hold it for a fine streete, but something addicted to Popery, for adoring the Crosse too much. . . . There are many vertuous and honest Women, some truly so, others are so for want of opportunity."[6]

Even a naive Jacobean spectator would see the false modesty of the goldsmith Touchstone's self-appraisal as "a poore *Cheapeside* Groome" in *EH* (4.2.234–35). More accurate is the reference to this street as *"famous for Gold & Plate"* (5.5.49) later in the play. In this scene the repentant apprentice Quicksilver bids *"Farewel Cheapside, farewel sweet trade"* (l. 113) and in his penitence desires "that I may goe home, through the streetes, in these [rags], as a Spectacle, or rather an Example, to the *Children of Cheapeside*" (ll. 202–4). This is similar to the Quarto text of *EMI*, where Matheo, Bobadilla, and their wretched poems are sentenced to public exposure in the "market crosse" (5.3.359), a punishment which does not appear in the Folio. In *Epic* Truewit advises politic wooers to give fruits for presents "and say they were sent you out o' the countrey, though you bought 'hem in *Cheap-side*" (4.1.115–17). On the attractiveness of his wife, John Littlewit declares in *BF*, "I challenge all *Cheapside*, to shew such another" (1.2.5–6). Iniquity promises Pug in *DA*, "I will fetch thee a leape / From the top of *Paul's*-steeple to the Standard in *Cheepe*" (1.1.55–56). Such a deed would certainly require supernatural aid, for if one assumes that Paul's Steeple was near the middle of the church (as contemporary views show), then Iniquity's jump would cover just under a quarter of a mile. In this same play the scheming Meercraft tells the goldsmith Guilthead that the latter's son Plutarchus, if properly schooled, may become an alderman, "and with his plume, / And Scarfes, march through *Cheapside*" (3.2.34–35). In *NI* the Host ascribes Lovel's lethargy to, among other things, "Cheape-side debt-Bookes" (1.3.147). Father Christmas in the epilogue to *CHM* sings, *"Now if the Lanes and Allyes afford / such an ac-ativitie as this: / At Christmas next, if they keepe their word, / can the children of Cheapside misse?"* (ll. 283–86). In *Und* 42, "An Elegie," the poet exposes the vanity of a City

6. Lupton, *London and the Countrey Carbonadoed*, pp. 28–30.

socialite who "would deride / Any Comparison had with his Cheap-side" (ll. 75–76).

CHELSEA FIELDS. The riverside area near Chelsea; in Jonson's time it was still a separate village about two and one-half miles southwest of Westminster.

Except that Sir Thomas More had his residence in Chelsea, this area's early literary associations are not very significant. H&S (11:38) limit their comments to citing John Norden's *Speculum Britanniae . . . Middlesex* (1593, p. 17) for the etymology of "Chelsea." According to Norden, it was so called "of the nature of the place whose strand is like the chesel which the sea casteth up of sand & pebble stones." Current London historians, however, list as many as five other possible origins for this name; K (p. 72) furnishes several alternatives.

In *For* 6, "To the Same [Celia]," the poet asks his beloved for as many kisses "till you equall with the store, / All the grasse that *Rumney* yeelds, / Or the sands in *Chelsey* fields" (ll. 12–14).

CHINA HOUSES. Shops in London where Eastern silks and porcelains were sold.

Both S (p. 117) and H&S (10:11) state that they were favorite resorts among fashionable women and often used for assignations. Their novelty in early Stuart times is apparent in a comment from Brome's *The Sparagus Garden*, "Though now you keepe a China-shop, and deale in brittle commodities (pots, glasses, Purslane Dishes, and more trinkets . . .) you must not forget your old trade of Barber Surgeon" (2.2). H&S also note an elaborate banquet given by the East India Company in 1609 where the guests were permitted to take home the fine china dishes in which the food was served.

In *Epic* Mrs. Otter is described as "the rich *China*-woman, that the courtiers visited so often" (1.4.27–28), to whom Lady Haughty pays a call "to see some *China* stuffes" (3.2.61–62). In the same play, Clerimont states that La-Foole has his lodgings in the Strand (q.v.) in order "to watch when ladies are gone to the *China*-houses, or the *Exchange* (q.v.)" (1.3.35–37). Later, Lady Haughty asks Epicoene to "goe with us, to *Bed'lem* (q.v.), to the *China* houses, and to the *Exchange*" (4.3.24–25). In *Alch* Subtle says that a countess deserves to have a splendid coach and equipage "to hurry her through *London*, to th' *Exchange, Bet'lem,* the *China*-houses" (4.4.47–48). In 1609 Jonson collaborated with Inigo Jones to produce an entertainment in honor of a visit by King James I and his family to the recently opened New Exchange in the Strand. According to documents among the Cecil papers at Hatfield House, "Over £96, or more than half the total cost of the royal visit, was spent on various Indian commodities, China commodities, and gold rings with poesies in them."[7]

COCK. A City tavern or hostelry, probably near Cheapside.

This sign was extremely popular with brewers; one recent study discovered twenty-five pre—Fire Cock breweries in the vicinity of Cheapside and Poultry, plus a Cock alehouse adjoining the church of St. Peter Cheap (in Wood Street just north of Cheapside).[8] According to John Taylor (*The Carriers Cosmographie*, 1637, sigs. B3, B4[v] [Spenser Society, 14]) commercial travelers from Hertfordshire and Buckinghamshire regularly lodged at the Cock in Aldersgate, off the west end of Cheapside.

In *EH* the usurer Security tells Quicksilver that his horse has been groomed by "the ostler a'th Cocke" (2.2.48). A number of the City scenes in this play are set at the home of Touchstone the goldsmith, who naturally would dwell in Goldsmiths' Row, Cheapside. The above lines were delivered at Security's house, which was probably not far off.

COCKPIT. A reference either to one of the several cockfighting resorts in early Stuart London or to one of two theaters built on sites previously occupied by such sporting centers.

S (p. 123) mentions a ring on the site of the later Phoenix Theater in Drury Lane. H&S (10:35—36) only quote an excerpt from an eighteenth-century travel narrative on the clamorousness of cockfights. Stow (2:102) points out a cockpit near Whitehall close to the royal tennis courts and bowling alleys. It was located in the western part of the palace and had an octagonal roof. Contemporary documents testify that it was used in the early Stuart years for both cockfights and dramatic productions. Under Charles I a comprehensive remodeling scheme was carried out according to a design by Inigo Jones. Many fascinating details about its new internal arrangements are furnished in a series of work orders and accounts preserved in the Public Records Office. The first play in this "new" Cockpit was staged on November 5, 1630.[9] The Cockpit (Phoenix) Theater in Drury Lane was

7. Scott McMillin, "Jonson's Early Entertainments: New Information from Hatfield House," *Renaissance Drama*, n.s. 1 (1968):166.

8. Kenneth Rogers, *Old Cheapside and Poultry* (London: Homeland Association, 1931), pp. 10, 98.

9. G. E. Bentley, *The Jacobean and Caroline Stage*, 6:270—71. On pp. 271—79 Bentley provides generous extracts of F. P. Wilson's transcript of P.R.O. E 351/3263—7 and discusses its significance. Jones's drawings are used by D. F. Rowan, "The Cockpit in Court," in Galloway, ed., *The Elizabethan Theatre—1*, pp. 89—102, where further doubt is cast on the presence of the "inner stage" as a typical feature of pre-Civil War staging and a positive case made for "an upper acting area" (pp. 98, 101). The Cockpit's entire history from 1630 to 1675 is furnished by Montague H. Cox and G. Topham Forrest, eds., *The Parish of St. Margaret, Westminister, Part 3*, Survey of London, 14 (London: London County Council, 1931), pp. 23—29.

one of the two main Caroline theaters. Constructed by John Best in 1609, it was used only for cockfights until 1616 when Christopher Beeston, the dominant figure in its history, leased and began converting the property. In March 1616/17 it had the misfortune to be the site of a Shrove Tuesday apprentices' riot, which nearly destroyed the place. The theater was repaired and had a most successful career in this increasingly fashionable part of London until 1649. Between 1617 and 1642 it was the home of Queen Anne's Men, Prince Charles's Men, Lady Elizabeth's Men, Queen Henrietta's Men, and Beeston's boy company.[10] In Nabbes's *Covent Garden* a character expresses delight at his master's move to this locale: "We shall then be neere the *Cockpit*, and see a Play now and then" (1.1).

Epic contains references to both types of entertainment offered by the Whitehall Cockpit. Lady Centaur speaks of lovers who "make *anagrammes* of our names, and invite us to the cock-pit, and kisse our hands all the play-time" (4.3.47—49). Morose includes "the cock-pit" in the catalogue of noisy places where he would do penance if rid of his "wife" (4.4.14). The former passage seems to refer to the dramatic productions at the Cockpit, the latter to the bird fights. Another time when Jonson employs a reference to the clamor at these sporting events is in *Volp* when the central character remarks about Lady Would-be's loud chatter, "The cock-pit comes not neere it" (3.5.7). According to H&S (9:163) Jonson's *TT* was first staged at the Drury Lane Cockpit in 1633. A court performance on January 14, 1634, according to Sir Henry Herbert's office book, was "not likt." The latter performance may well have been at the Whitehall Cockpit. Jonson's initial staging of this play at the Cockpit in Drury Lane may be explained by his tendency of presenting plays at theaters situated close to the settings of the plays themselves. This habit is especially evident in the cases of *Alch* and *DA* at the Blackfriars Theater (q.v.), *Epic* at the Whitefriars (q.v.), and *BF* at the Hope (q.v.). The setting of *TT* is the semirural locale northwest of the City, to which the Drury Lane Cockpit was the closest available theater. Also, the audience at this theater would find much of relevance in *TT*, for this play deflates pretensions to social eminence, a problem of much concern to residents in this newly fashionable quarter of London.

COLEHARBOUR (COLD HARBOUR). A sanctuary for vagrants and debtors composed of a number of small tenements in Upper Thames Street. Its site was in the vicinity of the present-day Cannon Street Station.

H&S (10:20) quote Stow (1:236—37) for historical background on this locale. S (p. 125) refers to Healey's translation of Joseph Hall, *Discovery of a*

---

10. Alfred Harbage, *Annals of English Drama*, rev. S. Schoenbaum (London: Methuen, 1964), p. 305. Bentley, *The Jacobean and Caroline Stage*, 6:47—77, provides a very full account of the Phoenix's history, closing with the reminder that it was one of the playing areas which figured in the beginnings of the Restoration theater.

New World (1605, p. 106), "And here is that ancient modell of *Cole-harbor*, bearing the name of *The Prodigalls' Promontorie*, and beeing as a Sanctuary unto banque-rupt detters." The place name, "Cole Harbour," is of fairly frequent occurrence in various parts of Great Britain; originally it meant a place where travelers could obtain shelter, but no food or fire.[11]

Seeking revenge against Clerimont, Morose in *Epic* warns that his nephew will soon degenerate to where he will "take sanctuary in *Cole-harbour*, and fast" (2.5.111). Morose's comment becomes especially pertinent when one realizes that it was on September 30, 1608, just at the time when *Epic* was being written, that Coleharbour's sanctuary privileges were abolished.[12]

COLEMAN STREET. A City thoroughfare running north from Gresham Street and Lothbury to London Wall.

While Stow (1:282, 284) and Kingsford (2:335–36) believe that this street was named after an early property owner, G. Bebbington (*Street Names of London*, London: Batsford, 1972, p. 94) maintains that it derives from the charcoal burners of pre-Conquest days. S (p. 125) terms Coleman Street a haunt of Puritans, but his evidence is of a later period than Jonson's era. H&S (9:371) note that the London historian H. B. Wheatley praised the quality of its shops and residences by calling it "the Bond Street of the period." In *The London Prodigal* (2.4.168) Lancelot is led to believe that Flowerdew has left him "two housen furnished well in *Cole-man* street."

Justice Clement's house, *EMI*, is located in Coleman Street (3.2.52–53), about in the middle of its course (3.5.98–99). Earlier, Kitely asked Cash to bring word of any visitors to him at the Exchange (q.v.) "or here in *Colman*-street, to Justice CLEMENTS" (3.3.119). Thus the location of Justice Clement's residence is virtually in the center of this play's real-life "stage," a neighborhood encompassing just a few City blocks (except for 1.1-3) and the adjoining open ground in Moorfields.

CORNHILL. A central London thoroughfare, running east from Poultry, past the Royal Exchange to Leadenhall Street. In Jonson's day its course was longer, extending east as far as Lime Street.

London's first corn market was held in Cornhill, and, as pointed out by S (p. 131) Cornhill was mentioned in such early works as *Piers Plowman* and "London Lyckpenny." Most memorable is the reference to Cornhill in *The Three Lords and the Three Ladies of London* (p. 397) as the place where the actor Dick Tarlton "hath toss'd a tankard . . . ere now." In Dekker's *The*

11. Henry A. Harben, *A Dictionary of London* (London: Jenkins, 1918), p. 161. The author cites Skeat, *Place-Names of Hertfordshire*, p. 68, for this detail.

12. Kingsford, "Historical Notes," p. 99.

Shoemakers' Holiday Sybil watched Lacey pass in his scarf and feathers "at our door in Cornehill" (2.1.29–30). H&S (10:387) state that in 1604 when James I rode through London on his official coronation day, the architect Stephen Harrison commented that "the *Conduits* of *Cornhill*, of *Cheape* [q.v.], and of *Fleetestreete* [q.v.], that day ran Claret wine very plenteously." Stow (1:94ff.) discusses Cornhill as a holiday center. A quintain [tilting post] was set up in this street near Leadenhall where this author saw "great pastime" made. At Christmas its standard (a pillar enclosing a conduit) was decorated with "Ivie, Bayes, and what soever the season . . . aforded to be greene." Also, the chief City maypole was erected here in front of St. Andrew's Church. According to W&C (1:458) the standard "was an object of such mark that distances throughout England were measured from it as the heart of the City."

Meercraft, *DA*, declares that Cornhill, like Cheapside, is a place where the goldsmith's son Plutarchus may fittingly display himself "with his plume, / And Scarfes, march through *Cheapside*, or along *Cornehill*" (3.2.34–35).

COUNTERS. City prisons for debtors and minor offenders. One Counter was located in the thoroughfare known as Poultry and another in Wood Street.

As S (p. 133) has noted, the Wood Street Counter was originally located in Bread Street but was moved in 1555 because of the keeper's cruelty and his habit of allowing thieves and strumpets to lodge there. An elaborate comparison between the Counters and a university is in Dekker and Middleton's *The Roaring Girl* (3.3.81–92), and in *Greene's Tu Quoque* (p. 563) there is a discussion of the costs of the various grades of accommodation in the Counters. H&S (9:360) cite William Fennor, *The Compters Commonwealth* (1617, p. 9), for a description of the Wood Street Counter. These editors also point out that both *EMO* and *EH* conclude in one of the Counters, or Compters, as they were also called. In addition, H&S, (9:478) briefly cite other contemporary dramas which illustrate life in these prisons. Stow (1:263, 350) provides background on the history of both City Counters, giving special attention to the Bread Street episode mentioned above. Ned Ward's 1698–99 description of conditions in the Counters, cited by K (p. 233) is memorable: "a mixture of scents from mundungus, tobacco, foul feet, dirty shirts, stinking breaths, and uncleanly carcases . . . far worse than a Southwark ditch, a tanner's yard, or a tallow chandler's melting-room."

Jonson's works contain many references to the Counters. In *EMO* Asper uses these institutions to make a memorable comparison: "The conscience / Is vaster then the ocean, and devoures / More wretches then the *Counters*"

(induction, ll. 43–45). At the close of the play, the courtier Fastidious
Brisk is committed to the Counter (5.7.16–17). Macilente mentions this
event to both Fallace (5.8.57–58), and to Deliro (5.9.23–24). Fallace
pays a visit to the prisoner (5.10.1–4). In *EH* the wayward apprentice
Quicksilver declares his aversion to penal institutions (2.2.263–66). But
the foolish behavior of Quicksilver and Sir Petronel Flash lands them in one
of the Counters (4.2.252–53, 322), a fact which is lamented by Sir
Petronel's wife Gertrude (5.1.22). This play's final scenes are set in the
Counter, where Quicksilver repents and even reforms a tough inmate
known as the "Bandog of the Counter" (5.2.61–65). To demonstrate his
own redemption, Quicksilver livens the play's closing moments with a song
promising that virtuous living will enable one to "*Scape* Tiborne [q.v.],
Counters, & *the* Spitle [q.v.]" (5.5.122). At the end of this song the
goldsmith Touchstone tells everyone, "This day shalbe sacred to *Mercy* &
the mirth of this *Encounter*, in the *Counter*" (5.5.153–54). The epilogue in
EH, wherein Quicksilver parades through the City, opens as he informs
Touchstone of what is to happen: "Stay, Sir, I perceive the multitude are
gatherd together, to view our comming out at the *Counter*" (ll. 1–2). In
both *EMO* and *EH* the Wood Street Counter seems to be the more
appropriate setting. In *EMO* it is closer to St. Paul's than is the jail in
Poultry. A stronger case may be made in *EH* where the site of the Wood
Street Counter (close to Goldsmiths' Row, the probable residence of
Touchstone) would much enhance the unity of act 5, where settings
alternate between Touchstone's home and the Counter. In *EMI* the pes-
simist Downright predicts that the merry youth Wellbred will end up in
the Counter (2.1.77–78), ill fortune which never happens. *DA* also
contains a goldsmith, this time named Guilthead, who boasts of how City
shopkeepers deal with customers whose desires are bigger than their purses:
"Wee drive 'hem up / In t'one of our two Pounds, the *Compters*, streight"
(3.1.19–20). In *Und* 15, "An Epistle to a Friend," Jonson cites "the
Counters, or the Fleete [q.v.]" (l. 105) as the destination for free-spending
materialists. Some of Jonson's works also contain references to the various
grades of accommodation in the Counters. In *EH* the Hole, Knight's Ward,
and Two-penny Ward are discussed by one of the keepers (5.2.42–49). A
fourth area is mentioned in *EMO* when Buffone remarks that Puntarvolo
walks "as melancholy as one o' the Masters side in the *Counter*" (5.6.36–
37). Finally, Macilente in this scene foresees the Two-penny Ward as where
Brisk's follies will land him (5.11.50–51).

COW LANE. A no longer extant thoroughfare just northwest of the
City, which ran from West Smithfield south to Snow Hill.
     S (p. 135) states mainly that both Awdeley's *Fraternitie of Vagabonds*

(1563) and the 1599 edition of *The Spanish Tragedy* were published in Cow Lane. Stow (2:29) declares that the prior of Semperingham had his lodgings in Cow Lane and that many newly built residences were also located there.

In *BF* Dame Purecraft got her desire for a mad husband after having her fortune told "by the Cunning men in *Cow-lane*" (1.2.47).

CRIPPLEGATE. One of the seven old City gates, lying between Moorgate and Aldersgate.

Stow (1.33) furnishes an etymology based on a tradition attesting to miraculous cures for crippled beggars in the area, which has been largely dismissed by later authorities such as S (p. 138). Besides pointing out derivations based on the topography of the Cripplegate area, H&S (9:418) refer to a popular legend attributing its etymology and construction to a lame malingerer who grew wealthy from his begging. These editors also note that just north of where this gate once stood is a church dedicated to St. Giles, the patron saint of cripples. As S has shown, writers were fond of puns utilizing this name and its traditional associations. In his *Seven Deadly Sinnes of London* (*Non-Dramatic Works*, 2:57), Dekker introduces Apishness as "prawncing in at *Cripplegate*" because of the "lame" imitations he gives of those whom he copies.

Jonson uses his audience's familiarity with Cripplegate's "history" to drive home a point in *EMO*. In this play Asper calls servile, halting poets "as lame / As VULCAN, or the founder of *Cripple-gate*" (induction, ll. 71–72). The Cripplegate locale contains several possible ties with Jonson. It was in the church of St. Giles mentioned above that Mark Eccles found recorded the baptism of "Joseph, the soñe of Beniamyne Johnson" on December 9, 1599. As H&S have pointed out in their discussion of this discovery (11:575), Jonson was then employed with the Lord Chamberlain's Men in an adjacent parish. Also in St. Giles's, John Payne Collier called attention to the marriage of "Beniamyne Johnson and Hester Hopkins" on July 27, 1623. H&S, as above, in connection with this information, note that T. Cooke's court bill of 1620 reprinted in H&S (1:235) described a messenger going "by Cripellgatt" requesting Jonson to attend Prince Charles.

CROOKED LANE. A City thoroughfare no longer extant, which in 1918 ran from near the corner of Cannon and King William Streets to Miles Lane.

In Jonson's time its course was longer and truly worthy of its name, as S (p. 138) and others have remarked, but construction of the approaches to the "new" London Bridge in the early nineteenth century obliterated its eastern portion. Other dramatists besides Jonson have made fascinating quips using this placename. Middleton, *No Wit, No Help, Like a Woman's*, has a character recount a fanciful tale of a maid whose marriage was thwarted by her "Crabb'd uncle, Cancer here, dwelling in Crooked Lane" (2.1.235). H&S (10:565) cite the reply of the Clown in *The Witch of Edmonton* (2.1.39–40) when he is asked to fetch bells, "Double Bells: *Crooked Lane*, ye shall have 'em straight in *Crooked Lane*."

Jonson plays upon this street name in *CHM* when he includes "Child Rowlan, *and a straight young man, / though he come out of Crooked-lane-a*" (ll. 236–37) in his Christmas procession.

CROYDON. Once a Surrey market town ten miles south of London Bridge, today a large suburb in metropolitan London.

Croydon was noted in Tudor-Stuart times for the production of charcoal and the holding of major fairs on July 6 and October 2. Most of the dramatic references to Croydon cited by S (p. 139) allude to one of these associations. H&S (10:323) remind us also of its prominence as a coaching stop and resort in a passage from John Taylor (*The World runnes on wheeles; Folio of 1630* pt. 2, p. 238, [Spenser Society, 3]), "Every *Gill Turnetripe*, Mistris *Fumkins*, Madame *Polecat* . . . with their companion Trugs, must be coach'd to Saint *Albanes, Burntwood, Hockley* in the *Hole* [q.v.], *Croydon, Windsor* [q.v.], *Uxbridge* [q.v.], and many other places like Wilde Haggards prancing up and downe."

In *NI* Pinnacia Stuffe describes the actions of her tailor husband, who first wears the clothes he makes for gentlefolk and "runnes / In his velvet Jackat thus, to *Rumford* [q.v.], *Croyden*, / *Hounslow* [q.v.], or *Barnet* [q.v.], the next bawdy road" (4.3.70–72).

CUCKOLD'S HAVEN. A point on the Surrey shore about three miles east of St. Paul's where the river begins a large loop to the south, today opposite Limehouse Reach and the West India Docks.

At Cuckold's Haven in Jonson's time stood a tall pole topped by a set of horns. The legend associated with this locale and its distinctive "monument" is given by S (p. 140). This monument, known to Elizabethans as the "tree," denoted the boundary of some lands granted by King John to a miller from Charlton, whom he had cuckolded. Jonson is the only dramatist who employs this locale as a setting, although others have used it figuratively such as Ford and Dekker in *The Witch of Edmonton*: "That confidence is a wind that has blown many a married man ashore at Cuckold's Haven" (2.2). H&S (9:666) cite *Pasquils Night-cap* (1612, p. 53) for information on the later association of butchers with Cuckold's Haven. It seems that certain roguish citizens kept tearing down the horns erected along the riverside. In time, London's butchers agreed to keep the "tree" continually thus furbished in return for perpetual title to the nearby fields. H&S also point out (p. 665) a parallel to Jonson's utilization of the "tree" below in Wentworth Smith's *The Hector of Germany*, where a shipwrecked character climbs a rock and tries to hail passing ships for his rescue.

Cuckold's Haven is the setting for act 4, scene 1 of *EH*. Perched atop the "tree," Slitgut, a butcher's apprentice, observes the misfortunes befalling some adventurers going downriver to Blackwall (q.v.), from where they had hoped to embark upon a voyage to the New World. Ironically, the ill-fated crew had earlier drunk toasts "to all that are going Eastward to night, towardes *Cuckolds haven*" (3.3.114–15) and "so to famous *Cuckolds haven* so fatally remembred" (l. 120). In this scene the usurer Security, whose wife is planning to run off with another man, has Cuckold's Haven much on his mind (ll. 168–70, 172–73, 184–85) before this unlucky trip. Appropriately, after Security pursues his wife downriver, the boat capsizes, and he is rescued; he comes ashore at Cuckold's Haven and is welcomed by Slitgut (4.1.40–44).

CURRIERS' HALL. The headquarters for this guild located in Jonson's day in London Wall near no-longer-extant Philip Lane. According to today's City topography, the hall would have stood on the east side of the intersection of Wood Street and London Wall.

According to S (p. 141), it was used as a Dissenters' meeting place "and even in the time of James seems to have been connected with Puritanism." H&S (10:560) only quote Stow's brief comments on its location (1:297): "Little Woode-streete runneth down to Cripplesgate, and somewhat East from the Sunne Taverne against the wall of the Citty is the Curriers Hall." S's statements on its Puritan associations are probably derived from W&C (1:485), who also make this point and note that the Curriers had been incorporated only since 1605.

The title figure of *CHM* introduces this work by admitting, "It was intended, I confesse, for Curryers Hall" (l. 21), but because good weather kept the liverymen too busy to see it, he deemed it "convenient . . . to fit it for a higher place" (ll. 24–25). This reference is appropriate in this masque, for it combines with some later remarks on the "papist" associations of Old and New Fish Streets (q.v.) to produce a strongly Protestant tone which Jonson appears to satirize, thereby urging folk to give up their sectarian prejudices for a few moments of uninhibited festivity.

CUSTOM HOUSE QUAY. The riverside area serving the Custom House in Lower Thames Street.

S (p. 141) cites a few dramatic references to this place of business. In act 4 of Rowley's *A New Wonder: A Woman Never Vexed*, George tells his employer that his wares have been conveyed "in carts to the Custom House, there to be shipped." H&S (1:362) point out that the mention of the Custom House in the Folio of *EMI* is a fine instance of Jonson's artistry as he revised the play. In this example, fully quoted below, a character makes his point by means of a vivid image of a familiar scene rather than with a wordy, learned allusion.

Wellbred, in the Folio text of *EMI*, tries to inspire his comrades by declaring that if Old Knowell can outwit them, "Would we were eene prest, to make porters of; and serve out the remnant of our daies, in *Thames*-street, or at *Custom*-house key, in a civill warre, against the carmen" (3.2.67–70). The maddening bustle, noise, and congestion so characteristic of this locale will be the "punishment" for their intellectual failure. Originally in the Quarto, Brainworm vowed, "May they [his wits] lie and starve in some miserable spittle, where they may never see the face of any true spirit againe, but bee perpetually haunted with some *church-yard Hobgoblin in secula seculorum*" (2.3.225–28). As H&S note (9:337), this parodies the conclusion of a familiar homily. The tactics of employees at the Custom House are mentioned in *DA*. Iniquity tells Pug that during their planned "infernal grand tour" of London they will "put in at *Custome-house* key there, / And see, how the Factors, and Prentizes play there, / False with their Masters" (1.1.63–65).

D

DAGGER TAVERN. A drinking spot noted also for its pies and frumenty. Jonson's plays contain references to Daggers in Holborn and possibly Cheapside.

Both S (p. 144) and H&S (10:60) cite Gascoigne, *Delicate diet for drinke mouthde Droonkardes* (*Complete Works*, 2:467), "But we must have March beere, dooble dooble Beere, Dagger ale, Bragget, Renish wine, White wine, French wine, Gascoyne wine." In Heywood's *2 If You Know Not Me* (*Dramatic Works*, 1:257), the Second Prentice says, "I must needs step to the *Dagger*, in *Cheape*, to send a letter into the Country unto my father." S notes that a "Dagger in Cheape" is mentioned in the anonymous *Penniles Parliament's* mandate number 32 as a meeting place.[1] H&S also state that the mince pies of the Dagger in Foster Lane, Cheapside, are referred to by R. Johnson, *The Pleasant Conceits of Old Hobson* (1607, sig. B2ᵛ). According to W&C (1:489), Dagger pies were "embossed with a representation of a dagger and a magpie on the point." Without giving any evidence, these authorities contend that all of Jonson's references to the Dagger were to "a low-class gambling house" located in Holborn. A recent study has located other Daggers in Cheapside (near Bow Lane) and the lower part of Friday Street (close to the famous Mermaid Tavern) (q.v.). The former appears to have been an eating place kept by a licensed victualler rather than only a tavern.[2] This Dagger cannot be the one in Foster Lane cited earlier because Foster Lane is several blocks west of Bow Lane and in another parish.

It is "In *Hol'bourne*, at the dagger" where Face meets Dapper, the gullible law clerk in *Alch* (1.1.191). This victim is later told that to please the Queen of Faery he must eat "no more *Wool-sack* [q.v.] pies, / Nor *Dagger* frume'ty" (5.4.41–42). The Dagger and Woolsack are also mentioned in *DA* as places where cheating apprentices spend their gains (1.1.66). The site of the Daggers mentioned in the act 5 quote from *Alch* and in *DA* may have been established by the recent discoveries that the Daggers in Foster Lane, in Cheapside, and in lower Friday Street all stood close to Woolsack taverns. This would explain why the Woolsack was named in conjunction with the Dagger in both of these references.[3]

1. *The Penniles Parliament* is reprinted in *The Harleian Miscellany*, ed. William Oldys and Thomas Park (London: John White, 1808), vol. 1; quote on p. 184.
2. Kenneth Rogers, *Old Cheapside and Poultry*, pp. 48–50.
3. Rogers, *Old Cheapside*, p. 51.

DEPTFORD. In Jonson's time a village four miles east of London on the south bank of the Thames, just west of Greenwich.

The site of a royal dockyard founded by Henry VIII, Deptford was a popular place for river crossings and also for robberies, as borne out by S's citations (p. 150). In 1593 at a house in Deptford occurred the altercation in which Marlowe was slain. Sir Francis Drake's ship was permanently moored at Deptford, and, as H&S (9:353) point out, this hero was knighted aboard his vessel in 1581. They also note (p. 664) that John Taylor, *Jacke a Lent* (*Folio of 1630*, pt. 1, p. 116 [Spenser Society, 2]), declared *"Sir Francis Drakes* Ship at Detford" to be among the "secret and unsuspected places" searched for illegal butchering during Lent. This ship, writes K (p. 245), was kept at Deptford in dry dock until it "literally fell to pieces through age."

In *EMI* Edward Knowell, in pointing out the impropriety of Stephen's actions, remarks, "It cannot be answer'd, goe not about it. DRAKES old ship, at *Detford*, may sooner circle the world againe" (1.3.120—22). With the presumption typical of Jonsonian overreachers, Sir Petronel Flash and most of his followers in *EH* decide to hold a prevoyage supper on this famed ship (3.3.149—51, 179—80), a plan which is literally scuttled by a storm on the river.

DEVIL TAVERN. A tavern with strong Jonsonian associations situated at 2 Fleet Street where Child's Bank now stands.

This haunt was close to the church of St. Dunstan in the West, and its sign depicted St. Dunstan tweaking the devil's nose with his pincers.[4] Early in Rowley's *A Match at Midnight* when a youth hesitates to "step to the Devil," he is assured that "he cannot hurt you, fool; there's a saint holds him by the nose." Although this tavern is mentioned by several other dramatists, as shown by S (pp. 151—52), its chief fame derives from Jonson's making its Apollo Room the regular site of convivial meetings with his friends. H&S (1:85—86; 11:294—300) furnish ample information on this subject, including the probable story behind Jonson's christening of the Apollo Room, the exact location of this room in the building, and the subsequent history of the tavern for the next several generations. H&S also call the reader's attention to Katherine Esdaile's detailed account of this tavern's past in *Essays and Studies of the English Association* 29 (1944,

---

4. Kenneth Rogers, *The Mermaid and Mitre Taverns*, p. 146, points out a 1608 entry in the court books of the Vintners' Company concerning the tavern's licensee, Simon Wadlow, "This day Simon Wadlowe was required to reforme his signe of St. Dunstan and the Divell and to put the Divell Cleane out of yt and to leave St. Dunstan aloane, and he hath promised so to reforme yt as in the Discretion of twoe of the Assistants of this Comp^e shalbe thought w^thin 14 dayes."

93–100). At Child's Bank two relics associated with Jonson's sessions at the Apollo Room—a wooden plaque bearing the poet's greeting to visitors and a bust of Apollo—have been carefully preserved. The board with the verse painted in gilt on a black background is exactly as described by Miss Esdaile in 1944, but the bust's appearance today differs considerably from when she saw it. In Miss Esdaile's account the bust was of black-painted terra cotta. Some years later, bank officials had the paint removed and discovered that the bust was made of alabaster rather than terra cotta. It has remained in this original state ever since, semitranslucent with a pinkish-gold tinge.[5]

The Devil Tavern is mentioned in two of Jonson's works. Among the things judged irrelevant to the poetic scene in the stage prologue to *SN* is whether the Devil or the Phoenix (q.v.) has better wine (l. 16). The Apollo Room at the Devil figures prominently in this play. Penniboy Junior is advised to "Dine in *Apollo* with *Pecunia*, / At brave *Duke Wadloos*" (2.5.127–28), and soon afterwards Madrigal hears of his decision to do so (ll. 134–37), making plans to join him there (3.3.6–8). Pecunia, under charge of the Broker, awaits Penniboy at the Devil (3.4.9–10, 15–17). The Apollo Room becomes the site for all four scenes of act 4 and is mentioned twice therein (4.3.62, 79). The antimasquers in *MA*, who hail from the breweries in the precinct of St. Katherine's, sing *"Nor the Vintry Cranes, / Nor St. Clements Danes, / Nor the Devill can put us down-a"* (ll. 187–89), a boast exalting the roistering abilities of the St. Katherine's folk over those of drinkers from two noted London taverns and a residential area heavily populated by law students. To guide and inspire his companions at the Devil Tavern, Jonson wrote a set of "house rules," the *Leges Convivales*, and a welcome, "Over the Door at the Entrance into the Apollo" (one of the relics described above). H&S (8:656–57) provide texts of both these writings.

DISTAFF LANE. A City thoroughfare which in Jonson's time ran between Old Change and Friday Street south of and parallel to Watling Street.

As S (p. 153) has explained, Jonson's Distaff Lane was absorbed long ago by the creation of Cannon Street. The present-day Distaff Lane, which runs south from Cannon Street, was known in the seventeenth century as Little

5. According to L. C. Steib, assistant manager of Child's Bank, experts at the Tate Gallery have attributed the bust of Apollo to Edmund Walker rather than Edward Marshall, the sculptor put forth by Miss Esdaile. A history of the property containing the Devil Tavern and several other businesses which ultimately became the premises of Child's Bank is provided in the pamphlet, "At the Sign of the Marygold," available upon request from Child's Bank. This account originally appeared in the *Three Banks Review* (September 1969).

Distaff Lane. H&S (10:565) cite only Stow's comments (1:345) on its etymology. Later on Stow states (pp. 351–52) that Little Distaff Lane was a thoroughfare which ran southward from Distaff Lane proper.

One of the many examples of wordplay using topographical references in *CHM* involves Distaff Lane. In this entertainment Father Christmas tells the audience that a member of the masquing procession is *"My Sonne Hercules, tane, out of Distaffe-lane, / but an active man, and a Porter"* (ll. 212–13). Jonson's topographical selectivity is explained by S, who reminds us of Hercules' brief adventure in woman's clothing armed with a distaff rather than a club.

CITY DITCH. Once a moat completely surrounding the City just outside its walls. However, by Jonson's time it had become a garbage dump and a building site.

H&S (11:155) note that Stow says nothing about the "New-Ditch" mentioned by Jonson below, discussing only (1:19) the already decayed "towne Ditch without the Wall of the citie." Stow (p. 20) goes on to complain that in his lifetime cleaning of the Ditch had been neglected, thus narrowing and dirtying its course: "Before the which time the saide ditch lay open, without wall or pale, having therein great store of verie good fish, of divers sorts, as many men yet living, who have taken and tasted them can well witness: but now no such matter, the charge of clensing is spared, and great profite made by letting out [erecting tenements on] the banks, with the spoyle of the whole ditch."

In *UV*, 35, "To Inigo Marquess Would be: A Corollary," the poet writes, "But when thou turnst a Reall Inigo; / Or canst of truth ye least intrenchm^t pitch, / Wee'll have thee styld ye Marquess of New-Ditch" (ll. 22–24). The details furnished by Stow about the old City ditch clearly indicate the sort of "domain" with which Jonson's bitter rival was to be endowed.

DOO-LITTLE LANE. A City thoroughfare which once ran north from Knightrider Street to Carter Lane, just south of St. Paul's. Its course today is occupied by Knightrider Court and Sermon Lane.

Authorities such as S (p. 154) and H&S (10:563) rely upon Stow's description (2:18), "a place not inhabited by Artificers, or open shop keepers, but serving for a neere passage from Knightriders street, to Carter lane," for their historical commentary on this thoroughfare. The only other contemporary dramatist to mention it is Middleton; in his *Family of Love* a character praises a local physician; neither "the wise woman in Pissing-Alley, nor she in Do-little-Lane, are more famous for goods deeds than he" (5.3.366–68).

In *ML* the "spirit" invented by the scheming Needle is said to have lived "in *Doo-little* Lane, a top o' the hill there" (5.5.22). In *CHM* Venus says of her son Cupid, "I had him by my first Husband, he was a Smith, forsooth, we dwelt in Doe-little lane then" (ll. 125–27).

DOWGATE TORRENT. A channel of floodwater carried to the bottom of Dowgate Hill, where was located one of the ancient watergates of London in the vicinity of today's Cannon Street Station.

Stow's commentary (1:230), which illuminates Jonson's references, is cited by S (p. 157) and given in full by H&S (9:481; who use the 1598 edition of Stow, p. 34): "*Downe* gate, so called . . . of the sodaine descending, or downe going of that way from *S. John's* Church upon Walbrooke into the River of Thames, whereby the water in the chanell there hath such a swift course, that in the year 1574 on the fourth of September after a strong shower of rayne, a lad (of the age of 18. yeares) minding to have leapt over the chanell, was taken by the feete and borne downe with the violence of that narrow streame, and caryed towarde the Thames with such a violent swiftnesse, as no man could rescue or stay him, till he came against a cart wheele, that stood in the water gate, before which time he was drowned, and starke dead."

This unleashing of natural power is used as the basis of courtly compliment in the epilogue to *EMO* presented before Queen Elizabeth. Here Macilente compares the soothing of his passions by the Queen's "ample, and unmeasur'd floud" of perfections to the diffusion of the Torrent's polluted strength by the Thames' relative purity and vastness (ll. 8–13). Later Jonson uses the image of the Torrent's unclean power to mock the achievements of Inigo Jones in *UV* 35. In this poem Jonson ridicules Jones's scene-designing abilities, citing his "Dowgate Torrent falling into Thames" (l. 16). As H&S (11:155) have noted, what Jonson had in mind was Jones's creation in *MBl* of an "artificiall sea . . . seene to shoote forth, as if it flowed to the land" (ll. 26–27).

E

EASTCHEAP. The continuation of Cheapside (q.v.) eastward from Cannon Street and Gracechurch Street to Great Tower Street.

Both S (p. 165) and H&S (9:435) rely on Stow's observations (cited by H&S from the 1598 edition, p. 170), "This Eastcheape is now a flesh Market of Butchers there dwelling, on both sides of the street, it had sometime also Cookes mixed amongst the Butchers, and such other as sold victuails readie dressed of all sorts." The earliest mention of this street pertains to rent from a meat-stall in the reign of King John; thus it is not surprising that Jonson's references to Eastcheap below are in connection with the butchering trade, as is Simon Eyre's comment in *The Shoemakers' Holiday*, "Have I not tane you from selling tripes in Eastcheape, and set you in my shop?" (2.3.60–61). Although the chief City meat market had by Jonson's time moved to Leadenhall, some butchers still worked in Eastcheap, as Stow's comments have testified. The Boar's Head Tavern immortalized by Shakespeare's readers is believed to have stood at the west end of Eastcheap, close to the site of a statue of King William IV pulled down in 1934.[1]

In *EMO* Carlo Buffone comments about a man whom he dislikes, "Well, and e'er I meet him in the city, I'le ha' him joynted, I'le pawne him in east-cheape, among the butchers else" (2.2.93–95). Slitgut, who from a lofty vantage point at Cuckold's Haven (q.v.) witnesses the shipwreck of *EH*'s adventurers, is apprenticed to a "poore Butcher of East-cheape" (4.1.4). The appropriateness of the linkage between his occupation and Cuckold's Haven is discussed by H&S (9:666).

EDMONTON. In Jonson's day a Middlesex village eight miles north of London.

This village, today a populous part of the metropolis, was the setting for two pre-Restoration dramas, *The Merry Devil of Edmonton* (c. 1602), attributed to Dekker, and Ford and Dekker's *The Witch of Edmonton* (1621). Later, Edmonton's Bell Inn figured in Cowper's amusing "Ballad of John Gilpin." The area was still semirural in the nineteenth century when Charles Lamb made his last home there, in a cottage near All Saints Church where he and his sister Mary are buried.

1. K, pp. 491–92, provides details on the site and history of the Boar's Head. He reminds us that this tavern is not mentioned by name in any Shakespearean play. It was first designated as the haunt of Prince Hal and Falstaff in Theobald's 1733 edition.

Both of Jonson's Edmonton references are to *The Merry Devil of Edmonton*, a sprightly comedy featuring a not-so-fearsome devil who is outwitted by a local conjurer, Peter Fabell. The prologue to *DA* asks the audience for the same favor shown to *"your deare delight, the* Divell *of* Edmunton" (l. 22). In *SN* the Gossips poke fun at this same figure, calling him *"an Asse"* who was *"coosen'd . . . with a candles end"* (first intermeane, ll. 67–70).

ELTHAM. A Kentish village approximately nine miles southeast of St. Paul's, where stood a royal residence occasionally used by King James I.

In 1610 a perpetual-motion machine was exhibited at Eltham Palace. Both S (p. 171) and H&S (10:43–44) refer to the diary of von Vendenheym (British Museum Add. MS. 20001), which records a visit to view this object. Invented by Cornelius Drebbel, who also introduced microscopes and telescopes into England, the mechanism consisted of a hollow glass globe that continued to revolve around a small ball at its center. Interestingly enough, the machine was not designed to exhibit the possibility of continuous movement, but to "prove" the validity of the Ptolemaic theory of the universe, for the central ball represented the earth. H&S also note that Peacham's preliminary verses to Coryat's *Crudities* mention "that heavenly motion of Eltham" as one of the leading local sights and that an engraving of the machine is contained in Th. Twynne, *A Dialogue philosophicall, wherein Natures secret closet is opened . . . Together with the wittie invention of an Artificiall Perpetuall Motion (*1612).

Charles I was the last sovereign to enjoy Eltham Palace. During the Civil War soldiers were quartered on its grounds, causing irreparable damage. By the Restoration many of its buildings had been demolished; the great hall was used as a barn and remained such until the mid-nineteenth century. Today the great hall, a fine piece of medieval domestic architecture, is cared for by the Ministry of Public Buildings and Works and is open to the public.[2]

Morose laments at a particularly trying moment in *Epic*, "I dwell in a windmill! The perpetuall motion is here, and not at *Eltham*" (5.3.62–63). Similarly, in *Epig* 97, "On the New Motion," the subject of the poem (courtly affectation) is deemed a greater curiosity than "the *Eltham*-thing" (l. 2).

ENFIELD. A Middlesex village about eleven miles north of London, today a very pleasant suburb.

2. Christopher Trent, *Greater London: Its Growth and Development through Two Thousand Years* (London: Phoenix House, 1965), pp. 111–12. The rest of the estate houses the Institute of Army Education and dates largely from 1931 when it was restored by Stephen Courtauld.

Enfield's manor house was one of the residences of Elizabeth while she was still a princess. Northwest of the town was Enfield Chase, a large forested tract which in King James's time was a royal hunting preserve well stocked with deer. In 1607 the king even traded his estate at Hatfield for one at Theobald's (q.v.) in order to be close to this sporting ground. The town and the chase both figure significantly in Dekker's *The Merry Devil of Edmonton*; the latter locale is once cited in his *Northward Ho*. In the early nineteenth century Charles Lamb moved to Enfield to escape the bustle of London.

Jonson's friend Sir Robert Wroth, who married Sir Philip Sidney's niece, had one of his principal residences, the estate of Durrants, in the Enfield area. Jonson praised the virtues of the country life, probably as represented at this estate, in *For* 3, "To Sir Robert Wroth."

EXCHANGES, ROYAL AND NEW. London's centers for financial and mercantile dealings. The Royal Exchange stood between Cornhill and Threadneedle Street. Its construction in 1566–68 was financed by the illustrious entrepreneur Sir Thomas Gresham. In 1609 the New Exchange, or "Britain's Burse," was opened in the Strand (q.v.), close to the London residence of the Cecil family.

The Royal Exchange, as S (pp. 185–86) and other historians have pointed out, contained a large central court for business transactions and a hundred small shops around an inner balcony. This institution is often mentioned in drama as a meeting place, emporium for divers artifacts, and source of female companionship.[3] H&S are concerned with aspects of the Exchange which are mentioned by Jonson. Hence their discussion of "Exchange time" (9:372); of its use as a gossip mart and meeting spot (10:262, 265); and of the instances where Jonson clearly differentiates between the Royal Exchange and its Jacobean successor (10:11, 356).

W&C (3:182–83) inform us that the Royal Exchange was similar in design to the Burse at Antwerp and that its building materials were brought

---

3. Contemporary writers often had low opinions about women who frequented or were employed at the Exchanges. Donald Lupton, *London and the Countrey Carbonadoed*, pp. 25–26, commented, "Here are usually more Coaches attendant, then at Church doores: The Merchantes should keepe their Wives from visiting the Upper Roomes too often, least they tire their purses, by attyring themselves. . . . There's many Gentle-women come hither, that to help their faces and Complexions, breakes their husbands backs, who play foule in the Country with their Land, to be faire; and play false in the City." Even more unflattering is the anonymous author of *The Ape-Gentle-woman; or, The Character of an Exchange-wench* (London: Pye, 1675), p. 1: "She's but one Story above a common Harlot, and when ever she falls from her Shop, drops into a Brothel-house. Her carriage is so equally divided betwixt a natural Levity and forc'd Modesty, that one would take her for a kind of Motly'd Christian, or a new interdisposition betwixt Lust and Charity."

Greater London Council

Interior facing west of the Royal Exchange, built by Sir Thomas Gresham between 1566 and 1571 (Wenceslaus Hollar, 1644).

from Flanders. It boasted a lofty bell tower surmounted by the grasshopper emblem of Gresham. Howes's 1631 edition of Stow's *Annales* (p. 869; cited by W&C, above) furnishes a full description of the retailing activities in the Royal Exchange: "For then the milliners or haberdashers in that place sold mouse-traps, bird-cages, shoeing-horns, lanthorns, and Jews' trumps, etc. There were also at that time [those] that kept shops in the upper pawn [corridor] of the Royal Exchange, armourers that sold both old and new armour, apothecaries, booksellers, goldsmiths, and glass-sellers."

The New Exchange was a project conceived and carried out by Robert Cecil, earl of Salisbury, who leased additional property next to his own residence in the Strand in hopes of stimulating economic growth in this part of London and enhancing his own reputation.[4] It was opened in 1609 with a layout similar to that of the Royal Exchange. Difficulty in renting out many of the one hundred shops on the upper floor led to the conversion of this area into private lodgings in 1627. Ten years later a more favorable economic climate caused the upper floor to be rededicated to commercial purposes, at which time also occurred an overall redesigning which cost £1,030. Between 1660 and 1680 the New Exchange enjoyed its greatest prosperity. Pepys's *Diary*, wherein it is mentioned several times, notes that the premises even included a milk bar popular with Westminster-bound lawyers.[5] Because of the ever-westward movement of the social and fashionable center of London, the New Exchange declined after 1680. It was pulled down in 1737, and eleven houses replaced it. This was exactly one hundred years after the death of Jonson, who had collaborated with Inigo Jones on an entertainment marking the New Exchange's official opening.

In *EMI* Kitely promises to meet a business acquaintance "on the *Exchange*, anon" (2.1.10). Later, when he asks "What's a clocke?" his clerk Cash replies "*Exchange* time, sir" (3.3.44). Kitely then instructs Cash to send any news of Wellbred's activities to him at this place of business (l. 118). In musing upon Cash's trustworthiness, Kitely admits, "But, should he have a chinke in him, I were gone, / Lost i' my fame forever, talke for th'Exchange" (3.3.61–62). In this same play, Captain Bobadil asserts that the Exchange is one of the places where swordsmen wishing to test his skill have accosted him (4.7.46). Brisk, the foppish courtier in *EMO*, discloses his plans to meet Puntarvolo "at a *Notaries*, by the *Exchange*" (4.2.65–66). We are informed that another would-be gallant, Sir Amorous La Foole of *Epic*, has his home in the Strand so that he may observe young ladies on their

4. All the following material in this paragraph is from Lawrence Stone, "Inigo Jones and the New Exchange," *Archaeological Journal* 114 (1957):106–21, passim.

5. *Diary of Samuel Pepys*, ed. Robert Latham and William Matthews. 6 vols. to date (London: G. Bell, 1970—), 4:164, 286; 5:133–34, 198, 269; 6:120. The citations given by Stone, p. 120, are from the Wheatley edition (1893–99).

way to the China Houses (q.v.) and the Exchange in order to later "acciden-
tally" meet them there (1.3.35–37). Here and in the next two citations the
reference is to the New Exchange in the Strand. Later in this play Madame
Haughty tries to persuade Epicoene to accompany the Collegiate Ladies "to
Bed'lem [q.v.], to the *China*-houses, and to the *Exchange*" (4.3.24–25). In
Alch Subtle's catalogue of the pleasures available to Dame Pliant includes a
coach driven by eight mares "to hurry her through *London*, to th'*Exchange,
Bet'lem*, the *China*-houses" (4.4.47–48). In *BF* Littlewit challenges the
Exchange, along with Moorfields (q.v.) and Pimlico Path (q.v.) to produce
the equal of Win's outfit for the fair (1.2.6–8). In *DA* the unscrupulous
Meercraft gives word to his accomplice, "Tell Mr. *Wood-cock*, I'll not faile to
meet him / Upon th' *Exchange* at night" (2.1.20–21). The Exchange in *SN*
is one of the sources of information for this news-gathering institution
(1.2.60; 1.4.15; 1.5.110). The Exchange emissary in *SN* is *"Froy Hans
Buz"* (1.2.70–71), a Dutchman. In *ML* Compass tells the devious lawyer
Practise to meet the Loadstone wedding party at Parson Palate's church,
which is located "Behind the old Exchange" (4.6.11), where once stood the
church of St. Bartholomew, Exchange. Jonson's references to this financial
institution are probably all to the Royal Exchange, except for the three
occasions in *Epic* and *Alch* as previously noted and the Britain's Burse
entertainment discussed below. People such as La Foole and the Collegiate
Ladies would be attracted by the novelty of the New Exchange, which was
located near their homes and offered more rare and exotic articles than did
Gresham's institution. Information recently discovered among the Cecil
papers at Hatfield House reveals that Jonson collaborated with Inigo Jones
to produce a modest entertainment presented before King James at the
opening of the New Exchange in 1609.[6] The script is lacking, but
documents remain which list payment to three performers: Nathan Field,
William Ostler, and Giles Gary. Finally, Jonson makes a few references to
the Exchanges in his poems. Denouncing materialism in *Und* 42, "An
Elegie," the poet remarks, "O, what strange / Varietie of Silkes were on
th'Exchange! / Or in Moore-fields, this other night!" (ll. 71–73). In *Und*
43, "An Execration upon Vulcan," among the matter deemed fitting for
this god's repast are "Captaine *Pamp*[*h*]*lets* horse, and foot, that sallie /
Upon th'Exchange, still, out of Popes-head-Alley [q.v.]" (ll. 79–80).

---

6. Scott McMillin, "Jonson's Early Entertainments," pp. 153–66. The actors are
discussed on pp. 159ff.

F

FENCHURCH STREET. A central London street which runs from the corner of Aldgate and Leadenhall west to Gracechurch Street.

This street figures prominently in the nocturnal merriment of *Englishmen for My Money*, from which S (p. 189) offers a citation. Also, the "Cripple of Fenchurch Street" is an important character in Heywood's *The Fair Maid of the Exchange*. The King's Head Tavern in Fenchurch Street was long reputed to have been where Queen Elizabeth had her first dinner upon release from the Tower of London. However, as has been noted by W&C (2:35), this tradition conflicts with a contemporary report quoted by Nichols, *Progresses* (1:8) that recounts how the young queen took a barge from Tower Wharf to Richmond and went from there to Windsor and Woodstock.

One of the triumphal arches for King James's progress to his official coronation in 1604, for which Jonson, Dekker, and Middleton wrote speeches of welcome and praise, was set up in Fenchurch Street. Jonson's comments were appropriate to this structure's lavish ornamentation, which represented "Londinium"; H&S (7:83–94) reprint Jonson's remarks uttered by characters representing "Genius" and "Tamesis" (see Thames). The former urged the city to raise "thy forehead high, and on it strive to weare / Thy choisest gems" because "thou now art blist to see / That sight, for which thou didst begin to be" (ll. 277–78, 284–85).

FETTER LANE. A thoroughfare running south from Holborn, joining Fleet Street near the middle of its course between Ludgate and the western limits of the City.

S (p. 190) declares that Fetter Lane appears to have been associated with pawnbrokers in the seventeenth century and cites an excerpt from Barry's *Ram-Alley*, "Take thou these books, / Go both to the broker's in Fetter-lane, / Lay them in pawn for a velvet jerkin / And a double ruff" (3.1). Stow records (2:39) that it was "so called of Fewters (or idle people) lying there . . . now of latter yeares on both sides builded through with many fayre houses." This etymology has been upheld by Kingsford (2:363), who refers to the *New English Dictionary* definition of "faitour" as "an imposter, a cheat, especially a vagrant, who shams illness or pretends to tell fortunes." It is thus not surprising, as W&C (2:37) have noted, that both the Holborn and Fleet Street ends of Fetter Lane were used as sites for public executions.

In *EMO* Fungoso, in debt to his tailor, asserts, "Fortie shillings more I can borrow on my gowne in *Fetter-lane*" (4.2.98–99).

The Londinium arch in Fenchurch Street which greeted James I on his coronation procession in 1604 (from the architect Stephen Harrison's *Arches of Triumph*, 1604).

FINSBURY. In Jonson's time generally a reference to the open area north of Moorfields (q.v.) often used for archery or recreative purposes.

There had earlier been a prebendal manor or lordship of Finsbury north of the City wall between Moorgate and Cripplegate. The above sporting ground (often referred to as Finsbury Fields) was once part of the manor and given later to the City for public use.[1] Later there came to be a Finsbury Square (laid out between 1777 and 1781) and a Finsbury Circus (1814).[2] In 1835 the overall area once comprising the prebendal manor was classified as a *division* of Ossulston Hundred, one of the six hundreds making up the county of Middlesex.[3] In 1899 this same general locale was re-formed into the metropolitan borough of Finsbury and remained so until 1966 when it was combined with Islington to form the new inner London borough of Islington.[4] No reference to the "Finsbury Hundred" which is significantly utilized by Jonson below has been found.

In several dramas it is apparent that Jonson, like many other playwrights, has the recreative "Finsbury Fields" locale in mind. In *EMI* Stephen complains of the provincial implications of his suburban home, "Because I dwell at *Hogsden* [q.v.], I shall keepe companie with none but the archers of *Finsburie*? or the citizens, that come a ducking to *Islington* ponds?" (1.1.47–50). In *BF* Quarlous says to Waspe just after he has discovered the theft of Cokes's marriage certificate, "Nay, Sir, stand not you fixt here, like a stake in *Finsbury* to be shot at" (5.6.93–94). In *DA* among the gentlemanly delights described by Meercraft are "*Finsbury* battells" with lead soldiers (3.2.41). H&S (10:240) point out that the site of these mock affrays, staged by the City Trained Bands, was Bunhill Fields, near where the Honourable Artillery Company (q.v.) has its present headquarters. In *TT*, however, Jonson seems to invoke Finsbury in a metaphorical rather than a literal sense. Although the action of the play is supposedly laid in "Finsbury Hundred," a careful reading shows that the scene is set about two miles northwest of the area known in Jonson's time as Finsbury. Also, as mentioned above, I have found no record of an administrative unit called "Finsbury Hundred." That the "Council of Finsbury" which attempts to govern "Finsbury Hundred" in *TT* (H&S, 3:9) has no actual counterpart in

1. Harben, *Dictionary of London*, p. 230; reaffirmed by Margaret McDerby, *Official Guide to the Metropolitan Borough of Finsbury* (London: Pyramid Press, 1963), p. 19.

2. W&C, 2:42, 44. These authorities also point out a "Finsbury Park" in the Hornsey district, over two miles from the area under consideration. It acquired this name in 1866 from the Metropolitan Board of Works. Clunn, *The Face of London*, p. 386, suggests that it was originally meant to serve the crowded Finsbury area.

3. Samuel Lewis, *A Topographical Dictionary of England*, 3 vols. (London: Lewis, 1835), 2: no pagination. Much earlier, Blaeu's map of Middlesex (ca. 1650) labels much of today's north and west London "Fynnesbury and Wenlaxbarne Liberties."

4. McDerby, *Official Guide to Finsbury*, p. 18; 1966 data (mimeographed list) available from the Greater London Council.

local government is entirely in keeping with Jonson's habit of making his satiric targets general types rather than specific individuals. The members of Jonson's imaginary civic body speak in a "rustic" dialect loaded with malapropisms. Many of their concerns, however, such as ancestral pride, social mobility, and antiquarianism are those in which London's would-be elite (and Jonson's audiences) were keenly interested. Thus it was not only artistically successful but also professionally prudent for Jonson to identify this comic and unflattering picture of local leadership with an imaginary governing body. Near the beginning of *TT* Canon Hugh tells Squire Tub that it was the Finsbury Council's idea to marry Audrey Turfe to John Clay (1.1.32–42). The council's most learned member, Diogenes Scriben, earnestly avows his unfamiliarity with "Sin Valentine" by saying that he has not seen any record of his existence "in *Finsbury* Bookes" (1.2.14). Constable Turfe is proud to call his prospective son-in-law "a *Midlesex* Clowne; and one of *Finsbury*" (1.3.34). Leading the wedding procession, Turfe cries out, "Presse all noises / Of *Finsbury*, in our name" (1.4.50–51). Dame Turfe speaks of "the wise-men all of *Finsbury*" (3.8.30). Tub's retainer, Basket-Hilts, addresses them as "the High Constables Counsell, here of *Finsbury*" and "wise men of *Finsbury*" (5.2.16, 18); a short time later Tub calls them "the foure wise Masters here, / Of *Finsbury* Hundred" (5.3.7–8), "Councell of *Finsbury*" (5.6.24–25), and again "the Wise of *Finsbury*" (5.7.57). In the play's final scenes Hilts invites a member of the Tub household to view Medlay's masque, "Come goe with me / To the sage sentences of *Finsbury*" (5.8.15–16). During the masque, which was contrived by one of the council, mention is again made of "the wise of *Finsbury*" (5.10.21). All of these references to the council's wisdom are, of course, ironic, because this group is for the most part composed of bungling, ignorant, and narrow-minded provincials whose ineptness is an important thematic motif in the play.

FISH STREET, OLD AND NEW. City thoroughfares existing concurrently but some distance apart in Jonson's time. Old Fish Street ran west from Bread Street (q.v.) to Old Change. New Fish Street was situated well to the east, below Old London Bridge, running south from Eastcheap (q.v.) to Lower Thames Street. Old Fish Street was absorbed into what is now Queen Victoria Street. New Fish remains under the name of Fish Street Hill.[5]

S (p. 192) informs us that Old Fish Street was the site of London's first fish market and was famous for the quality of the food and drink offered by

---

5. W&C, 2:45–46, are the most helpful in differentiating between these two thoroughfares. In addition, there was Old Fish Street Hill, of which a small portion still remains running north from Queen Victoria Street along the east side of St. Nicholas Cole Abbey Church.

its many taverns. The latter point also held true for New Fish Street. H&S (10:562) quote Stow (1:211) on this matter: "In new Fishstreete bee Fishmongers and fayre Tavernes." Until the period 1831–35 when King William Street was built, New Fish Street was the main approach to Old London Bridge. As noted by W&C (2:424), London Bridge then was located one hundred eighty feet farther down river than where the present bridge (built in 1825–31 and replaced in 1969–72) stands. W&C (2:45–46) point out that several trade tokens from taverns in Old Fish Street have been preserved.

In the *BF* puppet show, Hero comes *"over into Fish-street to eat some fresh herring"* (5.4.154), as promised by the synopsis which specifies this thoroughfare as Old Fish Street (5.3.124–25). Leander then journeys to woo her at a Swan Tavern (q.v.) in this area (5.4.156, 199–204). Later, Damon also seeks Hero in Fish Street (ll. 231–32). In *CHM* Father Christmas declares that no masquers from either Fish Street are to be admitted because of their associations with "Fish, and fasting dayes" (ll. 81–83, 85–86). These passages, along with the early reference to Curriers Hall (q.v.) in this masque may be regarded as satiric portrayals of hyper-Protestantism, through which Jonson rebuked those members of his audience whose sectarian prejudices permeated even their festive moments.

FLEET BRIDGE. One of the four bridges across the Fleet Ditch (q.v.), then connecting Ludgate Hill with Fleet Street (q.v.).

According to S (p. 194), this bridge built in 1431 was sometimes used by dramatists as a demarcation point between the City and more fashionable areas. In Mayne's *The City-Match* a law student exclaims, "I thought all wit had ended at Fleet-bridge" (1.4). K (p. 355) notes that in 1699 Fleet Bridge was a marketplace where nuts, gingerbread, oranges, and oysters were hawked from small, wheeled shops, often tended by disreputable-looking vendors. W&C (2:55) cite a comment from Gildon's *Comparison between the Two Stages* (1702, p. 67) which corroborates Jonson's reference below to this area, "Gad, there's not a year but some surprising monster lands: I wonder they don't first show her at Fleet Bridge, with an old drum and a cract trumpet—walk in and take your places—just going to show."

In *EMO* Sogliardo says, "They say, there's a new Motion of the city of *Nineveh*, with JONAS, and the whale, to be seene at Fleetbridge? you can tell, cousin? (2.3.146–48). H&S (9:730) cross-reference Jonson's mention in *Volp* of the "rare motion, to be seene in *Fleet-street*" (5.4.77) with the *EMO* citation above.

FLEET DITCH. The name applied by Jonson's era to the erstwhile river which flowed south from the near-rural northern villages of Hampstead and Highgate into the Thames just west of the old City wall.

In the thirteenth century this waterway was navigable up to Holborn (q.v.) Bridge, but fifty years later it had become choked by filth from tanneries and dumps. It was a common sewer in the sixteenth century, reported impassable for boats by 1652. S (p. 194), who provides this information, declares that enlargement of its course after the Great Fire was of no help and that by 1766 the Fleet Ditch was completely covered over. Dramatists usually regarded it unflatteringly, as in Davenant's *News From Plymouth*, where a character speaks of the "distress'd daughters of old Eve, that lie windbound / About Fleet-Ditch" (5. 1). H&S (11:30) note that for a short stretch north of Holborn Bridge the Ditch was known as Turnmill Brook and that Stow (1:26) records how the waterway had narrowed by his time. Stow also remarks (p. 13) that in 1589 a thousand marks were collected for the cleaning of the Ditch to no avail: "The Brooke . . . is now become woorse cloyed and [choken] then ever it was before." W&C (2:52) cite Fuller, *Worthies* (2:348), who declared, "It creepeth slow enough; not so much for age, as the injection of city excrements wherewith it is obstructed."[6]

Jonson makes unforgettably pungent and often witty use of the Fleet Ditch as the setting for his burlesque of a classical voyage to the underworld in *Epig* 133, "On the Famous Voyage," where two local adventurers decide to navigate from the Thames to Holborn in a wherry.

FLEET LANE. A narrow thoroughfare which runs from Old Bailey west to Farringdon Street. The latter now occupies the site of the Fleet Ditch (q.v.) mentioned below.

In Jonson's time this locale was chiefly occupied by taverns and cooking shops, as a passage cited by S (p. 194) and H&S (11:32) from Massinger's *The City Madam* bears out, "Fie on 'em! they smell of Fleet-lane and Pie-corner [see Bartholomew Fair]" (1.1.152).

The above associations are reinforced by Jonson's *Epig* 133, "On the Famous Voyage," where the dwellers along the banks of the Fleet Ditch include "*Fleet*-lane *Furies*; and hot cookes" (l. 143).

FLEET PRISON. A jail used for Chancery Court and Star Chamber (q.v.) offenses located east of the Fleet Ditch (q.v.) and a little to the north of Ludgate Hill.

On the treatment of inmates in the Fleet, S (p. 195) cites John Bradford's paraphrase of Psalm lxxix; *Writings* (1:289), "How miserably they handle thy bond-servants . . . the prisons of the King's Bench, Marshalsea, Fleet,

6. K, p. 354, notes an attempt to clean this waterway as early as 1307 when Henry Lacy petitioned for such action and also for the removal of a mill farther upstream. His petition was granted, but the river soon became filth-clogged again, and an official commission was this time appointed to supervise the job.

Newgate, and in many other places . . . doth presently to all the world cry out." Among the writers incarcerated in the Fleet in Johnson's era were Henry Howard, Thomas Nashe, and Thomas Dekker. A 1593 petition to Lord Burghley cited by K (p. 406) stated, "The place is a congregation of unwholesome smells of the town." Especially revealing are excerpts from letters in the *State Papers, Domestic, 1619–23* (pp. 68–69, 86) cited by W&C (2:58):

August 2, 1619—The Warden [of the Fleet] has put into the dungeon called Boulton's ward, a place newly made to exercise his cruelty, three poor men, Pecke, Segar, and Myners, notwithstanding the express command of the Council that they should be favorably dealt with till further orders; they are starving from want of food.

October 16, 1619—Sir John Whitbrook killed in the Fleet by Boughton, a fellow prisoner, of whose turbulence he had often complained.

In *Epig* 133, "On the Famous Voyage," a mournful accompaniment to the sights and sounds of this trip up the Fleet Ditch are "the out-cryes of the damned in the *Fleet*" (l. 172). The errant apprentice Quicksilver in *EH* boasts, "Let 'hem take their choice, eyther the *Kings Benche*, or the *Fleete* . . . I like none of 'hem" (2.2.263–66). In *SN* Penniboy Senior is warned that rash words against the government may land him in the Fleet with his ears cropped (2.3.51). In *Und* 15, "An Epistle to a Friend," the poet comments disapprovingly about ostentatious and expensive dress. A man who spends all his money "on his back, shall after blow / His body to the Counters [q.v.], or the Fleete" (ll. 104–5).

FLEET STREET. An important thoroughfare which runs west from Ludgate Hill to Temple Bar (q.v.) where it becomes the Strand.

    The Inns of Court (q.v.) were located in this vicinity, as were also the residences of some eminent persons and a multitude of taverns. A splendid conduit erected in 1388 stood in Fleet Street just west of Shoe Lane. It featured a stone tower topped by statues of St. Christopher and some angels with a chime of bells worked by internal engines. S (pp. 195–96), who supplies the above background, provides dramatic evidence for regarding this street as a center for fashionable display. In Beaumont and Fletcher, *Wit at Several Weapons*, Oldcraft says of his niece, "At first snap she's a Countess, drawn with six mares through *Fleet-Street*" (1.1), and in Mayne's *The City-Match* a young merchant says to some law students, "I deny not / But you look well in your unpaid-for glory, / That in these colours you set out the Strand / And adorn Fleet Street; that you may laugh at me" (1.4). H&S (10:387) note one of this street's festive moments when, according to the architect Stephen Harrison's account of James I's 1604 coronation progress through London, "The *Conduits* of *Cornhill* [q.v.], of *Cheape* [q.v.], and of *Fleetestreete*, that day ran Claret wine very plenteously." Wealthy Fleet Street dwellers, says Stow (1:18), had Thames water piped into their homes. W&C (2:61–62) and K (pp. 263–66) associate residences in Fleet Street with John Florio, Michael Drayton, James Shirley, Isaak Walton, and John Milton. A long tradition maintains that Prince Henry and Prince Charles held their councils as Princes of Wales in a still extant first-floor room at 17 Fleet Street.[7] According to W&C, above, puppet shows, waxworks, and other exhibitions were a common part of the Fleet Street scene from Elizabethan through Victorian times.

Downright, *EMI*, is conscious of protecting his public reputation when he avers, "'Sdeynes, and I swallow this, Ile ne're draw my sword in the sight of *Fleet-Street* againe" (2.2.20–22). Fleet Street's reputation as a showplace for the rare and curious is well maintained by two Jonsonian references. In *Epic* Dauphine relates how Morose, to escape his "bride's" garrulousness, has perched "over a cross-beame o' the roofe, like him o' the sadlers horse in *Fleetstreet*, up-right" (4.1.24–25). Peregrine, *Volp*, aptly comments of Sir Politic's attempt to hide in a large tortoise shell, "'Twere a rare motion, to be seene in *Fleet-street*" (5.4.77).

FORTUNE THEATER. A playhouse opened in 1600 which stood north of the city outside Cripplegate, between Golding (now Golden) Lane and Whitecross Street.

The building contract of the Fortune, financed by Philip Henslowe and Edward Alleyn, is still preserved among the Henslowe Papers at Dulwich College. The overall structure was eighty feet square and cost £520. As S (p. 199) and many other authorities have pointed out, it was destroyed in a 1621 fire and rebuilt soon after with brickwork on the outside and, according to James Wright's dialogue (*Historia Histrionica*, 1699), in the more common polygonal shape.[8] W&C (2:69) cite a 1621 letter from John Chamberlain to Sir Dudley Carleton where the Fortune is termed "the fairest playhouse in the town." The level of its dramaturgy, however, was by no means comparable. G. E. Bentley (*The Jacobean and Caroline Stage*, 6:146) states that during Charles I's reign it was "one of the lowest theatrical resorts in town" and documents its degeneration with evidence dating as early as 1612. The Admiral's Men, Prince Henry's Men, the

7. A full and objective account of the property, which is open to the public on weekday afternoons, is furnished in *No. 17 Fleet Street*, a pamphlet issued by the Greater London Council. The revised edition (1967) declares, "The evidence is therefore against any close connection between the Duchy of Cornwall [another title held by the Prince of Wales] and No. 17 though it is possible that on occasion the fine room on the first floor might have been hired for a Council meeting" (p. 10).

8. Bentley, *The Jacobean and Caroline Stage*, 6:155, while admitting that this tendency toward conformity seems plausible, maintains that "it would, however, be comfortable to have evidence earlier than Wright's."

Palsgrave's Men, the King's Revels Company, the Red Bull-King's Company, and Prince Charles's Men all used this theater before it was sacked by the Puritans in 1649 and mostly pulled down in 1661.[9]

A comment to the player Histrio in *Poet*, "You have *fortune*, and the good yeere on your side" (3.4.126–27), has caused scholars to judge this a reference to the rival Admiral's Company, as H&S (1:426n.) state. *Und* 43, "An Execration upon Vulcan," includes the 1621 fire in a catalogue of recent destructive blazes (ll. 153–55).

FRIDAY STREET. A City thoroughfare which today runs south from Cannon Street to Queen Victoria Street. In Jonson's time Friday Street's course was longer, extending south from Cheapside to Old Fish Street.

Like Jonson, Nabbes plays upon the "papist" associations of this street name in *The Springs Glory* when Shrovetide ridicules Lent as "this leane thin-gut starveling, begot by a Spaniard, and nurst at the lower end of Friday-Street" (p. 232). H&S (10:562) refer to Stow (1:351) for its etymology, "so called of fishmongers dwelling there, and serving Frydayes market."

In *CHM* no masquers from this area or from Fish Street are allowed entry into the festivities because of their "papist" tendencies (ll. 80–86). Here as in his earlier reference to Curriers' Hall (q.v.) in this piece, Jonson appears to be overemphasizing Protestant elements for comic and satiric effects.

FULHAM. Then a Thames-side village in Middlesex six miles southwest of the City, today very much a part of the metropolis.

S (p. 211) notes that besides boasting a palace used by the bishops of London, Fulham had associations with another sort of devotion, for according to the *New English Dictionary* it was a notorious hangout of gamesters. "Fulham," a canting term for loaded dice, may thus have derived from the topographical reference, as both S and H&S (9:453–54) suggest. Such is the basis for puns upon this village's name, of which Jonson's reference below is an excellent example. S cites some appearances of the gambling term in Tudor-Stuart drama. In *Nobody and Somebody* an inquisitive character is told that in a particular bale of dice, "These are called high Fulloms . . . those low fulloms" (sig. G3^v). In *The Merry Wives of Windsor* Pistol exclaims, "Let vultures gripe thy guts; for gourd and fullam holds, / And high and low beguiles the poor" (1.3.94–95).

In *EMO* Carlo boasts about Shift, "Who? he serve? Sbloud he keepes high men, and low men, he; he has a faire living at *Fullam*" (3.6. 154–55).

9. Bentley, p. 178, citing William Maitland, *History of London* . . . (1739), 2:1370, states that as late as 1739 some of the ruins were still to be seen in the Golding Lane neighborhood.

G

GARDINER'S LANE. A thoroughfare in Westminster which once extended from 20 King Street to Delahay Street. All these streets were obliterated around 1906 when a large block of government offices was erected between Parliament Street and St. James's Park.[1]

Little of note seems to be associated with Gardiner's Lane, although H&S (10:281) record that the eminent seventeenth-century engraver Wenceslaus Hollar had his last residence there.

During the third intermeane in *SN*, Gossip Mirth declares, pleased with the sources of news available to her cohorts, "*I, my Gossip* Tatle *knew what fine slips grew in* Gardiners-lane" (ll. 24–25). The remark of S (p. 214) on this comment—that Jonson puns on "slips" to create a reference to illegitimate children in the area—appears to be accurate. Like the other places mentioned in this part of the play, Gardiner's Lane was close to the poet's own residence in Westminster at this time; hence this comment may be viewed as a subtle jest about his neighbors' behavior—or perhaps even his own.

GLASSHOUSE. A glassmaking factory. Records remain of one such establishment located in the district vacated by the Crutched Friars (near Fenchurch Street station today) and another in Blackfriars.

S (p. 223) declares that visiting the glasshouses was a fashionable amusement in Jonson's day and cites examples of this habit from *Westward Ho* and *The Parson's Wedding*, as well as a memorable reference by Dekker in *Jests to Make you Merrie* (*Non-Dramatic Works*, 2:305) to the continual fires in these establishments, "O envy . . . wash thine eies that lookes flaming like the ceaselesse fire of the Glashouse," H&S (11:80) point out that Stow records (1:148) that the glasshouse in Crutched Friars burned down in 1575 when stocked with forty thousand billets of wood. The glasshouse in Blackfriars stood close to today's thoroughfare of Playhouse Yard, near the Blackfriars indoor theater. As W&C (2:115) have noted, Dekker used this glasshouse in *Newes from Hell* (reissued as *A Knight's Conjuring; Non-Dramatic Works*, 2:97–98): "For like the Glass-house *Furnace* in Blackefriers, the bone-fiers that are kept there, never goe out, insomuch that all the Inhabitants are almost broylde like Carbonadoes with the sweating sickness."

---

1. Clunn, *The Face of London*, p. 258.

In *Und* 43, "An Execration upon Vulcan," the poet asks for just punishment of the errant deity, "A Court of *Equitie* should doe us right, / But to confine him to the Brew-houses, / The Glasse-house, Dye-fats, and their Fornaces" (ll. 178–80).

GLOBE THEATER. A principal early London theater located in Southwark on the south side of Maid Lane (now Park Street) at or near where it is today crossed by Southwark Bridge Road.[2]

Cuthbert and Richard Burbage built the Globe in 1598–99 with timbers from London's first public playhouse, the Theater. At the Globe performed Shakespeare's company, the Chamberlain's / King's Men. In 1613 this theater was destroyed by fire during a performance of *Henry VIII*. As S (p. 224) has pointed out, John Taylor (*The Sculler; Folio of 1630*, pt. 3, p. 31 [Spenser Society, 4]) viewed this catastrophe optimistically, "As gold is better that's in fire tride, / So is the Bankside *Globe* that late was burn'd; / For where before it had a thatched hide, / Now to a stately Theater 'tis turn'd." H&S (11:79) refer to the eyewitness account of the fire provided by Sir Henry Wotton. The conflagration started when cannon wadding used during a festive scene lighted in the thatched roof, burning the structure to the ground in less than an hour. Another account of this blaze occurs in a letter from John Chamberlain to Sir Ralph Winwood, as cited by W&C (2:116–17).[3]

The Globe was the scene for early performances of *EMO* (1599), *Sejanus* (1604), and *Volp* (1606). The induction to *EMO* contains what H&S (9:424) feel is a reference to its construction. Here Cordatus is termed "a well-timbered fellow" who "would ha' made a good columne, and he had beene thought on, when the house was a building" (ll. 327–29). The revised Quarto conclusion to this play entreats applause from "the happier spirits in this fair-fild Globe" (l. 24). A less idealized version of this playhouse is offered in *Poet*, where Captain Tucca angrily tells Histrio, "And you stage me, stinkard; your mansions will sweat for't . . . your *Globes*, and your *Triumphs*" (3.4.199–201). Similarly, the faults of Everill, according to Meercraft in *DA*, include "haunting / The *Globes*, and *Mermaides* [q.v.]! wedging in with *Lords*" (3.3.25–26). In *Und* 43, "An

2. Roberts and Godfrey, *Bankside*, p. 75. The editors cite W. W. Braines. *The Site of the Globe Playhouse* (1924) and a 1618 map of Southwark at the Guildhall.

3. Bentley, *The Jacobean and Caroline Stage*, 6:179n., calls this disaster "one of the most fully attested occurrences in the early seventeenth-century theatre" and notes that on the next day two ballads on the fire were entered at Stationers' Hall. Besides Taylor, Wotton, and Chamberlain, contemporary recorders of the fire include Thomas Lorkin, cited in Birch, *The Court and Times of James the First*, 1:253, and Edmund Howes's continuation of Stow's *Annales* (both 1615 and 1631), Iiii.

Execration upon Vulcan," the poet declares that he saw the burned-out
Globe with "nothing but the piles / Left! and wit since to cover it with
Tiles" (ll. 137–38).

GOLDSMITHS' ROW. A block of splendid shops and residences on the
south side of Cheapside (q.v.) which extended from Bread Street to the
Cross opposite the end of Wood Street.

S (p. 226) reports that these buildings were built in 1491 by a
goldsmith, Thomas Wood, and that they were chiefly occupied by others of
that trade until the seventeenth century, when Howes complained in 1631
that goldsmiths were moving to more fashionable quarters farther west,
leaving the Row open for booksellers and linen drapers. A 1634 edict
attempting to limit tenancy in the Row to goldsmiths was ineffective. H&S
(10:244) cite Stow (1:345), who describes this locale as "the most beautiful frame of fayre houses and shoppes, that bee within the Walles of London,
or else where in England. . . . It contayneth in number tenne fayre
dwelling houses, and fourteene shoppes, all in one frame, uniformely
builded foure stories high, bewtified towardes the street with the
Goldsmithes armes." Kingsford (2:351–52) calls attention to Paul
Hentzner's account of the Row; this traveler mentioned that its ornamentation included "a gilt tower, with a fountain that plays." W&C (2:125) cite
John Chamberlain's comments on City conditions after James's latest
money-raising project in 1622, "But it was remembered how impoverished
it is since the last loan, and it is a strange sight to see meaner trades creep
into Goldsmiths' Row, the glory and beauty of Cheapside."

It is logical to assume that Touchstone the goldsmith in *EH*, who
overmodestly refers to himself as a "poore *Cheapside* groome" (4.2.234–35)
dwells in the Row. Also, Fitzdottrel's reference in *DA* to a present shortage
of gold in the Row (3.5.2–3) shows Jonson's awareness of the above shift of
tenants.

GOOSE FAIR. A yearly festival held on Whit Monday in the village of
Stratford atte Bow (q.v.) a few miles east of the City.

S (p. 71) furnishes a witty exchange from Middleton's *A Chaste Maid in
Cheapside*. When the Porter tells the goldsmith Yellowhammer, "If I see
your worship at Goose-fair, I have a dish of birds for you," the latter replies,
"Why, dost thou dwell at Bow?" "All my life, sir," replies the Porter, "I
could ever say bo to a goose" (1.1.81–85). H&S (9:555) point out that
John Taylor (*Taylor's Goose; Folio of 1630*, pt. 1. p. 110 [Spenser Society,
2]) describes this fair's activities, among which was the eating of young
geese.

In *Poet* Captain Tucca threatens to reduce Histrio to the state where he will "march in a tawnie coate, with one sleeve, to Goose-faire, and then you'll know us" (3.4.134–35).

GRACECHURCH STREET. A City thoroughfare running south from the junction of Cornhill and Leadenhall to Eastcheap.

Both S (p. 229) and H&S (10:667) note that it was originally called Grass Street, being the site of London's first fodder market. The parish church was called Grass Church and later Grace Church; this street name followed suit. By Stow's time it was a center of the poultry trade (1:186), as several dramatic references cited by S testify. Also in this street was the Saba Tavern, kept by the Elizabethan comedian Richard Tarlton. W&C (2:136) point out that at the Cross Keys Inn, a Gracechurch Street establishment, Bankes exhibited the feats of his "wonder horse" Marocco.

In the antimasque portion of *Nep Tr* Jonson displays his knowledge of this street's associations, as his cast includes "a plump Poultrers wife, in *Graces* Street," who "playes Hen with egges i' the belly, or a Coney" (ll. 299–300).

GREENWICH. Then a Thames-side village five miles east of St. Paul's. Its palace was the birthplace of Henry VIII, Mary Tudor, and Elizabeth, while James I and Charles I often resided there.

S (pp. 235–36) states that the royal park at Greenwich, covering almost two hundred acres, was first enclosed in 1433 and that the view from Greenwich Tower was held to be one of the best in Europe. John Taylor (*Honourable and Memorable Foundations*, 1636, p. 12 [Spenser Society, 21]) praised Greenwich "for situation and prospect a Paradise of pleasure."

James I attempted to heighten its attraction by commissioning Inigo Jones to build the "Queen's House" for his Anne of Denmark. She died, however, before its completion, which was put off until Charles had the desire and funds to see the project through. Like so many other royal residences, Greenwich passed through difficult times during the Commonwealth, but prospects brightened again with Charles II's hopes for an entirely new palace planned by Jones's nephew John Webb. Lack of funds thwarted part of this effort also, and James II had little interest in developing this site for the monarchy. He proposed instead that a naval hospital be set up at Greenwich, and his son-in-law William III made it a reality. In 1873 the buildings became the home of the Royal Naval College, as they remain today, except for the Queen's House. Since 1937 this has served as part of the National Maritime Museum.

Jonson pays tribute to the reputation Greenwich enjoyed as a beauty spot by ranking it with St. James's Park (q.v.) and Theobald's House (q.v.) as one of "the finer walled places" (ll. 94–95) in *GM*. The sorry progress of the

"Virginia voyagers" in *EH* is revealed by Goulding's statement that they may have been shipwrecked "o' this side *Greenwich*" (4.2.87). In his "Epithalamium" celebrating the Weston-Stuart marriage, *Und* 75, the poet notes that this occasion "Hath fil[l]ed, with *Caroches*, all the way, / From *Greenwich*, hither, to *Row-hampton* gate" (ll. 11–12). This was quite a compliment, for even as the crow flies it is ten miles between Greenwich and the wedding site at Roehampton (q.v.) Chapel.

GUILDHALL. The civic hall of the Corporation of London, standing at what is now the north end of King Street, two blocks north of Cheapside.

In this building sit the Court of Aldermen, Court of Common Council, Court of Hustings, Lord Mayor's Court, and the Sheriff's Court. In Rowley's *A New Wonder: A Woman Never Vexed*, as cited by S (p. 238), young Stephen rises to where he is "now the Sheriff of London, and in council / Set in the Guildhall in his scarlet gown" (5.1). The foundation of the present building was laid in 1411, although lord mayors have been installed in earlier structures since 1191. The annual custom of electing and ceremoniously installing lord mayors and sheriffs at the Guildhall is still observed today. Throughout its history, one of the Guildhall's most prominent ornamental features has been a pair of giant statues known as Gogmagog and Corineus, which represent the enmity between the original Celtic inhabitants of Britain and the legendary Trojan invaders. During the midsummer pageants of the sixteenth and seventeenth centuries, these statues were paraded around London. The current models, carved in limewood and over nine feet tall, replace those destroyed in the 1940 Blitz which devastated much of this section of the City.

In *EMI* Wellbred's letter to Edward Knowell ends with the promise, "*If the worst of 'hem* [gulls] *be not worth your jorney, draw your bill of charges, as unconscionable, as any Guild-hall verdict will give it you*" (1.2.87–89). In *EH* Touchstone muses, "I wonder I heare no news of my sonne *Goulding!* He was sent for to the *Guild-hall*, this Morning betimes, and I marvaile at the matter" (4.2.29–31). Soon after, it is revealed that this diligent apprentice has been appointed deputy alderman in his ward and has also been made one of the worshipful commoners of the City (ll. 38–43).[4]

---

4. This sort of rapid advancement could only have happened in a play with the satiric overtones of *Eastward Ho*. Frank Foster, "Merchants and Bureaucrats in Elizabethan London," *Guildhall Miscellany* 4, no. 3 (October 1972):158, comments, "Regardless of status, wealth, or influence, a candidate for the Court of Aldermen required a considerable amount of experience in City politics. There was a traditional though not rigid hierarchy of positions in which most rulers held a number of the same offices or served in the same capacities."

H

HACKNEY. In Jonson's time a village about three miles northeast of St. Paul's.

S (p. 240) terms Hackney "in the sixteenth century a fashionable country suburb where many noble families resided" and declares that Queen Elizabeth and her court entourage frequently visited it. Norman G. Brett-James (*The Growth of Stuart London*, p. 111) states that during the reign of James I, the proprietor of a brick kiln at Hackney was ordered to close down his works, as the noxious smell offended both the lord mayor, whose country seat was at Hackney, and King James, who regularly passed by on the way to his estate at Theobald's (q.v.). Hackney was a pleasure spot for ordinary citizens as well. In Webster, *Cure for a Cuckold*, a character asks, "Did he not dance the *Hobby-horse* in *Hackney*-Morrice once?" (2.3.13–14).

Jonson, in *Epig* 129, "To Mime," portrays his rival for court favor, Inigo Jones, as addicted to the petty pleasures of the time, "There's no journey set, or thought upon, / To *Braynford* [q.v.], *Hackney*, *Bow* [see Stratford atte Bow], but thou mak'st one" (ll. 3–4).

HAMMERSMITH. A village now an integral part of London, about six miles west of St. Paul's.

S (p. 242) remarks that Jonson, as illustrated below, was rather accurate in his comical antiquarian associations with this area, for twentieth-century scholarship has turned up some reasons for fixing Caesar's crossing of the Thames described in *De Bello Gallico* at Brentford, about four miles away.[1]

In *TT* To-Pan the tinker boastfully claims descent from one of the "Gentlemen" who landed with "Mad *Julius Caesar*" and marched from Dover to London beating England's first kettle-drum, "Which peice [*sic*] of monumentall copper hangs / Up, scourd, at *Hammer-smith* yet; for there they came / Over the *Thames*, at a low water marke" (1.3.52, 55–57). Hammersmith also may have been where Jonson reentered the London area after his walk to Scotland. An Inigo Jones poem, "To his false friend Mr. Ben Johnson," H&S (11:385) avows, "I never went to Scotland, nor did meete / thee att returne my selfe alone or with / my friends but soe far of a [s] Hammersmith" (ll. 24–26).

1. The place where Caesar crossed the Thames has never been definitely ascertained. Recently, Ralph Merrifield, *Roman London* (New York: Praeger, 1969), p. 16, included the Brentford site in his review of possible crossing points.

HAMPTON COURT. A royal palace on the Thames about fifteen miles southwest of central London.

Hampton Court's early eminence was associated with Cardinal Wolsey, whose hope of constructing a grandiose residence containing five courtyards and utilizing both medieval and Renaissance architecture was halted by his fall from power. In 1526 the estate was handed over to Henry VIII, who delighted in its pleasures and improved the grounds and buildings. In late Elizabethan and early Stuart times the great hall became a common setting for plays and other noble entertainments. Much of Hampton Court today results from Sir Christopher Wren's architectural genius, under the generous approbation of William and Mary. It continued as a popular royal residence until George III removed the ruling family's main country seat to Windsor and began the practice still followed of using Hampton Court as the home of royal officials, their widows, or important visitors.

As H&S (3:605) point out, Hampton Court is associated with Jonson in a fascinating manner, for it was from a performance of Samuel Daniel's *Vision of the Twelve Goddesses* in its great hall that Jonson and his friend Sir John Roe were ejected for unmannerly behavior. Jonson was probably chuckling at the ponderous and dull attempts of one of his rivals, whom he termed in the *Conversations With Drummond* (H&S, 1:132) "a good honest Man . . . bot no poet." Jonson pays tribute to Hampton Court when he uses it as the scene for thoughts about his lady in *Epig* 126, "To his Lady, Then Mrs. Cary." The poem opens, "Retyr'd, with purpose your faire worth to praise, / 'Mongst *Hampton* shades, and PHOEBUS grove of bayes."

HAMSTED (HAMPSTEAD). In Jonson's time an outlying parish five miles northwest of St. Paul's, composed of one important manor and its nearby village.

After the Dissolution, Hampstead Manor, once owned by Westminster Abbey, was given to Sir Thomas Wroth. His grandson, Sir Robert Wroth, husband to Mary Sidney (Sir Philip's niece), was lord of this manor from 1606 to 1614. To settle his debts, Sir Robert made over this estate and his other Middlesex property to three relatives all named John Wroth.[2] In

2. John J. Park, *The Topography and Natural History of Hampstead*, p. 115. The Wroths' connections with their Hampstead property are difficult to determine. Monica Carolan, "A Short History to 1900," in Mavis and Ian Norrie, eds., *The Book of Hampstead*, p. 160, states that Sir Robert Wroth "presumably lived at Hampstead." Earlier, J. Kennedy, *The Manor and Parish Church of Hampstead and Its Vicars* (London: Mayle, 1906), p. 53, declared, "The Wroths cared nothing for Hampstead, and sold it just when it was becoming valuable." The Wroths were good friends with Jonson, who dedicated *Alch* to Mary Wroth and *For* 3 to Sir Robert. The latter is a companion piece to his Penshurst poem in its similar praise of the "good life" in the country. However, as H&S, 11:35, remind us, the estate associated with this poem is the Wroth manor near Enfield (q.v.), several miles north of Hampstead.

1620 Hampstead Manor was sold to Sir Baptist Hicks, an eminent City merchant whose move to this area is a fine example of the northwesterly direction of London's most significant seventeenth-century growth.[3] Previously, the village of Hampstead was where the clothes of the city's gentry and nobility were brought to be washed. By the latter part of James I's reign, this area was in a transitional stage of social prestige, coming truly into its own as a resort and residential area after the accession of Charles II when the rolling fields and salubrious waters of Hampstead's spas fulfilled a much different need among prominent people.[4] A trade token issued during the Restoration from one of these Hampstead establishments has been preserved.[5]

Jonson's references to Hampstead in *TT* emphasize the still strongly rural characteristics of this area for comic and satiric effects. Rasi Clench, a blacksmith and member of the bumbling Council of Finsbury (q.v.), resides here (persons, l. 14). This is reiterated by Canon Hugh (1.1.35) and in his own assertion, "I am old Rivet still, and beare a braine, / The *Clench*, the Varrier, and true Leach of *Hamsted*" (1.2.27—28; also scene interloping, ll. 12—13). Clench is again associated with Hampstead as preparations are made for the "masque" which concludes this play (5.2.15). The "robbery" of the fake Captain Thums was said to have occurred "betwixt this and *Hamsted*-Heath" (3.9.17). Later we are reminded of the recreative qualities of the Hampstead area in Hilts's insult to the servile clerk Miles Metaphor, "Thou, that when last thou wert put out of service, / Travaild'st to *Hamsted* Heath, on a *Ash-we'nesday*, / Where thou didst stand

3. Sir Baptist was said to be the first City merchant who ran his shop after being knighted. He was one of the City aldermen commissioned to consider the renovations necessary for St. Paul's. He also personally financed construction of a judicial meeting house in Clerkenwell north of the City wall and gave many charitable bequests. A less admirable facet of his career was his costly, bitter fight over questions of precedence caused by his elevation to knight commoner in 1608. Hicks's life is summarized in J. Preston, *The Story of Hampstead* (London: Staples Press, 1948), pp. 17—18. A full account of the precedency conflict is contained in William Maitland, *The History and Survey of London from Its Foundation to the Present Time*, 2nd ed., 2 vols. (London: Osborne, 1756), 1:287—89.

4. Additional evidence of Hampstead's associations with the eminent during the early Stuart period was found in a chicken house located near Pilgrims' Lane, in a backyard off Rosslyn Hill. It contained a set of stained-glass windows, one bearing a portrait of King James, the other of Buckingham. The inscription on the former read, "Icy, dans cette chambre coucha nostre Roy Jacques premier du nom le 25me Aoust, 1619." By the late nineteenth century the windows were at Dagnam Park, Romford, the seat of Sir Thomas Neave, whose family owned the Hampstead property. See Preston, p. 67; also Barratt, *Annals of Hampstead*, 1:105—7.

5. Warwick Wroth, *The London Pleasure Gardens of the Eighteenth Century* (London: Macmillan, 1896), pp. 177—83; J. Norris Brewer, *London and Middlesex* (London: J. Harris et al., 1816), 4:190—91, also provides a full discussion of Hampstead's post-Fire social eminence.

sixe weekes the *Jacke* of *Lent*, / For boyes to hoorle, three throwes a penny, at thee" (4.2.47–50).

HARROW ON THE HILL. A village in Middlesex twelve miles northwest of London in Jonson's day, now well within the metropolitan area.

As S (p. 243) has noted, the village achieved prominence by the seventeenth century in two diverse areas. The famous public school at Harrow was founded in 1571; at about the same time one of its taverns was exposed as a haunt of rogues and vagabonds by Thomas Harman in his *Caveat for Common Cursitors*. The village's topography made it an excellent rendezvous for highwaymen because the crest of the hill which it occupies is the highest ground in Middlesex. The views from the summit, especially to the south and west, embrace several counties.[6]

Jonson's awareness of these conditions is apparent in a comment from *EMO*, where Puntarvolo asks Shift and Sogliardo, "You knew signior CLOG, that was hang'd for the robbery, at *Harrow* o' the hill?" (4.6.31–32). The comic butt in much of *BF*, Bartholomew Cokes, is described as an "Esquire" from the village (persons, l. 8; 1.1.3–4; 5.4.79–80). When Cokes makes an utter fool of himself, his overseer, Humphrey Waspe, wishes himself back in Harrow (3.5.230).

HEAVEN AND HELL TAVERNS. Drinking spots situated near Westminster Hall. The former stood on the site of the House of Commons committee rooms, and the latter was beneath the old Exchequer Chamber.[7]

Heaven, according to S (p. 244), was originally a private residence, while Hell (p. 246) began as a debtors' prison. H&S (10:112) cite a passage from Overbury's *Characters* (5th ed., 1614, sig. F3) attesting to their popularity among lawyers' clerks. They also note that John Taylor provides a witty sketch of Hell in *Part of this Summers Travels, or News from Hell, Hull, and Halifax* (1639, pp. 33–35, Spenser Society, 7). In a description of midsummer conditions at Westminster, the anonymous author of *St. Hillaries Teares* comments, "On both sides of the Hall they complaine, At Heaven they say ther's not a Lawier no Clerke comes neare them: And at hell where they had wont to flock like Swallowes to a Reede bush, they come but dropping in now and then one, as opportunity of businesse makes them able."[8] W&C (2:201) state that Hell, appropriately enough, "was of meaner grade." These authorities also point out that nearby stood "Purgat-

---

6. Clunn, *The Face of London*, p. 571.

7. Reverend MacKenzie Walcott, *Westminster: Memorials of the City . . . Streets, and Worthies* (London: Masters, 1849), pp. 220–21.

8. *St. Hillaries Teares Shed upon All Professions . . .* (London, 1642), sig. A3.

ory," a temporary prison where the ducking stool was kept, and also that Heaven was a favorite dining place of Pepys's.

The popularity of these resorts in Jonson's day is evident in Doll Common's monition to Dapper in *Alch*, that to keep his good-luck charm working he must not "breake his fast, / In *heaven*, and *hell*" (5.4.42–43).

HIGHGATE. A village on the main road to London, five miles northwest of St. Paul's. Today a popular residential quarter, it stands on one of the two chief hills just north of the City, three hundred and fifty feet above sea level.

Because of Highgate's location, there were numerous taverns and alehouses in its main street. These catered to not only bona fide travelers, but also to Londoners out for a Sunday excursion. It is as a holiday resort, as S (p. 250) illustrates, that Highgate is often mentioned in the drama. Several prominent court and City personages resided in this area; among them was Sir William Cornwallis, uncle of the essayist by the same name. In 1593 Queen Elizabeth paid a visit to this gentleman's Highgate estate, and King James repeated the gesture eleven years after. For the latter occasion Jonson provided a graceful entertainment fully discussed below. The scene for this presentation was described in 1593 by the geographer John Norden: "Upon this hill is most pleasant dwelling, yet not so pleasant as healthfull, for the expert inhabitants there, report that divers that have beene long visited with sicknes, not cureable by Physicke, have in short time, long repayred their health by that sweete salutarie aire. At this place —————— CORNEWALLEYES esquire, hath a verie faire house from which he may with great delight beholde the stately Citie of *London, Westminster, Greenewich*, the famous river of *Thamyse*, and the countrey towardes the south verie farre."[9]

Jonson significantly utilizes references to Highgate in two of his works. In *TT* he plays upon its associations with merriment and perhaps illicit revelry when one of the foolish "Council of Finsbury" (q.v.) says of "Zin" Valentine, "Hee was a deadly *Zin*, and dwelt at *High-gate*" (1.2.8). Soon after, it is revealed that this notorious figure "kept brave house" (l. 20) at the Cock and Hen Tavern in this village. In a similar vein, it is appropriate that Father Rosin, the chief musician at Audrey Turfe's wedding in this play, also hails from Highgate (1.4.35; 2.1.50). In the entertainment written to celebrate King James's 1604 visit to Cornwallis at Highgate (H&S, 7:136–44), Jonson displays a thorough knowledge of this area's topography and connotations. Details relating to the setting are employed in a graceful compliment to Jonson's patron and to this section of greater

9. *Speculum Britanniae . . . Middlesex* (1593), p. 22. H&S, 10:398, furnish the second sentence cited above in their notes.

London as well. Cornwallis's hilltop home is transformed into the dwelling place of Mercury on the Arcadian hill Cyllene. The poet recognizes Highgate's popularity with London citizens in his comments: "Here for her moneth, the yeerly delicate *May* keepes state; and from this *Mount*, takes pleasure to display those valleyes, yond' lesser hills, those statelier edifices, and towers, that seeme enamour'd so farre off, and are rear'd on end, to behold her, as if their utmost object were her beauties. Hither the *Dryads* of the valley, and *Nymphs* of the great river come every morning, to taste of her favours; and depart away with laps fill'd with her bounties" (ll. 74–82). A large part of this entertainment is devoted to a jovial drinking bout led by Pan, which is appropriate not only to Highgate's reputation as an imbibing center, but also to the court's pre-eminence in such matters.[10] Highgate is briefly mentioned in *NI*, when Barnaby the coachman explains why he is hatless, "The wind blew't off at *High-gate*, and my Lady / Would not endure mee, light, to take it up, / But made me drive bare-headed i' the raine" (4.1.15–17). Such treatment is to be expected from Barnaby's mistress, the haughty Pinnacia Stuffe, who with her tailor husband makes a habit of journeying through the towns near London dressed in clothes ordered by their customers. Apparently the Stuffes have driven up from the south in this scene, as Highgate lies several miles south of Barnet (q.v.), where this play takes place. See the Hounslow entry for a complete discussion of the Stuffes' sartorial fetish.

HOCKLEY IN THE HOLE. In the late sixteenth century both a village in Bedfordshire between Dunstable and Fenny Stratford and a locale just outside the city, northwest of Clerkenwell Green.

S (p. 251) comments that the former place was a notorious spot for robberies, being situated on an important thoroughfare en route to London. Dramatic references bear out this conclusion. In *The Birth of Merlin* the Clown says to the title figure, "Our standing-house is Hocklye i' the Hole and Layton Buzzard [a town four miles away]" (3.1.127). H&S (9:467) inaccurately associate Jonson's reference below with the Clerkenwell Hockley, which during the poet's lifetime was a settlement of no special significance. During the eighteenth century it gained fame as the site of a bear garden. The context of Jonson's quotation also makes it apparent that he had the Bedfordshire Hockley in mind.

In *EMO* Sogliardo says mockingly of Macilente, "He has been the only *Bidstand* [highwayman] that ever kept *New-market, Salisbury-plaine, Hockley* i' the hole, *Gads-Hill:* all the high places of any request" (4.5.36–

10. See the correspondence of Sir John Harington, as cited by Mary Susan Steele, *Plays and Masques at Court* (New Haven: Yale University Press, 1926), pp. 150–51.

38). All of these locales offered excellent prospects for thievery, with the reputation of Gadshill being the most memorable, for it was here that Falstaff performed his "heroics" against a multiplying band of rogues clad in "Kendal green" in *1 Henry IV*.

HOGSDEN (HOXTON). In Jonson's time a semirural village north of the City; today a working-class neighborhood north of Old Street and west of Kingsland Road.

S (p. 251) cites Stow's description of Hoxton as "a large streete with houses on both sides" and points out that it was a popular recreative spot with Londoners, for it had extensive open fields and several noted places where ale, cakes, and cream could be obtained. His assertions are borne out in Beaumont's *The Knight of the Burning Pestle:* "March out and shew your willing minds by twenty and by twenty, / To Hogsdon or to Newington, where Ale and Cakes are plenty" (4. interlude, ll. 53–54). In Shirley's *The Wedding* Captain Loudly exclaims, "They point a duel! / At Hogsden, to shew fencing upon cream / And cake-bread . . . / Or some such daring enemy" (4.1). Stow also notes (2:76) that Moorgate (q.v.) was constructed "for the ease of the Cittizens to walke that waye uppon Causeyes towardes Iseldon [see Islington] and Hoxton."

Jonson's own associations with Hoxton almost proved fatal, for his duel with Gabriel Spencer took place in its open fields. This affray, in which his opponent died, resulted in Jonson's wounding and arrest. In his works Jonson utilizes the recreative, slightly provincial connotations of this district. In *Alch* Lovewit declares that people have been seen flocking to his "deserted" Blackfriars home as if it were "a second *Hogs-den*, / In dayes of *Pimlico* [q.v.], and *Eye-bright*" (5.2.19–20). Later, Face sardonically remarks on how Mammon would have spent his alchemical gains, "I, he would ha' built / The citie new; and made a ditch about it / Of silver, should have runne with creame from *Hogsden*" (5.5.76–78). Satan deflates Pug's achievements in *DA* by declaring, "Some old Ribibe [old woman], about *Kentish* Towne [q.v.], / Or *Hogsden*, you would hang now, for a witch" (1.1.16–17). An understanding of London's small size at the close of the sixteenth century is essential for an appreciation of Stephen's complaint to Knowell in *EMI*, "Because I dwell at *Hogsden*, I shall keepe companie with none but the archers of *Finsburie* [q.v.]? or the citizens, that come a ducking to *Islington* ponds?" (1.1.47–50). At that time Hoxton was the equivalent of today's greenbelt suburbs. Hoxton's suburban status is also apparent in Wellbred's comment in his letter to Edward Knowell: *"Doe not conceive that antipathy betweene us, and* Hogs-den; *as was betweene* Jewes, *and* hogs-flesh" (1.2.74–75).

HOLBOURNE (HOLBORN). A chief London street running west from the junction of Old Bailey and Newgate Street to Drury Lane. The portion west of the Fleet Ditch (q.v.) was in Jonson's time a steep ascent and known as Holbourne Hill.

Because the route from Newgate Prison to the Middlesex gallows at Tyburn was along Holborn, many grim jokes and references are associated with it. S (p. 252) calls attention to *A Game at Chesse*, where the Black Bishop says he tried to cure Gondomar's fistula "with a High Holbourn halter" (2.2.47). H&S (10:188) note a reference to the "heavy hill" en route to Tyburn soon after the start of the fourth act of Dryden's *The Kind Keeper, or Mr. Limberham*. Holborn was an important road leading out of London and thus the site of many inns and taverns; John Taylor's *The Carriers Cosmographie* (1637, Spenser Society, 14), alphabetically lists the usual lodging places of commercial travelers serving London.

Jonson utilized both the pleasant and malefic associations of Holborn in his works. In *BF* Ursula warns Knockem that he may be arrested for cutting purses and at day's end be heard to "groane out of a cart, up the heavy hill" (2.3.5). Feigning ignorance of her meaning, he replies "Of Holbourne, *Ursla*, meanst thou so?" In his commendatory verses prefixed to Coryat's *Crudities*, *UV* 10, Jonson gives prospective readers of this travel narrative a preview of its contents, in places clarifying his meaning with a local English reference, as in his comment, "Here, not up *Holdborne*, but down a steepe hill, / Hee's carried 'twixt *Montrell* and *Abbevile*" (ll. 12–13). The poet has Holborn's convivial aspects in mind when he makes it the destination of his adventurers in *Epig* 133, "On the Famous Voyage" (l. 38), which describes a trip up the noxious Fleet Ditch in a wherry. Late in this burlesque epic, as his heroes near their goal, Jonson points out one of the strange denizens of this locale, "Behold where CERBERUS, rear'd on the wall / Of *Hol'borne* ([the] three sergeants heads) lookes ore, / And stays but till you come unto the dore" (ll. 176–78).

HOLLOWAY. A district in North London extending north from High-bury to Highgate.

H&S [9:285–86] are quite informative regarding Jonson's mention of Holloway in *TT*, where he alludes to one "blind George" of this area. The editors point out that in Jonson's time this saying was attributed to an actual London personage. They cite passages from John Taylor's *Pennyles Pilgrimage* and from a contemporary travel narrative through this district. H&S also note that by 1678, according to Ray (*Proverbs*, 2nd ed., p. 268), the phrase, "That would I fain *see* said blind *George* of *Hollowee*," is termed "proverbial."

W&C (2:227) state that because Holloway was on the main road to the north, many inns and taverns were located there. On September 24, 1661, Pepys stopped to drink in Holloway "at the sign of a woman with Cakes in one hand and a pot of ale in the other."

In *TT* the family retainer Hilts declares his defiance of another servant's bluster with "That would I fain zee, quoth the blind *George / Of Holloway*" (2.2.25–26).

HONEY LANE. A minor City thoroughfare running north from Cheapside (q.v.) just opposite Bow Church.

Both Stow's and Kingsford's comments are furnished by H&S (10:565). Stow writes (1:271), "Then neare to the Standarde in Chepe is Honey lane so called not of sweetenes thereof, being very narrow and somewhat darke, but rather of often washing and sweeping, to keepe it cleane." Kingsford however, contends (2:333) that its name probably was derived from the sale of honey and that "Huni lane" appeared in records as early as 1207.

In *CHM* "New yeares gift" is described as *"With Orenge on head, and his Gingerbread,* Clem Waspe *of Honey-lane 'tis"* (ll. 224–25).

HOPE THEATER. A combination playhouse and bear pit erected on Bankside by Henslowe and his associates in 1613 on the site of a previous bear garden.

H&S (10:174) point out that the Hope was built on trestles to facilitate conversion into an amphitheater. Plays were acted on Monday, Wednesday, Friday, and Saturday; bears were the main attraction on the other weekdays. Its building contract specified that the Hope was to be equal in size to the Swan, another Bankside playhouse. Part of the new house was brickwork, costing £80 out of the total bill of £360. Its site, just a few feet south of the old bear ring, has been determined thanks to the testimony of a witness in a 1620 lawsuit.[11] Conflict of interest with the managers of the bearbaiting caused the dissolution of the resident company, the Lady Elizabeth's Men, as a regular acting troupe; their successors, Prince Charles's Men, did not remain long at the Hope. Bearbaiting then became the dominant but not sole entertainment at the Hope during the 1620s, as the leading acting companies tended to avoid this theater. In conjunction with occasional plays, there were also presented prize fights, fencing matches, and wild animal exhibitions. By 1632 the pamphlet *Holland's Leaguer* declared that *"wild beasts* and *Gladiators*, did most possesse it" (sig. F2ᵛ). Still, the Hope cannot be denied its considerable longevity as an entertainment center; after

11. Roberts and Godfrey, *Bankside*, pp. 69–70.

being largely pulled down and the bears shot in 1655/56, it was rebuilt a short distance south during the Restoration. Known as the "bear garden," it was visited several times by Pepys and last mentioned in a 1682 advertisement.[12]

BF had its premiere at the Hope on October 31, 1614, as stated in the induction's "Articles of Agreement," (ll. 64–68). The audience is reminded of its pungent staging conditions in the Stage-Keeper's remark that this theater is "as durty as *Smithfield* [q.v.], and as stinking every whit" (ll. 159–60).

HORN'S ORDINARY. Possibly the popular tavern at what is now 164 Fleet Street (q.v.); its full name was the Horn on the Hoop.

S (p. 256) furnishes two references to the spot from Middleton's *Father Hubburd's Tales* (1604; *Works*, 8:67): "They were to dine together at the Horn in Fleet-street, being a house where their lawyer resorted" and (p. 77) where would-be gallants are advised their "eating must be in some famous tavern, as the Horn, the Mitre [q.v.], or the Mermaid [q.v.]." S also suggests that the "Horn's Ordinary" mentioned by Jonson below may be a comic reference to a brothel. H&S (9:464) identify it with the Fleet Street tavern, citing in addition to the Middleton reference above, a passage from *Maroccus Extaticus* (1595, ed. F. E. Rimbault, p. 7) praising the excellence of the Horn's muscadine. The prominence of the Horn in Fleet Street is illuminated by several local and literary records. In 1553 it was one of three Fleet Street taverns permitted a license. According to Machyn's *Diary* (p. 151), the Spanish ambassador stopped at the Horn for a drink on September 16, 1557. In 1624 the place was owned by the Goldsmiths' Company, who leased it to a vintner for twenty-one years for a fine of £250 and a promise to provide the company "one good fat buck of the season and 1 tierce of wine . . . and one other buck on a subsequent occasion."[13]

In *EMO* Sogliardo is termed "a lieger at *Hornes* ordinarie yonder" (4.3.82–83), where he has been puffing tobacco from a pipe for over a day. The Horn in Fleet Street would fit in well with this play's other London references, chiefly to St. Paul's and to one of the City Counters (q.v.), both of which were fairly near.

---

12. Bentley, *The Jacobean and Caroline Stage*, 6:208–14, discusses the Hope's changing fortunes, the citation from *Holland's Leaguer*, and the activities of 1655–56 (p. 214). Roberts and Godfrey, *Bankside*, p. 70, discuss the Restoration bear garden.

13. *Diary of Henry Machyn*, ed. J. Gough Nichols, Camden Society, 42 (London: The Society, 1848); also Kenneth Rogers, *Mermaid and Mitre Taverns*, pp. 16, 154. Rogers cites William Prideaux, *History of the Goldsmiths' Company,* on the Horn's tenancy during Stuart times.

HOSPITAL (CHRIST'S). A school originally for poor children founded by Edward VI, occupying part of the former Grayfriars Monastery, just east of Newgate. In 1902 the school moved to near Horsham, Surrey.

As S (p. 118) has made apparent, this institution and its blue-uniformed students frequently figured in dramatic references such as in Middleton's *The Widow*, where a suitor congratulates himself that his two bastards are "well provided for, they're i' the Hospital" (2.1.203). H&S (9:359) comment that this institution also educated sons of City freemen and other London residents, as well as foundlings. These editors point out (10:386–87) the prominent role its students sometimes assumed in City celebrations, as recorded in Stephen Harrison's account of James I's coronation progress through London in 1604: "The first *Object* that his Majesties eye encountred (after his entrance into *London*) was part of the children of *Christs Church Hospital*, to the number of 300. who were placed on a Scaffold, erected for that purpose in *Barking Church-yard* by the *Tower*." Londoners, according to Donald Lupton in 1632, saw the hospital as "a good means to empty their streetes of young beggars, and fatherlesse Children: She [London] doth no more then the Lawes of the Land seeme to enjoyne, to keepe those that were borne within her."[14] Christ Church, where the students of the Hospital worshipped, was formerly one of the glories of Grayfriars Monastery and also one of the largest churches in England. Each summer during Bartholomew Fair (q.v.) its precincts were taken over by vendors of food and petty luxuries.[15]

In *EMI* Kitely informs us that his man Cash was a foundling and "since bred him at the Hospitall" (2.1.18). As stated in the induction to *BF*, Littlewit "dwels about the *Hospitall*" (ll. 5–6), and the play's first act is set at his home, which according to 1.3.140–41, is quite close to Newgate Market (q.v.). The Middleton quote cited earlier is echoed in *NI* when Tiptoe asserts about Burst's upbringing, "He had no Father, I warrant him, that durst own him; / Some foundling in a stall, or the Church porch; / Brought up i' the *Hospitall*; and so bound Prentise" (4.2.7–9). An allusion to the quite secular activities at times carried on in Christ Church may well be contained in a taunt made in *EH*, "His mother sould Ginger-bread in Christ-church" (1.1.115–16). S (pp. 117–18) feels that this merely refers to the woman's earning a living by selling this treat to the schoolboys. H&S (9:649–50) suggest a more insulting (and satirically pertinent) meaning in their comments which point out that the post-Dissolution amalgamation of the parishes of St. Nicholas, St. Ewin, and part of St. Sepulchre resulted in a parish known as Christ Church, within which Bartholomew Fair was held.

14. Lupton, *London and the Countrey Carbonadoed* (1632), p. 64.

15. E. H. Pearce, *Annals of Christ's Hospital* (London: Methuen, 1901), p. 162, cites Pepys's diary for August 31, 1662.

One should also remember, as noted above, that there is evidence for believing that small wares were also sold within this church itself. In either instance the reference to Christ Church would associate the mother with the often disreputable vendors at Bartholomew Fair.

HOSPITAL (ST. BARTHOLMEW'S). The earliest hospital in London, started in 1123 by Rahere (who also founded St. Bartholomew's Priory) and located just east of Smithfield (q.v.).

According to W&C (1:118) the hospital was seized by Henry VIII during the Dissolution and at the behest of Sir Richard Gresham, father of Sir Thomas Gresham, given to the City to operate in 1547. Here Sir William Harvey served as physician for thirty-four years, formulating many principles of organization and treatment followed for hundreds of years after. In *The Wonderfull Yeare* (*Non-Dramatic Works*, 1:112) Dekker observes that during the plague "every house lookt like S. *Bartholmews* Hospitall."

In *BF* Ursula inveighs against the crude attempts of her colleagues to ameliorate the pain of her scalded leg, "Would you ha' me i' the Hospitall, afore my time?" (2.5.183–84). There is also a slight possibility that the Stage-keeper in this play is referring to St. Bartholomew's in his statement that Littlewit "dwels about the *Hospitall*" (induction, ll. 5–6). However, because Littlewit works as a clerk in the Court of Arches (q.v.) located in Bow Church, Cheapside, it is more logical to assume that the "Hospitall" Jonson had in mind was Christ's Hospital (see preceding entry), a school located closer to Littlewit's place of work.

HOUNDSDITCH. A thoroughfare on the site of the old municipal moat between Aldgate and Bishopsgate, in Jonson's time chiefly tenanted by old-clothes dealers, known as "brokers."

S (p. 257) states that originally this name was given to the entire circuit of the moat and that this restricted meaning began during the sixteenth century. Dramatic references to the ill nature of Houndsditch tradesmen are common, as in Dekker's *Seven Deadly Sinnes* (*Non-Dramatic Works*, 2:81), where Cruelty calls the Houndsditch brokers his "deerest Sonnes." H&S (9:375) give a forceful citation from W. Parkes (*The Curtain-Drawer of the World*, 1612, p. 4), who stated that during the age of innocence, "Not one Broker had all *Hounds-ditch*, which now is able to make ten Juries, and cloath all the naked Savadges in *Virginia*, with the skins or cases that the unwily serpents of our age have cast or rather have been puld from, and stript, by creeping into too narrow Angles and corners." Stow declares (1:128) that in past times "much filth (conveyed forth of the Citie) especially dead Dogges were there layd or cast." W&C (2:236–37) add

ANN COLEMAN,

At the Sign of the *Porter* and *Dwarfe*, *Hand* and *Shears* and *Queen's Head*, upon the *Common-Shore*, in *Houndsditch*, *L O N D O N*:

SELLS all sorts of Linnen Goods, in the Piece or Made up as Dowlas, Garlicks, Ilinghams, Irish and Ruffia Cloth; fine Bag and rough Hollands; fine Cambricks, and Muslins, plain and strip'd Dimities, Dutch Flannels, Lindfeys, Coventry Stuffs, &c. She likewise sells all sorts of Womens and Girls Gowns ready Made up, as Stuff, Cotton, &c. Quilted & Flannel Pettycoats, Mens Flannel Waistcoats, and all manner of Seamen's Apparel Good Whalebone & Cane Hoop-Pettycoats, Stockings & Childrens Coats; likewise all sorts of Child-bed Linnen New or Second-hand, Wholesale or Retail at reasonable Rates.

N. B. She Furnisheth Parishes, with all forts of Poor's Clothing, Cheap and Reasonable.

Rag and second-hand clothing dealers flourished in Houndsditch.

that the kennels of the hounds used in City hunts were located in this district. They state, however, that according to John Taylor the name of the area resulted from popular hatred of the brokers. This idea is seconded in 1632 by Donald Lupton: "Here are Suites enough for all the Lawyers in *London* to deale withall . . . *Broke-Curs* they are in two respects, most of them were broke before they set up, & Currs for biting so sore ever since they set up."[16]

With all the above associations in mind, Brainworm, the decrepit soldier in *EMI*, wearing a coat obtained "of a *Hounds-ditch* man" (3.5.31), must have been memorable in his shabby disarray.

HOUNSLOW. A Middlesex village on the Great West Road about thirteen miles from the City.

According to S (p. 257), the heath adjoining this town was a noted haunt of highwaymen. Also in keeping with its commercial prominence, Hounslow boasted many excellent taverns which apparently were well known to Londoners, as attested to by a passage from *Thomas Lord Cromwell*, where some of the persons attending the hero at the height of his power are "my honest Host of Hounslow and his wife" (4.2.46).

In *EMO* Shift, boasting of his prowess in taking tobacco, declares he will teach Sogliardo to be so adept at discharging his "whiffes" that he may "take his horse, drinke his three cups of *Canarie*, and expose one at *Hounslow*, a second at *Stanes* [q.v.], and a third at *Bagshot*" (3.6.147–49). In *NI* Hounslow is one of the places where the tailor Nick Stuffe and his wife show themselves off in clothes meant for their customers. According to her, "He runnes / In his velvet Jackat thus, to *Rumford* [q.v.], *Croyden* [q.v.], / *Hounslow*, or *Barnet* [q.v.], the next bawdy road" (4.3.70–72). Both of the above citations expose the grossness of these characters' presumptions by the magnitude of the distance involved in their boasts. The tobacco-spouting journey envisioned by Shift is a simple southwest run, ending at a Surrey coaching town thirty miles from London, no brief jaunt, considering the circumstances, and it makes us aware of the emptiness of his vaunts. Stuffe's sartorial promenade forms nearly a complete circle through what is today part of greater London. It encompasses about sixty miles, beginning in the Essex village of Romford thirteen miles northeast of London and concluding almost due north of the city at Barnet. Here the circle's usual symbolic denotation of perfection suggests the total commitment of the Stuffes to their selfish idiosyncrasies.

HYDE PARK. A greenbelt between Green Park and Kensington, northwest of Westminster, which first gained prominence as a resort at about the start of Charles I's reign.

16. Lupton, *London and the Countrey Carbonadoed*, pp. 56–57.

Originally the park also included Kensington Gardens and was taken by Henry VIII from Westminster Abbey for use as a hunting ground. As S (p. 259) has shown, many stage references testify to its popularity in pre—Civil War days. It provided the title and several scenes for one of Shirley's most felicitous comedies. H&S (10:231) point out a passage in Mayne's *The City-Match*, where a lady aspiring to social eminence stipulates, "Then I'll have / My footmen to run by me when I visit, / Or take the air sometimes in Hyde Park"(5.2). Hyde Park remained stocked with game during this time, as is apparent from a letter written by John Chamberlain to Sir Dudley Carleton on October 30, 1619, telling of the execution of some deer stealers in this region.[17]

Jonson uses the park to call attention to the selfish urge for display which possesses many of his characters. In *DA* Fitzdottrel plans to hire a coach for Wittipol's assignation with Mrs. Fitzdottrel so that the pair may "take the ayre" and visit Hyde Park and Blackfriars (1.6.214–16). In the stage prologue to *SN*, the author does not deem "how many Coaches in *Hide-parke* did show / Last spring" (ll. 14–15) an important matter for discussion. According to the Second Herald in *NFNW*, the Moon offers to intrigue-minded travelers "above all the *Hide-parkes* in Christendome, farre more hiding and private" (ll. 250–51). Finally, in *Und* 15, "An Epistle to a Friend," Jonson warns against the fop who changes clothes thrice a day "to teach each suit he has, the ready way / From *Hide-Parke* to the Stage" (ll. 108–9).

---

17. *Calendar of State Papers, Domestic, 1619–23*, p. 88; such criminals are also mentioned on p. 86.

I

INNS OF COURT. London's "legal universities," of which Lincoln's Inn (q.v.), Gray's Inn, and the Inner and Middle Temples are the chief constituents. Lincoln's Inn stands just south of Holborn, near the north end of Chancery Lane; Gray's Inn is north of Holborn and west of Gray's Inn Road, and the Inner and Middle Temples are between Fleet Street and the Thames. Also prominent in Tudor-Stuart times were several subsidiary Inns of Chancery, now defunct.[1]

S (p. 268) supplies several dramatic references to the reputation of London's legal apprentices. In *Ram Alley* a character amazedly asks, "Come you to seek a virgin in Ram-Alley? / So near an inn-of-court? (3.1). In Glapthorne's *Wit in a Constable*, Knowell speaks of girls having "wit sufficient to withstand the assaults / Of some young Innes-acourt man" (3.1). John Earle (*Micro-cosmographie*, p. 12) defined a tavern as "the Innes a Court mans entertainment." As Philip J. Finkelpearl has pointed out in *John Marston of the Inner Temple* (p. 5), the Inns of Court constituted "the largest single group of literate and cultured men in London." Most students were from the landed gentry and were usually between the ages of seventeen and thirty. From 1550 until 1700 study at one of the Inns was expected of many an upper-class youth in preparation for full-time responsibilities and privileges. Many students, however, simply regarded the Inns of Court as a convenient place to live while indulging in the many pleasures and vices available in London and Westminster. Lord Clarendon wrote that at the Middle Temple "there was never an age, in which, in so short a time, so many young gentlemen . . . were insensibly and suddenly overwhelmed in that sea of wine, and women, and quarrels, and gaming, which almost overspread the whole Kingdom, and the nobility and gentry thereof."[2]

Jonson dedicated *EMO* to the Inns (H&S, 3:421), terming them "the Noblest Nourceries of Humanity and Liberty / In the Kingdome." The Oxford editors (1:22–23) declare that this play's content and theme were of special pertinence to such an audience. In *EMO* Sogliardo's nephew Fun-

---

1. According to Philip J. Finkelpearl, *John Marston of the Middle Temple* (Cambridge: Harvard University Press, 1969), p. 4, the Inns of Chancery affiliated with the four main institutions were the following: Lincoln's Inn—Furnivall's Inn and Thavie's Inn; Inner Temple—Clifford's Inn, Clement's Inn, and Lyon's Inn; Middle Temple—New Inn and Strand Inn; Gray's Inn—Staple Inn and Barnard's Inn.

2. Finkelpearl, p. 15, cites *Life of Edmund, Earl of Clarendon . . . Written by Himself* (Oxford, 1827), 1:76.

goso, a student at the Inns (1.2.69–70), is described in the cast list as *"one that has revel'd in his time, and followes the fashion a farre off, like a spie"* (ll. 71–72). In *EH* the butcher's apprentice Slitgut bids farewell to his lookout spot on the Cuckold's Haven "tree" after witnessing the wreck of the sea voyage planned by Sir Petronel and his followers. Slitgut's comments are prompted by the shape of the "tree"—which is a pole topped with a pair of horns. At one point he declares, "Farewell thou horne of hunger, that calst th' Inns a court to their Manger" (4.1.291–92). H&S (9:668) believe that Slitgut is alluding to the nightly dinner horn at the Inns. According to Face in *Alch*, an "innes of court man" is a good judge of horseflesh (4.4.7–9). In the induction to *BF* the Stage-keeper says that it would be a good idea to have a pump set on the stage and to set a slut on her head nearby so she would be "sous'd by my wity young masters o' the *Innes o' Court*" (ll. 34–35). In the same play Quarlous takes pity on Grace's predicament as a ward, "Would I had studied a yeere longer i'the Innes of Court, and't had beene but i' your case" (3.5.279–80). In *DA* the City goldsmith Plutarchus tells his son Guilthead that he will learn more in a year from Justice Eitherside than in twenty "at *Oxford*, or at *Cambridge*, / Or sending you to the *Innes* of *Court*, or *France*" (3.1.7–8). The "Epistle to Sir Edward Sackville," *Und* 13, denounces "Pyrats" who "man out their Boates to th' Temple, and not shift / Now, but command; make tribute, what was gift" (ll. 83–84). This of course refers to greedy lawyers who demand more than their share of fees. The Inns of Chancery were subordinate institutions to the Inns of Court, training young men for the Court of Chancery. Jonson was involved as a witness in a 1623 Chancery suit (discussed by H&S: 11:582–83) on behalf of Lady Raleigh. While preparing for the masque in *TT*, In-and-In Medlay praises the play's protagonist, Squire Tub: "Hee is a learned man; / I think there are but vew o' the Innes o' Court, / Or the Innes o' Chancery like him" (5.7.60–62). Medlay's comment is pure flattery of his employer, for Tub, though a pleasant fellow, has shown himself a weak-willed and easily led young gentleman. In the "Execration upon Vulcan," *Und* 43, the futile cry is raised, "Lyes there no Writ, out of the *Chancerie*, / Against this *Vulcan?*" (ll. 174–75).

ISLE OF DOGS. A peninsula on the north bank of the Thames, between Limehouse and Blackwall, a few miles east of the City.

Popular tradition held that the royal hounds were kept there, and as S (p. 154) has noted, most dramatic references to the area play on canine associations. The heroine of Dekker and Middleton's *The Roaring Girl* says of a gallant, "He hath bene brought up in the Ile of doggs and can both fawne like a Spaniell, and bite like a Mastive" (5.1.111–13). Most authorities find the above etymology highly unlikely. W&C (2:266) cite a Crown Works account of 1623–24 for work done at the "King's Majesty's Dog House" at Deptford directly across the river and contend that the hounds were kept there instead. Another suggestion—that the name is a corruption of "ducks"—is mentioned by K (p. 400).

The Isle of Dogs was a play apparently containing politically offensive matter on which Jonson collaborated with Thomas Nashe in 1597. The venture resulted in a brief sojourn in the Marshalsea Prison for Jonson and several actors. Nashe escaped by fleeing to Great Yarmouth, as noted by H&S (1:15–16). The Isle is also the setting for one of the rescues in *EH*, where a gentleman with a Scottish accent informs the bedraggled would-be voyager Sir Petronel Flash of the limited scope of his journey (4.1.173–74). Ever pompous, Sir Petronel assumes that he has landed in France, until told otherwise by the above thankfully anonymous northern gentleman who also recognizes him as "one of my thirty pound knights" (l. 178). That the Scottish King James's court was across the river at Greenwich when this play was first produced in 1605 should make the satiric emphasis in this scene quite clear indeed. Later, after his arrest, Sir Petronel declares that he would rather have starved on the Isle (4.2.183).

ISLINGTON. A large parish, later a metropolitan borough, extending north from the City boundary at Clerkenwell to the district of Highbury. In the early seventeenth century "Islington" usually denoted the small settlement about half a mile beyond Moorfields (q.v.).

As apparent in S's compilation (p. 274), Islington was frequently cited by many types of writers. The village was commonly invoked in diminutive comparisons with London. In 1550 Bishop Latimer exhorted, "For what was Nineveh? A noble, a rich and wealthy city. What is London to Nineveh? Like a village, as Islington or such another in comparison of London." Robert Laneham's account of the entertainment of Queen Elizabeth at Kenilworth included a travesty of heraldic affectation given by a "squire of Islington." During the early years of Stuart rule Islington was perhaps the most popular of London's recreational locales. Nearby were the archery fields and bowling greens of Finsbury (q.v.). "Ducking-ponds," on which ducks were hunted for sport, were a special feature of the Islington area. One long series stretched north from what is now Exmouth Market in Clerkenwell to Ducking Pond Field off the present Liverpool Road.[3] The ponds are discussed by Middleton, Davenant, and Pepys—who regretted, "They are so altered since my father used to carry us to Islington . . . to eat cakes and ale . . . that I did not know which was the ducking-pond nor

3. Walter Mingard, *The Story of Islington and Finsbury* (London: Laurie, 1915), p. 57.

On the North fide of London.   *Wollar delin: et sculp: 1665.*

The City as approached from the open fields to the north, in the area then known as Islington. Old St. Paul's is in the distance. The church tower to the left, over the large shed, is St. Mary le Bow, and the one immediately to the right of St. Paul's is St. Sepulchre's. The ditch in the foreground may be an overflow from the nearby New River Head on its way to the Fleet Ditch (Wenceslaus Hollar, 1665).

where I was."[4] Stuart dramatists frequently spoke of the opportunities for merrymaking near Islington. In Massinger's *The City Madam* a character mentions "Exchange-wenches, / Coming from eating pudding-pies on a Sunday / At Pimlico [q.v.], or Islington" (4.4.37–39). Valentine, in Glapthorne's *Wit in a Constable*, declares, "You . . . can have your meetings / At Islington, and Green Goose faire [q.v.], and sip / A zealous glasse of Wine" (2.1). In Brome's *A Mad Couple Well Match'd*, Careless offers to escort his aunt to "*Islington, Newington, Paddington* [q.v.]. *Kensington*, or any of the City out-leaps for a spirt and back againe" (2.1).

Because Jonson in *TT* identifies his literary antagonist Inigo Jones with Islington, it is pertinent to survey further its historical background and seventeenth-century associations. Of the six manors which composed the parish of Islington, two are of special interest. The manors of Canonbury and Barnsbury were tenanted by such luminaries as Lord Mayor Sir John

4. *Diary*, ed. Latham and Mathews, 5:101.

Spencer and the eminent juror Sir Thomas Fowler.[5] Although the exact
location of her home is not known, Queen Elizabeth's cousin, Margaret
Douglas (countess of Lennox) lived in Islington.[6] The partly aristocratic
nature of this district during Jonson's time is a common assertion made by
local historians. Islington's open fields, however, were haunted by duelists,
robbers, and vagrants. The queen herself, while once riding there, was
"environed with a number of begging rogues (as beggars usually haunt such
places) which gave the Queen much disturbance. . . . The same night did
the Recorder send out warrants into the same quarter, and into Westminster and the Dutchy [the liberty of the Savoy Hospital]; and in the morning
he went abroad himself and took that day seventy-four rogues."[7] Later in
the same year (1581) Fleetwood the Recorder stated that the "chief nursery
of all those evil people is the Savoy and the brick kilns near Islington."[8]

In *EMI* the would-be sophisticate Stephen shows disdain for this locale,
"Because I dwell at *Hogsden* [q.v.], I shall keepe companie with none but
the archers of *Finsburie?* or the citizens, that come a ducking to *Islington*
ponds? a fine jest i' faith! Slid a gentleman mun show himselfe like a
gentleman" (1.1.47–51). Jonson glosses a reference to magic spells in *MQ*
(H&S, 7:285), with an elaborate note which in one part tells about the
discovery of "certayne pictures of waxe found in a dunghill, neare *Islington*,
of o[r] late *Queenes*." Finally, this author's most significant use of the Islington
area is in *TT*, where Inigo Jones is caricatured as In-and-In Medlay, a joiner
and would-be masque maker, who is several times designated as residing

5. The elopement of Spencer's daughter with Lord William Compton was one of the
noted escapades of the era. Thomas Coull, *The History and Traditions of Islington* (London:
Miles, 1864), pp. 7–8, reprints a letter from the new Lady Compton to her spouse
outlining "what allowance were meetest for me" with suggestions rivaling the dreams of
Jonson's most acquisitive characters. At Barnsbury, Sir Thomas Fowler served as deputy
lieutenant of Middlesex, high commissioner of the Verge, and justice of the Quorum.
Islington's other manors were Clerkenwell, St. John's, Highbury, and what is generally
referred to as the "prebendal manor of Islington," which remained in church hands throughout Jonson's era. Clerkenwell was located just north of the City wall and was thoroughly
built up by 1600. During the seventeenth century many distinguished persons lived there.
The remains of the Priory of St. John had a similar history. In the northern part of Islington
lay the manor of Highbury, whose tenants included the wealthy and dashing Sir William
Compton noted above.

6. Lady Margaret was the mother of Henry, Lord Darnley, and Charles Stuart (Mary
Stuart's second husband, and the father of Arabella Stuart). In 1571 Lady Margaret brought
Charles to London. While in Islington she wrote to Lord Burghley asking him to receive the
youth into his home as a ward (*Calendar of State Papers, Domestic, 1547–80*, p. 428).

7. Sir Walter Besant, *London North of the Thames*, pp. 525–26, and J. Norris Brewer,
London and Middlesex, 4:228–29n., are among the many authorities who cite this incident.
Their source is Strype's continuation of Stow's *Survey* (1720), 2:61 (book 4).

8. Quoted by W. J. Pinks, *The History of Clerkenwell* (London: Pickburn, 1865), p. 282.

here (persons, l. 13; 1.1.36; 5.2.14, 32; 5.8,14–15). The association of Medlay with Islington is appropriate in two respects. As mentioned earlier, Islington was a most popular recreational area for the less discriminating Londoner. Medlay's artistry is similar. As the "masque" presented in *TT* shows, Jonson viewed Jones as a mere stage mechanic rather than a poet. Second, having his satiric target hail from an area inhabited by a number of upper-class folk (or aspirers) enabled Jonson to satirize those (like Jones) whose pretensions exceeded their accomplishments.

IVY LANE. A modest City thoroughfare which once ran north from Paternoster Row to Newgate Street, parallel to and just west of today's Pannyer Alley.[9]

H&S (10:701) refer to Stow's comments (1:342) that it is "so called of Ivie growing on the walles of the Prebend Houses, but now the lane is replenished on both the sides with faire houses, and divers offices be there kept, by registers, namelie, for the prerogative court of the Archbishop of Canterbury, the Probate of Willes, and for the Lord Treasurers remembrance of the Exchequer, &c."

In Jonson's *MO* one of the birds is described as a London cuckold who "had like to have beene ta'ne / At his shop in Ivy-lane" (ll. 93–94). H&S add to their above historical note the comment, "Jonson seems to have used the name to suggest an owl in the ivy, as in l. 73." In this line Jonson said that he found this nest of owls "in the ivy." Another possibility is that the poet chose this locale as a satiric thrust at the prosperous and probably complacent occupants of its "faire houses and divers offices."

---

9. Ivy Lane is not to be confused with Ivy Bridge Lane, which formed the old boundary between the duchy of Lancaster and Westminster and ran south from the Strand to the river (S, p. 280).

J

JUSTICE HALL. Another name for the Old Bailey, London's central criminal court. See the latter entry for information on Jonson's one reference to "Justice Hall."

K

KENTISH TOWN. In Jonson's time a village in the parish of St. Pancras (see Pancridge) a few miles northwest of St. Paul's, accepted by historians as the oldest settled part of the parish.[1]

S (p. 292) terms it "a rustic village" in the sixteenth century. Besides Jonson's references, S cites Dekker, *A Rod for Runaways* (*Non-Dramatic Works*, 4:296), where Kentish Town is described as a village near Old St. Pancras Church. Here Dekker tells of how some London holiday-makers bound for Kentish Town were kept from hearing services at this church by "a company of Hobnayle fellowes, with Staves." In Jonson's time this now heavily populated district was strung out along the Kentish Town Road beginning one and a quarter miles northwest of Old St. Pancras Church. The exact site of the manor house associated with Kentish Town has been disputed, but current authorities believe that it occupied the site of the "Old Farm House" on today's Caversham Road.[2] This would accord with earlier historians who declared that Queen Elizabeth used a building on that site for hawking expeditions. Records show the Manor House still standing in the manorial surveys of 1567 and 1649. Not long after this the house became dilapidated, and between 1650 and 1727 the lord of the manor moved away.[3]

Kentish Town is one of the suburban hamlets which figure importantly in *TT*. At Kentish Town lives Audrey Turfe, object of the vigorous, if not impassioned, rival wooing that is the basis of the plot. Throughout this play, Jonson informs his audience of the specific location of nearly every scene. Thus, because of its associations with a major character, Kentish Town is mentioned often. Audrey's father, Toby Turfe, is constable of the region (persons, 1. 9; 1.1.26–27; 2.2.52–53, 73). Lady Tub unsuccessfully seeks him out here (3.4.1–4). Later, Turfe signals a coming change of scene with "Let's back to *Kentish*-Towne, and there make merry" (3.6.38). Similarly, Tub asks, "Shall we to *Pancridge*, or to *Kentish-Towne*,

1. On the age of Kentish Town, see C. H. Denyer, ed., *St. Pancras through the Centuries* (London: Le Play House, 1935), pp. 16, 55; also Samuel Palmer, *St. Pancras . . .* (London: Palmer, 1870), p. 60. William Elliott, *Some Account of Kentish Town* (London: Bennett, 1821), p. 61, states that by the mid-eighteenth century, Kentish Town had about a hundred houses, chiefly detached from each other. Among its residents were two or three gentlemen who kept coaches.

2. Denyer, ed., *St. Pancras*, p. 56, notes the chief settled areas in Kentish Town and also, p. 23, provides evidence on the location of the manor house.

3. Denyer, ed., *St. Pancras*, pp. 22, 57–58.

Hilts?" Hilts replies, "Let *Kentish-Towne*, or *Pancridge* come to us, / If either will" (4.2.3–5), not caring what direction they turn next (ll. 13–16). During her perambulations north of the city, Lady Tub decides "to leave the way to *Totten* [see Tottenham Court] / And turne to *Kentish-Towne*, againe, my journey" (4.5.21–22). She reiterates this when she confronts Tub and Audrey (5.3.46–48). This important decision is again mentioned in the masque at Tub's house which reviews the day's hilarity (5.10.76–78). In *DA* Satan mocks Pug about his limited talents, "Some good Ribibe [old woman] about *Kentish* Towne / Or *Hogsden* [q.v.], you would hang now, for a witch" (1.1.16–17). Turfe's association with Kentish Town is appropriate in several respects. As authorities tend to agree that Kentish Town was the chief settlement in this district, it would be practical for the high constable of the area to dwell there. Second, the available evidence suggests that Kentish Town's inhabitants (excluding the tenants of the manor house) were definitely not aristocratic. Hence Turfe's repeated attempts to enhance his social and professional status would be most amusing to a contemporary audience. Similarly, by associating Pug with this somewhat provincial village, the *DA* reference is a derisive thrust at his demonic prowess.

KILBORNE (KILBURN). In Jonson's time a hamlet lying southwest of Hampstead about five miles northwest of St. Paul's.

Kilburn has few literary associations; its chief claim to literary prominence is that the hermitage dwelt in by the three virgins associated with the Ancren Riwle stood in this area. Most authorities place the site of the hermitage and later nunnery at the south end of Kilburn High Road. During the eighteenth century, though, the Kilburn area achieved some social recognition because of several healthful wells located there.[4]

In *TT* Audrey's intended husband, the tile-maker John Clay, is from Kilburn (persons, l. 12; 1.1.42, 51; 1.3.31; 1.4.4). This is an appropriate association because of Kilburn's etymology, tracing back to the Old English *cylenburna*, or "stream by a kiln."[5] Near the start of the play Constable Turfe tries to enhance Clay's status by calling him "Commander of foure smoking Tile-kils" and "Captaine of *Kilborne*" (1.4.12–13). There is a bit of wordplay on Clay's home district and occupation when a character boasts, "You shall see / The Tile-man too set fire on his owne *Kill*" (2.3.43–44). In trying to dissuade Audrey from this match, Tub stresses

4. Warwick Wroth, *London Pleasure Gardens of the Eighteenth Century*, pp. 194–96; also E. B. Chancellor, *The Pleasure Haunts of London during Four Centuries* (London: Constable, 1925), p. 372, who comments, "As the waters were of a bitter saline taste, people apparently came to prefer the diseases, as they ceased frequenting Kilburn and its wells during the closing years of the eighteenth century."

5. Eilert Ekwall, *Concise Oxford Dictionary of English Place-Names*, 4th ed. (Oxford: Clarendon Press, 1960), p. 275.

Clay's shortcomings as a lover, calling him "the *Kilborne* Clay-pit; that frost-bitten marle" (2.4.63) and later telling her that she must hate "*Clay*, and *Kilburne*" (l. 73). Stressing his innocence when accused of robbery, Clay bursts out, "I take the towne to concord, where I dwell, / All *Kilburne* be my witnesse; If I were not / Begot in bashfulnesse, brought up in shamefac'tnesse" (3.1.67–69). Clay demonstrates a notable lack of fortitude in his refusal to endure being suspected a criminal, "Alas, / That ever I was borne! I will not stay by't / For all the Tiles in *Kilburne*" (3.2.10–12). Turfe's attitude towards his daughter's wooer has changed considerably by the time he says to a friend, "I must goe now, / And hunt out for this *Kilburne* Calfe, *John Clay*" (3.8.42–43).

KING STREET. Formerly the chief thoroughfare from the court at Whitehall to Westminster Palace. It was obliterated in the rebuilding of Westminster between St. James's Park and Parliament Street at the turn of the present century.[6]

S (p. 294) notes that King Street was poorly paved even though it was a prominent street. H&S (10:281) furnish only topographical details as above, commenting inaccurately that part of its course still remains. In Tudor-Stuart times many eminent men lived on King Street. W&C (2:338) point out that in 1611 and 1613 Sir Henry Wotton dispatched letters from his lodgings here to Sir Edmund Bacon and Sir Dudley Carleton. Also, this street was the home of Lord Admiral Effingham, where Queen Elizabeth's privy councilors often held meetings.

The important state business conducted in King Street probably had its juicy sidelights, because this locale is one of the sources of the better news which Gossip Tatle, *SN*, declares she can get on her own (third intermeane, ll. 22–23). Also, though the story is now regarded as "incredible" by such scholars as H&S (1:161), contemporaries and credulous later readers accepted Drummond's statement from the *Conversations* (H&S, 1:137) that according to Jonson, the poet Spenser "died for la[c]ke of bread in King Street."

KING'S BENCH PRISON. A municipal debtors' jail located in Jonson's time on the east side of Borough High Street, Southwark, a short distance north of the Marshalsea Prison.

S (p. 294) mentions that the King's Bench was by the sixteenth century already the destination for some fictional unfortunates. This is illustrated by passages in John Skelton's *Colin Clout* (*Complete Poems*, p. 284) and *Hickscorner* (ed. J. S. Farmer; *Six Anonymous Plays*, Early English Dramatists, 1st ser., London, 1905, p. 143). K (p. 408) points out that

6. Clunn, *The Face of London*, p. 258.

the notable prisoners incarcerated there included the Protestant martyr John Bradford in 1554 and the theologian Richard Baxter in 1670. The King's Bench was rebuilt a short distance to the southwest in 1758 and soon earned a reputation as the most comfortable debtors' prison in England, as several of K's references testify.

The errant apprentice Quicksilver in *EH* is unconvinced of its merits in the early seventeenth century, asserting, "Let 'hem take their choice, eyther the *Kings Benche*, or the *Fleete* [q.v.] . . . for by the Lord I like none of 'hem" (2.2.263–66). He gets his wish to avoid both these jails, but as act 5 shows, ends up in one of the City Counters—debtors' prisons located near the heart of London, in Wood Street and in Poultry.

KING'S HEAD TAVERN. A popular tavern name in London, making the decision as to the location of Jonson's reference somewhat difficult.

S (p. 294) calls attention to three King's Head Taverns preserved through dramatic allusions: one in New Fish Street (today's Fish Street Hill), another in Fleet Street, and one in Smithfield. These were mentioned in *The London Prodigal* (2.4.12–13), *Ram Alley* (5.1), and *The Parson's Wedding* (2.3), respectively. H&S (10:353) note only the King's Head in New Fish Street and comment that its site is now marked by King's Head Court. Stow refers to a King's Head in Cheapside (1:257) and also says (2:62) that one of the many "fayre Innes" in Southwark bore this name. Recent scholarship has placed the King's Head in Fleet Street on the north side, at the east corner of Chancery Lane. This corrects W&C's and others' slight error (2:345) made earlier in locating the house.[7] Current research has also added to our knowledge of the King's Head at the southern end of New Fish Street (then known as Bridge Street). It was situated in the only thoroughfare into the City connecting with the south side of the Thames and stood close to London Bridge. Annual suppers held at this tavern by leading members of the Goldsmiths' Company attest to the high quality of its fare.[8]

Dr. Rut in *ML* advises Sir Moth Interest, "But feed you on one dish still, ha' your Diet-drinke, / Ever in Bottles ready, which must come / From the *King's-head*" (3.5.57–59). Without giving any reason, S thinks Jonson had the King's Head in Fleet Street in mind. H&S offer no opinion. The case for the King's Head in New Fish Street is strengthened by the prominence of

7. Kenneth Rogers, "On Some Issuers of Seventeenth-Century London Tokens," *Numismatic Chronicle*, 5th ser., 8 (1928):77–78.

8. Kenneth Rogers, *Signs and Taverns round about Old London Bridge*, pp. 77–78. Rogers also, "On Some Issuers," p. 86, found a King's Head Tavern at the corner of Old Fish Street and Lambeth Hill, which featured a rarely portrayed monarch (Henry VII) on its sign. Mid–seventeenth-century churchwardens' accounts from the nearby church of St. Mary Magadelen record payments for wines and dinners there.

this house, which would make it an apt place for the ambitious miser Interest to display himself favorably.

KINGSTON BRIDGE. A causeway leading to the town of Kingston upon Thames, about thirteen miles west of London on the south bank of the river.

S (p. 295) notes that Kingston Bridge was the first bridge above London as late as Elizabethan times and that in Kingston's marketplace Saxon kings were crowned between 901 and 978.

The above facts clarify the boast of To-pan the tinker in *TT*, who brags that his worthy ancestors came "over the *Thames*, at a low water marke; / Vore either *London*, I, or *Kingston* Bridge— / I doubt were kurzind [christened]" (1.3.57–59).

L

LAMBETH. Roughly the area on the south bank of the Thames opposite Westminster.

Lambeth in the seventeenth century was the site of two important bishop's palaces and an extensive amount of marshland. S (p. 297) provides ample dramatic evidence for regarding this area as the haunt of whores and pickpockets. In Glapthorne's *The Hollander* prostitutes are termed "maids of Lambeth Marsh" (3.1). Londoners reached Lambeth by taking a ferry from Millbank, south of Whitehall, to a landing near Lambeth Palace. The tolls went to the Archbishop of Canterbury. The above information was provided by H&S (10:67), who label the Marsh "a disreputable quarter." They also quote from J. H., *The House of Correction* (1619, sig. D2ᵛ, who writes of a whore "gone to *Lambeth* to take the ayre."

Jonson's awareness of Lambeth's reputation is apparent in several plays. Dol Common, *Alch*, points out that the undesirable customers hovering about Lovewit's house include "your giantesse, / The bawd of *Lambeth*" (1.4.2–3). The title figure in *Epig* 12, "On Lieutenant Shift," is described as "not meanest among squires, / That haunt *Pickt-hatch* [q.v.], *Mersh-Lambeth*, and *Whitefryers* [q.v.]" (ll. 1–2). During the antimasque portion of *FI* Master Skelton informs the audience that among the worthies he can conjure up is the noted virago Long Meg of Westminster, who "turnes home merry, / By *Lambeth* Ferry" (ll. 409–10).

LINCOLN'S INN. One of the Inns of Court (q.v.), located south of Holborn near the north end of Chancery Lane.

This site was assigned to the Dominican Order upon its establishment in London and was later used by lawyers after about 1300. In 1580 the legal profession bought the grounds outright. According to Stow (2:90), the name of this area derives from Henry Lacy, earl of Lincoln, who "builded his Inne [mansion], and for the most parte was lodged there." As noted by H&S (11:509), Thomas Fuller originated the tradition (*Worthies*, 2:425) that Jonson's early bricklaying experience was connected with improvements at Lincoln's Inn. As H&S (11:571) have pointed out, the research of Mark Eccles in the Black Books of Lincoln's Inn (*RES* 12, 1936, p. 263) has shown that 1588 was the most likely year for Jonson's employment there, because of a large outlay for new construction. According to Eccles (p. 264), the work was done under the direction of a bricklayer named Thomas Brett. This surname was borne by at least one of the residents of Hartshorn

Lane, the thoroughfare which has the earliest associations with Jonson (also according to Fuller, above). A property conveyance of 1586 lists among other details a garden near a ditch in Hartshorn Lane recently built by one Robert Brett.[1] In the earliest rate book of this parish (St. Martin in the Fields, 1597), a Robert Brett is listed as a contributor.[2] Finally, a Robert Brett was cited by Eccles (p. 264) as overseeing some repairs made on Lincoln's Inn in 1590 and 1591. That the Brett family had closer connections with Jonson's life than merely the above coincidental details is a possibility which merits further investigation.

In *DA* Wittipol remarks to Lady Fitzdottrel about how her husband has neglected her because of his obsession with satanism, "Whole nights, sometimes, / The Divell-given *Elfine* Squire, your husband, / Doth leave you, quitting heere his proper circle, / For a much-worse i' the walkes of *Lincolnes Inne*" (1.6.94–97). Lady Fitzdottrel tells Pug later that she wishes Wittipol would "for-beare his acting to mee, / At the Gentlemans chamber-window in *Lincolnes-Inne* there, / That opens to my gallery" (2.2.52–54). As shown in the above lines, the setting of the play is quite close to Lincoln's Inn. Metaphorically it serves as an ironic comment on life, for the play is largely devoted to illegal activities. It parallels the situation which ultimately ensnares the real devil Pug, where the infernal visitor is put to shame by the deeds of "innocent" humans.

LOLLARDS' TOWER. See the St. Paul's entry.

LONDON BRIDGE. The only bridge over the Thames in London until Westminster Bridge was opened in 1750.

S (pp. 316–17) provides an ample survey of London Bridge's history. Begun in 1176, it took thirty-three years to complete and was 926 feet long with a width of forty feet. It then rested on nineteen stone arches with a wooden drawbridge to allow for the passage of ships.[3] At each end was a gate over which the heads of traitors were exhibited. Houses and shops lined its course; one building, Nonesuch House, was four stories tall. S furnishes comments by Paul Hentzner and Fynes Moryson revealing the admiration which Elizabethan travelers had for the bridge. H&S provide several illuminating notes on Jonson's references to it, especially their discussion (10:223) of the falls and rapids which were created after the waterway was

1. Sir George Gater and E. P. Wheeler, eds., *The Strand*, p. 22.

2. These records are held by the City of Westminster Library, Buckingham Palace Road, London, S. W. 1.

3. Apparently the drawbridge had wooden supports, which explains why Stow, 1:26, and his followers, including H&S, 10:14, stated that there were twenty arches. This point is explained by W&C, 2:418. S, p. 316, and K, p. 50, give the figure as nineteen, the number of stone arches.

narrowed by the many stone arches. "Shooting the bridge" was dangerous, even for experienced watermen, and impossible at low tide. Passengers often alighted at the Old Swan Stairs and walked to a wharf, usually Billingsgate, below the bridge to reembark. H&S (10:270) also cite an excerpt from Middleton's *Black Book* (*Works*, 8:21–22) on the constant need for repairs to the bridge. The bridge's often sorry condition was, as Stow notes (1:24), a problem for Londoners as far back as 1289 when "the Bridge was so sore decayed for want of reparations, that men were afraid to passe thereon."

Many strange events occurred near London Bridge. Stow records (1.25) that when Isabel, the eight-year-old queen of Richard II, visited the Tower in 1396, nine people were pressed to death among the crowd assembled on the bridge to glimpse her. Then in 1481 one of the houses built on the bridge fell through, drowning five men. The rapids described above were increased by the wooden "starlings"—platforms which protected the piers of the arches. A number of boating calamities are listed by K (pp. 51–52). Cardinal Wolsey never took risks with the rapids, but Henry VIII did. Mrs. Anne Kirke, a lady of the bedchamber to Queen Henrietta Maria, drowned when the queen's barge overturned on London Bridge. John Temple, son of Sir William Temple, committed suicide by jumping overboard after he told a boatman to shoot the bridge. Narcissus Luttrell's diary records that on November 25, 1693, fifteen persons drowned near the bridge. Finally, K describes a visit by a "Monster of prodigious size" to London in 1240. It swam through one of the bridge arches and was pursued by sailors with ropes, slings, and bows. After a long fight, it was killed a few miles upriver at Mortlake.

In *TT* To-Pan the tinker boasts about one of his ancestors who lived before the building of London Bridge (1.3.52–59). Truewit, *Epic*, marvels at Morose's decision to marry, declaring that one would expect him to commit suicide rather than risk matrimony in such licentious times. Among the quick ways of self-slaughter Truewit recounts is to jump from "*London*-bridge, at a low fall, with a fine leape" (2.2.22). As H&S (10:14) have noted, this would be a plunge during ebb tide, a certainly fatal act. To be rid of his garrulous "wife," Morose later avows that he would do penance at "*London*-bridge, *Paris* Garden [q.v.], *Belins*-gate [q.v.], when the noises are at their height and lowdest" (4.4.15–16). The noise near the bridge was caused not only by the rush of water dropping from one level to another, but also by the working of the forciers or watermills constructed in 1582 to meet the city's growing water needs. In *DA* one of the London pleasures which Iniquity suggests to Pug is to "shoote the *Bridge*, childe, to the Cranes i' the *Vintry*" (1.1.70). Because the Three Cranes Tavern was upstream from the bridge, this would be an impossible task for mortals, as

H&S (10:223) have stated. Penniboy Senior in *SN* is denounced as an "ungrateful wretch" who "minds / A curtesie no more, then *London*-bridge, / What Arch was mended last" (2.4.99–101). Two of Jonson's plays have references which associate London Bridge with some rarely seen marine visitors. In *EH* Sir Petronel is warned not to attempt his Virginia voyage by a sailor who declares, "The skie is overcast, & there was a Porcpisce, even now seene at London bridge, which is alwaies the messenger of tempests" (3.3.139–41). After the storm which wrecks the adventurers' plans in this play, the butcher's apprentice Slitgut remarks about the river from a lofty vantage point downriver, "It runnes against London-Bridge (as it were) even full butt" (4.1.18–19). In *Volp* Sir Politik asks Peregrine if among the omens he has observed there were "three porcpisces seene, adove the bridge." "Sixe, and a sturgeon, sir" (2.1.40–41), is Peregrine's reply.

LONDON WALL. The old fortification around the City, measuring a little over two miles in circuit, not including the riverside portion which had been subverted since before the reign of Henry II.

S (p. 317) notes that the seven gates which punctuated its course were closed each night until the seventeenth century. The gates then remained standing for another hundred years. One of the few mentions of London Wall in drama occurs in Brome's *The City Wit*, as Crasy tries to recall where he met Doll Tryman, "About *London-Wall* was it?" (3.3).

According to Brainworm, *EMI*, Cob's house is "by the wall" (4.6.46). Earlier, Cob said that he was a neighbor of Justice Clement (who lives in Coleman Street) and that he dwelled "at the sign of the water-tankard, hard by the greene lattice" (3.7.10–11). This would put Cob's house close to the conduit at the corner of Curriers' Row and Coleman Street, just inside Moorgate. As H&S (9:379) have noted, a window of lattice work was a common designation for an inn. Cob's address today would still be "London Wall." A thoroughfare by this name runs west from Bishopsgate to Wood Street along the course of the old wall. In *Alch* Subtle and Face have a brief dispute as to whether their master was delaying his return until the plague death rate eased "within the walls" or "within the liberties [areas outside the walls but under City jurisdiction]" (4.7.116–18).

LONG LANE. A City thoroughfare which runs from Smithfield (q.v.) to Aldersgate Street north of St. Bartholomew's Church; like Houndsditch (q.v.), it was in Jonson's time chiefly occupied by old-clothes dealers and pawnbrokers.

The citations of S (p. 318) support the above details. In Nabbes's *Covent Garden* Ralph speaks of the players at the Cockpit Theater (q.v.): "They are men of credit. . . . they make no yearly Progresse with the anatomy of a

Sumpter-horse, laden with the sweeping of Long-Lane in a dead Vacation and purchas'd at the exchange of their owne whole Wardrobes" (1.1). Stow (2:28) declares, "This lane is now lately builded on both the sides with tenements for brokers, tiplers, and such like." H&S (9:477) furnish similar comments from Dekker and Webster's *Northward Ho* (2.1.13–15). W&C (2:439) add the statement of Nashe in *Pierce Penilesse* (*Works*, 1:182), "The times are daungerous, and this is an yron age; or rather no yron age, for swordes and bucklers goe to pawne a pace in Long-lane." The unflattering comments by Donald Lupton on Houndsditch were intended also to apply to Long Lane and are furnished in that entry.

Jonson's one reference to this area comes in the Quarto text of *EMO*, where Buffone remarks, "I referre me to your usurous Long-lane *Cannibals*, or such like" (5.5.73). The specific reference to Long Lane is omitted in the Folio, perhaps a concession to local business interests.

LORD CHANCELLOR'S TOMB. See the St. Paul's entry.

LORD MAYOR'S BANQUETING HOUSE. An edifice which stood in Tudor-Stuart times on the site of today's Stratford Place in New Oxford Street, west of the City. It was taken down in 1737.[4]

S (p. 318) mentions that it was a favorite spot for mayoral dinners held after visits to inspect conduit-heads west of London. Its proximity to the gallows at Tyburn was wittily used by Edmund Gayton, *Pleasant Notes upon Don Quixot* (1654, p. 119), who remarked that condemned men would tell their friends that they were invited to feast at the Banqueting House for a year and a day.

The Tyburn-Banqueting House connection is used by Jonson to provide a powerful contrast in *DA*, when Ambler tells Meercraft of the circumstances leading to the theft of his clothes. These include an assignation where he "got the Gentlewoman to goe with me, / And carry her bedding to a *Conduit-head*, / Hard by the place toward *Tyborne*, which they call / My L. Majors *Banqueting-house*" (5.1.26–29).

LOTHBURY. A City street running from Coleman Street east to Throgmorton Street.

S (p. 319) is among the modern authorities who disbelieve Stow's punning etymology (1:277), "This streete is possessed for the most part by Founders, that cast Candlestickes, Chafingdishes, Spice mortars, and such

4. W&C, 3:327, furnish this date and also point out that the conduit head adjacent to the Banqueting House was covered over at this time as well. Stratford Place runs north from New Oxford Street starting at a point almost directly across from the Bond Street Underground station.

like Copper or Laton workes, and do afterwarde turn them with the foot
. . . making a loathsome noice to the by-passers . . . and therefore by them
disdainedly called Lothberie."[5] Both S and H&S (10:632) cite dramatic
references to the noisiness of this quarter caused by the above trades, as in
Davenport's *A New Trick to Cheat the Divell*, where a wife threatens to make
her husband's home as noisy "as if you were to lodge in *Loth-bury* where they
turne brazen Candlestickes" (2.1). Stow also notes that the founders had not
changed their work areas, as had other trades recently, commenting (1:81),
"The Founders remaine by themselves in Lothberie."

In Jonson's *Alch*, Mammon, in collecting the dross metal to be converted
by Face and Subtle, says he will send to Lothbury for the copper (2.1.33–
34). Among the sensory offenses from which the masquers in *GM* pray to be
delivered are "The Candlesticks of *Lothbury* / And the loud pure wives of
Banbury" (ll. 1347–48). The town of Banbury, eighty miles northwest of
London, was a notorious dwelling place of Puritans. Rabbi Busy of *BF* was a
"Banbury *man*" (persons, l. 5).

LOVE LANE. One of several City thoroughfares by this name in Jonson's
time. One ran south from Eastcheap to Lower Thames Street, just east of
Pudding Lane; another's course was from Wood Street to Aldermanbury,
near the Guildhall. A third led off from Coleman Street in the same general
area.[6]

S (p. 320) argues that the context of Jonson's quote below indicates that
he had the first-mentioned thoroughfare in mind. H&S (10:563) quote
Stow's description (1:210) of this Love Lane, "of old time called Roape
Lane, since called Lucas Lane, of one *Lucas* owner of some part thereof, and
now corruptly called Love lane, it runneth up by the east end of a parish
church of . . . Saint *Andrew* in East Cheape." Stow also mentions the Love
Lane in Aldermanbury (1:296), "so called [because] of wantons." Kingsford (2:311) calls attention to the fact that there is a 1428 reference to "le
Stuehouse" in the Love Lane near Eastcheap. Concerning the third Love
Lane, off Coleman Street, Stow merely states (1:284) that it held many
tenements. Without explanation W&C (2:443) associate Jonson's reference with the Love Lane between Wood Street and Aldermanbury.

5. Kingsford, 2:334, conjectures that this name derived from a property owner. W&C,
2:442, also disagree with Stow and suggest a geographical source. Harben, *Dictionary of
London*, p. 370, is of a similar opinion, arguing for its origin from "lode," meaning "a cut or
drain leading into a large stream." This would be appropriate because of the street's
proximity to the extinct City waterway, Walbrook.

6. Both the Love Lane near Pudding Lane and the Love Lane near Wood Street are still
extant. The former, however, is presently known as Lovat Lane. Nothing remains of the Love
Lane off Coleman Street, which Stow described as being near the north end of that
thoroughfare.

According to Venus in *CHM*, her son Cupid is "Prentise in Love-lane with a Bugle-maker" (l. 119). Because the Love Lane off Eastcheap is near Pudding Lane, from where Venus is said to hail (l. 118), it appears that S's view, geographically speaking, is the correct one, even though the Wood Street Love Lane also had some erotic associations.

LUDGATE. One of the seven old City gates, once located at today's intersection of Old Bailey and Ludgate Hill.

Its construction was traditionally ascribed to the mythical King Lud, who was depicted on the gate standing during Jonson's time. H&S (9:427) point out the employment of the term "Ludgathians," used by Jonson below, by Dekker, *Seven Deadly Sinnes* (*Non-Dramatic Works*, 2:18), and Edward Sharpham, *Cupids Whirligig* (1607, sig. E3). Stow (1:39) comments that in 1378 it was converted into a prison for debtors and bankrupts. Stow also differentiates between Ludgate and Newgate (q.v.) prisons. The latter was used for felons and traitors rather than for solely monetary offenders. W&C (2:446) shed further light on the unfortunate residents there, citing Strype's continuation of Stow's *Survey* (1720, 2:175), "Formerly Debtors that were not able to satisfy their debts, put themselves into the prison of Ludgate for shelter from their creditors. And these were Merchants and Tradesmen who had been driven to want by losses at sea."

In *EMO* Carlo Buffone warns Sogliardo, "Mary this, alwaies beware you commerce not with bankrupts, or poore needy *Ludgathians*" (1.2.121–22). Later, Fallace emphasizes Deliro's miserliness, declaring, "He kept a poore man in *Ludgate* once, twelve yeere, for sixteene shillings" (5.10.20–21).

M

MARIBONE (ST. MARYLEBONE). A parish and later metropolitan borough two and one-half miles northwest of St. Paul's.

Dramatic references to this region are chiefly to Marylebone Park, which was a popular spot for assignations, as S (p. 336) has shown. Laxton, a gallant in Dekker and Middleton's *The Roaring Girl*, has his coachman drive "to the hither end of Marybone parke, a fit place for *Mol* to get in" (3.1.3–4). In Brome's *The Northern Lass* a character surmises that her sister has come "to fetch me forth into the aire of Hidepark (q.v.) or Marybone" (2.1). St. Marylebone history dates from 1400 when a church was dedicated to St. Mary on the banks of the Ty-bourne, one of several rivers running down to the Thames from the heights north of London. In Jonson's day the principal part of the old village was near the present junction of Marylebone Road and Marylebone High Street.[1] The old manor house of St. Marylebone was built in the reign of Henry VIII and utilized by both Mary Tudor and Elizabeth. In February, 1600–1601, Marylebone was the scene of a hunting party given by the crown for some ambassadors from the emperor of Russia.[2] Lease of this manor (also known as the manor of Tyburn) was granted to the Forset family by King James I, who retained crown control of the extensive woodlands of Marylebone Park, a practice continued by King Charles until 1646.[3] By the outbreak of the Civil War, London's expansion had provided this district with a growing number of wealthy residents.[4]

St. Marylebone is one of several locales for scenes in *TT*. The conniving, selfish Justice Preamble (alias Bramble) is identified with this area (persons, l.4; 3.9.21). His servile clerk "borrows" the uniform of a royal messenger who also lives in Marylebone in order to engage in some trickery for Preamble (1.5.39–41). Late in the play another character corroborates the

1. Gordon Mackenzie, *Marylebone: Great City North of Oxford Street* (London: Macmillan, 1972), pp. 19–20, discusses Marylebone's early years; Thomas Smith, *A Topographical and Historical Account of the Parish of St. Marylebone* (London: John Smith, 1833), p. 161, describes the old town center.

2. George Clinch, *Marylebone and St. Pancras* (London: Truslove & Shirley, 1890), p. 5, cites Nichols, *Progresses*, 3:519.

3. Mackenzie, p. 21; James, "noted for his addiction to hunting," probably used the park quite often (p. 23).

4. Smith, *Topographical and Historical Account*, pp. 64–65, reprints early church memorials to prominent residents and, pp. 161–62, traces Marylebone's origins as a drinking and sporting resort back to the mid-seventeenth century.

actions of a friend: "I, upon record! The Clock dropt twelve at *Maribone*" (5.2.5–6). The association of this play's leading authoritarian character with Marylebone accords with this district's actual associations with royal and civic leaders. As mentioned above, Marylebone Park remained in crown control throughout Jonson's era. Also nearby was the Lord Mayor's Banqueting House where City officials gathered after inspections of the water supply from conduits west of London. As an authoritarian figure who betrays the public trust, Preamble is much worse than Justice Overdo in *BF* because he is consciously and willingly unscrupulous. Thus by his association with an area commonly identified with royal and civic control, he represents an implicit Jonsonian comment on the worsening conditions in local and national government in early Caroline times.

MEDLEY'S ORDINARY. A then popular eating spot in Milford Lane, which runs south from the Strand (q.v.), just opposite St. Clement Danes.

This rendezvous is briefly discussed by H&S (10:260), who cite a letter by Sir Henry Wotton (1628) telling of "when we were last merry together at Medley's" and another by Nathaniel Bacon recounting a quarrel at this establishment.

Jonson mentions it in the stage prologue to *SN*, where the playwright does not deem it worthy of his concern "what fare to day at *Medleyes* was" (l. 15).

MERCHANT TAYLORS' HALL. Located on the south side of Threadneedle Street (q.v.), between Finch Lane and Bishopsgate Street. The present building dates from 1671.

The Merchant Taylors were one of the oldest and most prominent of the London livery companies. S (p. 341) cites a comment from Dekker's *Guls Horne Booke* (*Non-Dramatic Works*, 2:210) describing the golden age, "Taylors then were none of the twelve Companies: their Hall, that now is larger than some Dorpes among the *Netherlands*, was then no bigger than a Dutch Butchers shop." H&S (10:360) point out that one of the most memorable banquets at this hall occurred early in King James I's reign when he entertained the king of Denmark. This event was celebrated in "A Delightful Song of our four famous Feasts of England" (1606), which is reprinted in W. Herbert, *The Twelve Great Livery Companies of London* (London, 1836, 2:432–33). The Merchant Taylors' Hall also was the scene of a play, masque, and banquet which the City, upon James's insistence, provided for the notorious Carr-Howard wedding in 1613.

Considering the above testimony to the eminence of the Merchant Taylors' Company, it is a tribute to Jonson that in 1607 he was called upon to write an entertainment for King James and Prince Henry at a banquet in this hall. The records of the Company's Court of Assistants help to recon-struct the occasion: "And at the upper end of the hall there was sett a chayer of estate where his Ma[jes]^{ty} sate and viewed the hall, and a very proper child well spoken being clothed like an Angell of gladnes, with a taper of ffrancinnsence burning in his hand, deliv'ed a shorte speech . . . devised by Mr. Beniamyn Johnson the Poet wch pleased his Ma[jes]^{ty} marvelously well."[5] The Hall is mentioned in *ML* to enhance the ego of Sir Moth Interest in his plottings. This schemer, boasting of his acquaintance with a "lady" who supposedly buried a fortune in Lady Loadstone's well, declares, "Wee met at Merchants-Taylors-hall, at dinner, / In *Thred-needle* street" (5.7.86–87).

MERMAID TAVERN. A famous tavern associated with eminent seventeenth-century figures. There were many taverns by this name in London, but recent scholarship has reasonably well determined that it stood in lower Bread Street (q.v.), not far from the Thames.

Both S (p. 341) and H&S (10:178) held that its site was near the north end of Bread Street with extra entrances from Friday Street and Cheapside. The fact that this was an error, resulting from there being a Mermaid Tavern in Cheapside and another farther south in Bread Street, has been recently pointed out. Kenneth Rogers has shown that the traditional idea of the above three entrances to the Mermaid is not backed by documentary evidence but based upon a misreading of a tradesman's token.[6] Rogers cites evidence from the Hustings Rolls attesting to the existence of a Mermaid Tavern between Bread Street and Friday Street, close to where Old Fish Street formerly ran. In addition, Rogers discovered the identities of the vintners who kept the Mermaid during the seventeenth century and who also served excellent seafood dinners.[7] Rogers believes that this Mermaid was the one celebrated by Jonson, Coryat, and others because of its good food and convenient access to Blackfriars (q.v.) and the stairs for river crossings. The Mermaid in Cheapside, with which it was long confused, evidently adjoined the east side of Saddlers' Hall, near Foster Lane. Accord-ing to Rogers (pp. 36–37), this tavern was situated well back from the north side of Cheapside and had a long, narrow entrance from that street.

5. *Collections III: A Calendar of Dramatic Records in the Books of the Livery Companies of London 1485–1640*, ed. Jean Robertson and D. J. Gordon (Oxford: Malone Society, 1954), pp. 169–70; Jonson was paid £20 "for inventing the speech to his Ma^{ty}", and for making the songs, and his direccons to others in that business" (p. 174). H&S, 11:586–87, also provide these details, as set forth by C. M. Clode, *The Early History of the Guild of Merchant Taylors* (London: Harrison, 1888), 1:280, 290.

6. Kenneth Rogers, *The Mermaid and Mitre Taverns in Old London*, pp. 7–9.

7. Rogers, pp. 9–27; the vintners during Jonson's time are discussed on pp. 21–27 and Jonson's references to the Mermaid on pp. 29–34.

Rogers found no evidence of its patronage by dramatists and believes that this Mermaid was frequented more by City business folk than by players and gallants.

In *BF* Littlewit declares, "A poxe o' these pretenders to wit! your *Three Cranes* [q.v.], *Miter* [q.v.], and *Mermaid* men" (1.1.33–34). In *DA* Meercraft tells Everill of his spendthrift faults, which include "haunting / The *Globes* [q.v.], and *Mermaides*! wedging in with *Lords*, / Still at the table" (3.3.25–27). In *Epig* 101, "Inviting a friend to Supper," the poet effuses, "But that, which most doth take my *Muse*, and mee, / Is a pure cup of rich *Canary*-wine, / Which is the *Mermaids*, now, but shall be mine" (ll. 28–30). The mock-epic adventurers of *Epig* 133, "On the Famous Voyage," make their decision to embark up the Fleet Ditch (q.v.) after a merry dinner "at *Bread-streets* Mermaid" (l. 37). Thomas Coryat's *Greeting from the Court of the Great Mogul* (1616) was addressed to "the Sireniacal Gentlemen, that meet the first Fridaie of everie Moneth, at . . . the Mere-Maide in Bread-streete" and contained specific greetings to Jonson (pp. 35, 43) as well as to Sir Robert Cotton, Inigo Jones, and John Donne.

MILE END. A village one mile east of Aldgate (q.v.) along the Whitechapel Road. Its green was used as a training ground for London's militia and as a staging area for civic shows and fairs.

S (p. 346) provides numerous dramatic citations of Mile End's associations with the London militia. These include the exhortations of the Grocer's Wife in Beaumont's *Knight of the Burning Pestle*, who counsels Ralph, "I would have thee call all the youthes together in battle-ray, with drums, and guns, and flags, and march to Mile-end in pompous fashion" (5.1.57–59). H&S (9:368) cite Stow, *A Summarie of the Chronicles of England* (1604, p. 420), who notes that on August 27, 1599, "3000 Citizens, householders and subsidy men, shewed on the Miles end, where they trained all that day and other untill the fourth of September." H&S also here note a comment from B. Rich, *The Fruites of long Experience* (1604, p. 33), where Captain Skill, arguing with Captain Pill, says, "God blesse me, my Countrey and friendes, from his direction that hath no better *Experience* then what he hath atteyned unto at the fetching home of a Maye-pole, at a Midsomer fighte, or from a trayning at *Milende-Greene*." Stow (1:103) describes the Midsummer Watch of 1539, when "a great muster was made by the Cittizens, at the Miles end all in bright harnesse with coates of white silke, or cloath and chaines of gold, in three great battailes, to the number of 15000."

In *EMI* Brainworm, disguised as a soldier, vows to abuse Knowell's patience so much that "hee will hate the musters at Mile-end for it, to his dying day" (2.5.143–44). His disguise works so well that later on, Formal asks Brainworm to recount his war experiences, for "they say they be very strange, and not like those a man reades in the *Romane* histories, or sees, at *Mile-end*" (4.6.71–73).

MILK STREET. A City thoroughfare running north from Cheapside (q.v.) to Gresham Street between Wood Street and Lawrence Lane; today the southern end of Milk Street is wide enough for pedestrians only.

S (p. 347) states that originally London's milk and butter market was held in this street and that Dekker mentions it in *Jests to Make You Merrie* (*Non-Dramatic Works*, 2:323) as one of the areas where "our worthiest citizens" resided. H&S (10:563) cite Stow (1:295), who writes that this street was "so called of Milke sold there, there bee many fayre houses for wealthy Marchantes and other." Sir Thomas More was born in Milk Street in 1480, the son of an eminent lawyer.

In Jonson's *CHM* one "*John Butter* o' Milke-street" asks to come in. He is allowed to "slip in for a Torch-bearer, so he melt not too fast, that he will last till the Masque be done" (ll. 87–90).

MILL. Believed from the dramatic context given below to have been situated in Westminster close to the Thames south of Whitehall.

H&S (10:281) believe that Jonson's reference was to a water mill owned by the abbot of Westminster at the end of College Street. Today's thoroughfare named Millbank in this area carries on these associations. A 1565 entry in the overseers' book of the parish of St. Margaret, Westminster, cited by W&C (1:232), also helps to locate this structure. Here is listed "the Myll next to Bowling Alley [q.v.]." From all extant evidence it appears that the Bowling Alley also was situated very near today's College Street and could be listed as "next to" the Mill.

In the third intermeane of *SN*, Gossip Mirth remarks that Gossip Tatle knows all kinds of news, including "*how much griest went to the* Mill, *and what besides*" (ll. 27–28). The geographical proximity of the Mill and Bowling Alley is maintained by Jonson's reference to the Bowling Alley in the line immediately preceding his mention of the Mill. Thus it appears that Jonson was adhering closely to local geography as he pointed out the "newsworthy" spots in the neighborhood of his final residence (see Westminster).

MITRE TAVERN. A common London tavern name. As in the case of the Mermaid (q.v.), recent scholarship has made relatively accurate judgments about to which of the many London Mitres Jonson referred.

S (p. 348), and H&S (9:449), and W&C (2:551–52) have adhered to the traditional belief in two or three Mitres with literary associations during the seventeenth and eighteenth centuries: a Mitre in Bread Street at the corner of Cheapside (or with entrances from there) and one or two Mitres in Fleet Street (q.v.).[8] Of the latter pair, one was associated with Dr. Samuel Johnson; the other was prominent during the seventeenth century. Kenneth Rogers's research, however, has changed matters considerably. First, he has shown that there were Mitres in early Stuart times in both Cheapside and Bread Street. He has also revealed that previous authorities had either confused or transposed the locations of the Fleet Street Mitres.[9] Rogers points out that the Mitre in Cheap, like nearly all the taverns bearing this name, was originally associated with a religious house—in this case the Hospital of St. Thomas of Acon, which it adjoined. This Mitre stood close to the Great Conduit and St. Mary Colechurch at the northeast end of Cheapside by Mercers' Hall. The present site is marked by 83–85 Cheapside. Confusion of this place with a "Mitre Court" on the south side of Cheapside helped to create the misconception which resulted in the idea of a Mitre in Cheapside with an entrance from Bread Street. The real Mitre in Bread Street was situated away from the bourgeois bustle of Cheapside. This tavern, near the south end of Bread Street, gained much trade from the nearby landing places at Queenhithe and Three Cranes.[10] The locations of the Fleet Street Mitres were ascertained by using parish lists and John Rocque's 1745 map of London. Rogers's work (pp. 132–37, 140) led to the conclusion that the seventeenth-century Mitre stood in Mitre Court, close to the notorious Ram Alley (q.v.). Dr. Johnson's Mitre was situated about twenty paces farther west, where at 39 Fleet Street Hoare's Bank now stands. Rogers (pp. 103, 107–8, 114) puts forth logical evidence for locating the Mitre which figures in *EMO* (5.4) as either the Bread Street or Cheapside establishment discussed above. These City taverns are better candidates than the Fleet Street Mitres to the west because the next scene in the play is set at one of the City Counters (q.v.).

The Mitre in *EMO* is first mentioned by Puntarvolo, who declares that there is "no better place, then the Mitre" (3.3.73), and "Your Miter is your best house" (3.6.161). Later on he asserts, "Carlo shall bespeake supper, at the Mitre, against we come backe" (4.8.106–7). Macilente next mentions the locale, "Our supper at the Mitre must of necessitie hold to night" (5.3.79–80). Scenes 4 through 7 take place at the Mitre, as the choric figures remind us (5.3.92–93). During one of these scenes (5.4.4) Carlo calls out to a drawer named George, prompting H&S to surmise (9:474)

8. H&S, 9:449, cite no authority for their assertion that the Bread Street Mitre later moved to Fleet Street. S, p. 348, treats the associations of the two Fleet Street Mitres as pertaining to only one such establishment.

9. *Mermaid and Mitre*, pp. 83, 132. K, p. 494, follows S, above, while W&C, 2:551–52, transpose the sites of the Fleet Street Mitres. The errors of the latter authorities have been followed by other modern writers.

10. Rogers, pp. 83–85, 109.

that Jonson had a real person in mind, for "*George* the drawer at the Miter" is also mentioned in Dekker and Webster, *Westward Ho* (4.1.62). Finally, toward the close of the play, Macilente recalls to the others where their last meal was (5.8.27). Among the changes from the Quarto to the Folio of *EMI* was the alteration of a tavern reference from "Mitre" to "Star" (4.2.68–69). This shift would be in keeping with the topographical unity which Jonson imposed upon the Folio, where nearly all the action takes place in the neighborhood of the Old Jewry (q.v.) and Coleman Street (q.v.). A Star Tavern has been located in Coleman Street, which would better have served Jonson's needs than the Mitre. Both the Mitre in Cheap discussed earlier and a lesser-known Mitre in Fenchurch Street would not be as suitable to the new geographical range of *EMI*.

MOORFIELDS. A stretch of erstwhile marshland running north between Bishopsgate and Cripplegate north of the City. By Jonson's time it had been reclaimed and was being laid out in parks and walkways. During the eighteenth and nineteenth centuries this area was built up, leaving the greenery of Finsbury Circus and Finsbury Square the sole remaining open spaces.

As illustrated by S (p. 353), Moorfields was the scene of activities ranging from laundry-drying to military practice to duelling. It was notorious as a beggars' quarter. In Field's *A Woman Is a Weather-cocke* a character exclaims, "Godamercy, zoones methinkes I see my selfe in *Moorfields*, upon a wodden leg, begging three pence" (4.2.119–20). Not only indigent citizens but also licensed mad folk frequented Moorfields because of its proximity to Bedlam (see Bet'lem) Hospital. H&S (10:67) cite Stow's list (2:145–47) of the lazar (leper) houses in London and comment that apparently lepers were allowed to beg in Moorfields as well. On the pleasanter side, H&S (10:179) refer to a contemporary account of that portion of Moorfields newly converted into a civic recreational ground.[11] Stow (2:78) was displeased by citizen encroachment upon these grounds before they were publicly developed. He remarks how Moorfields was despoiled "by meanes of inclosure for Gardens, wherein are builded many fayre summer houses, and as in other places of the Suburbes, some of them like Midsommer Pageantes, with Towers, Turrets, and Chimney tops, not so much for use or profite, as for shewe and pleasure." Current authorities, such as K (p. 369) believe that the erection of the Roman wall

11. Richard Johnson, *The Pleasant Walkes of Moore-fields* (London, 1607). Written as a dialogue between a citizen and a countryman, this treatise is an encomium rather than a debate; for a discussion of this work as part of the tradition of London encomia, see Louis B. Wright, *Middle-Class Culture in Elizabethan England* (Chapel Hill: University of North Carolina Press, 1935), pp. 37–38.

over the Walbrook, a onetime stream near the City, created the marshy nature of this locale. Edmund Howes's 1631 edition of Stow's *Annales* (p. 1021) cited by W&C (2:560), gives another comment on conditions in Moorfields, "This field, untill the third year of King James, was a most noysome and offensive place, being a generall laystall . . . burrowed and crossed with deep stinking ditches and noysome common shewers, and was of former times held impossible to be reformed."

Jonson's awareness of the many associations borne by this area is evident in his wide employment of Moorfields references. In *EMI* Moorfields figures in Brainworm's plan to gull Knowell. This locale is along Knowell's route to the City from his home in the northern suburbs and a superb place for Brainworm's begging-soldier ruse (2.4.8–9; 4.6.2–3). In *EH* Golding predicts the results of Quicksilver's improvidence in a sketch suggesting close observation on Jonson's part, "Mee thinks I see thee already walking in Moore fields without a Cloake, with half a Hatte, without a band, a Doublet with three Buttons, without a girdle, a hose with one point and no Garter, with a cudgell under thine arme, borrowing and begging three pence" (1.1.137–41). Another vivid Moorfields picture is offered in *Alch*, where Subtle tells how he "envisions" Mammon utilizing the elixir which the quacks have promised him, "walking *more-fields* for lepers; / And offring citizens-wives pomander-bracelets, / As his preservative, made of the *elixir*" (1.4.20–22). Later, Face derisively remarks that, had their project worked, Mammon would have installed a cream-filled, silver-lined ditch around London, "That, every sunday in *More*-fields the younkers [young men], / And tits, and tom-boyes [both young girls] should have fed on, *gratis*" (5.5.79–80). After the civic development of Moorfields, this area became a popular place for outings and the display of new fashions. In *BF* Littlewit challenges "*Morefields, Pimlico* [q.v.] path, or the *Exchange* [q.v.], in a sommer evening" (1.2.6–7) to outshine his wife's holiday attire. Not long after this, in a typically Jonsonian juxtaposition of the beautiful and grotesque, the audience is reminded of the Bedlamites in this area when Win states that according to "tother man of *More-fields*" (l. 52) it must be a "Gentle-man Mad-man" (l. 51) that will make a proper husband for the widowed Dame Purecraft. Finally, in *Und* 42, "An Elegie," Jonson remarks, "O, what strange / Varietie of Silkes were on th' Exchange! / Or in Moore-fields, this other night! sings one" (ll. 71–73).

MOORGATE. An opening in the City wall made in 1445 between Bishopsgate and Cripplegate to gain access to Moorfields (q.v.). Its position today is marked by the junction of Moorgate Street and London Wall.

S (p. 353) provides added historical information and a dramatic citation referring to the presence of a ducking stool at Moorgate from W. Rowley, *A*

New Wonder: A Woman Never Vexed (2.1). Stow's brief remarks (1:32) include his observation that Moorgate was located "neare unto *Coleman-streete*." This reinforces the topographical unity of *EMI*, as discussed below.

Justice Clement's house in this play is located in Coleman Street, and Moorgate is mentioned in connection with characters' visits to the City area near it. Early in the play, Young Knowell asks Stephen to accompany him on his visit to Wellbred, "I am sent for, this morning, by a friend i' the old *Jewrie* [q.v.] to come to him; It's but crossing over the fields to *More-gate*" (1.3.92–94). With his typical affected camaraderie, Stephen replies, "You shall command me, twise so farre as *More-gate* to doe you good, in such a matter" (ll. 97–99). The worthlessness of this avowal would be apparent to Jonson's audience, as the distance from the Knowell home in Hoxton (see Hogsden) to the City boundary at Moorgate was only about a mile.

N

NEWGATE MARKET. Located in Jonson's time in the center of Newgate Street, near its junction today with Warwick Lane, just west of St. Paul's.

W&C (2:590), gaining their information from Stow (1:343), state that Newgate Market was once primarily devoted to the sale of grain. After the Great Fire the market relocated a short distance southward, on the site of today's Paternoster Square. In 1869 this enterprise was "dismarketed" because of the establishment of the Central Meat Market at Smithfield.

During a visit to Littlewit's house in *BF*, Quarlous declares of Rabbi Busy, "He has undone a Grocer here, in Newgate-market, that broke with him" (1.3.140–41). The location of Newgate Market would thus fit in with the geographical consistency of the play, because the market was very close to Christ's Hospital (the probable site of Littlewit's house) and but a few hundred yards from the fairground in Smithfield (q.v.), the sites for all of the play's action.

NEWGATE PRISON. A prison during Jonson's era occupying one of the City's seven main gates, located in Newgate Street east of today's Giltspur Street.

S (pp. 363–64) states that Newgate housed criminals since 1200. In the brief fragment of Chaucer's "Cook's Tale" we learn that the wayward apprentice Perkin Revellour was "somtyme lad with revel to Newgate." For a long time Newgate held both felons and debtors; finally in 1815 it was given over exclusively to felons in the expanded quarters just to the south into which it had moved in 1770. The prison was finally dismantled in 1903.

In *DA* the hapless Pug's efforts to corrupt society land him in Newgate (5.6.3). Additional references to Newgate are contained in the marginal notes to the text, where there is mention of the "great noise" heard there when Pug escapes (H&S, 6:262) and the direction, "Enter the Keeper of Newgate" (p. 268). One of the jailers then laments, "O! such an accident falne out at *Newgate*, Sir" (5.8.123).

O

OLD BAILEY. London's central criminal court, located today in the street by this name which runs from Ludgate Hill north to Newgate Street.

S (p. 375) explains its etymology; the building once lay behind the ancient bailey (outer court) of the city wall, specifically between Ludgate and Newgate Prisons. The "bells of Old Bailey" mentioned in the famous nursery rhyme were probably the bells of the church of St. Sepulchre (q.v.) nearby, where a knell was always rung for condemned felons.

The Old Bailey was also known as Justice Hall, which explains the outcry of one of the jailers after Pug's explosive escape from Newgate Prison in *DA*, "A piece of *Justice Hall* / Is broken downe" (5.7.1–2). In addition, a crucial episode in Jonson's career occurred at the Old Bailey, where he was tried in 1598 for slaying Gabriel Spencer in a duel, discussed by H&S (1:18).

OLD JEWRY. A City street which extends north from Poultry to Gresham Street (in Jonson's day to Lothbury [q.v.]).

S (p. 376) cites Fuller's description of the Jews in his *Church History* (2:221), "But their principal abode was in London, where they had their arch-synagogue at the north corner of the Old Jewry, as opening into Lothbury." According to S, this building later became the Windmill Tavern (q.v.), which figures prominently in *EMI*. After the expulsion of the Jews in 1291, this district became occupied by prosperous City merchants. One grand residence noted by W&C (2:614) was that of Sir Robert Clayton, a Lord Mayor during the Restoration. His home featured a cedar-wainscoted banqueting room adorned with frescoes depicting battles between classical gods and giants.

Although not of Clayton's stature, Kitely in *EMI* is described by a servant as "the rich merchant i' the old *Jewrie*" (1.2.57). Cob, the local water carrier, describes one of the houses he services as "one master KITE-LY'S, i' the *old Jewry*" (1.4.71–72). In this area also resides Wellbred, whose letter to Edward Knowell (1.2.70–71) asks if Edward has forgotten his friends dwelling in the Old Jewry. Soon afterward, Edward tells his cousin Stephen, "I am sent for, this morning, by a friend i' the old *Jewrie* to come to him" (1.3.92–93).

P

PADDINGTON. In Jonson's day a village three and one-half miles west of St. Paul's and half a mile north of the gallows at Tyburn.

As S (p. 384) has noted, a number of springs which furnished London with water were located in this area. Paddington was somewhat of a resort for Londoners. Both Brome's *A Mad Couple Well Matched* (2.1) and his *New Academy* (2.1) refer to it as frequented by citizens out for an afternoon stroll. In Shirley's *The Ball* Barker asserts that he is no false flatterer: "I write no odes / Upon your mistress, to commend her postures, / And tumbling in a coach towarde Paddington; / Whither you hurry her to see the pheasants" (4.1). From the time that King Edgar gave large tracts of land in this locale to the monks of Westminster, through the Elizabethan era and later, much of Paddington was owned by ecclesiastical authorities and leased out almost totally for agriculture. Even in the early nineteenth century this district had a rural independence that made its proximity to the City hard to believe.[1] H&S (9:288), in conjunction with one of Jonson's references to Paddington, below, confine their comments to information about the Red Lion Inns of the area.[2]

Paddington was but a mile or two from the main settings of *TT*. It is mentioned in this play as part of the "evidence" in one of Squire Tub's plots. Tub's disguised servant charges that the robbery suspect, John Clay, be taken to Paddington, where his "victim" is lodged (2.2.160–62), to which Constable Turfe agrees (l. 176; 2.3.26–27). Later, Squire Tub, after discovering Justice Preamble's plot to marry Audrey, declares, "Ile post to *Paddington*, t'acquaint old Turfe [Audrey's father], / With the whole busines" (2.6.43–44). Clay then flees, and when he is discovered in hiding, explains his action, "Hearing your newes *Ball Pupy*, / You ha' brought from *Paddington*, I ene stole home here" (4.6.99–100). More specifically, the "Captain" whom Clay purportedly robbed is said to be resting at the Red Lion Inn at Paddington (2.3.29–30; 3.1.11–12). This inn is again mentioned soon after when Puppy tells of the trick that

1. Harold P. Clunn, *The Face of London*, p. 472, writes, "As recently as 1820 Paddington, although joined to the metropolis, still possessed many rural spots which appeared as secluded as though they had been a great distance from town" and "as late as 1830 [it] was still regarded by many people as a rustic village."

2. William Robins, *Paddington Past and Present* (London: Robins, 1853), pp. 181–82, points out one Red Lion Inn near the junction of the Edgeware and the Harrow Roads, at which Shakespeare is said to have acted, and another farther out on the Harrow Road; Robins also records a tradition that Jonson often visited the "Wheat Sheaf" in the Edgware Road.

separated him from Audrey. Puppy was instructed to inform the Turfes that "the Captaine lay at the *Lion*, and before / I came againe, *Awdrey* was gone with the serving-man" (3.2.24–25).

PANCRACE OR PANCRIDGE (ST. PANCRAS).

A parish and later metropolitan borough two miles northwest of St. Paul's, best known in Tudor-Stuart times for its recreational opportunities and also for the disreputable associations of its parish church.

As illustrated by S (p. 387), references to the St. Pancras area during this period are plentiful. Many deal with its pleasures or humorously compare its chief features to City counterparts. In Nashe's *Lenten Stuffe* (*Works*, 3:214), the author comments that lawyers seldom remember "their owne privy scapes with their laundresses or their night walkes to Pancredge." The Clown in Heywood's *The Royal King* remarks that "our organ of *Powles* is much bigger and better than yours of *Rixham* [Wrexham, a Welsh town famous for its church organ], by as much as *Powles* Church is bigger and better than Saint *Pancridge*" (1.1). The reputation and history of Old St. Pancras Church are of special interest here because the vicar of this institution plays an important role in Jonson's *TT*. By Jonson's time this church appears to have been the Gretna Green of the London area, judging from the dramatically substantiated assertions of S and H&S (9:275) that "Pancridge Parson" denoted a cleric willing to perform sudden or irregular marriages. In Field's *A Woman Is a Weathercocke* a fake minister involved in an amorous episode is denounced as "Thou *Pancridge* Parson" (2.1.92). A character in Middleton's *A Fair Quarrel* tries to defend the legitimacy of his child, "For we were married by the hand of heaven / Ere this work was begun" (5.1.372–73). To this comes the sardonic reply, "At Pancridge, I'll lay my hand on't" (l. 374). Lent, in Nabbes's masque, *The Spring's Glory* (*Works*, 2:232), boasts, "Besides, I couple more than the Parson of *Pancrace:* I meane City woodcocks, with Suburb-wagtailes." A surprise turn of events in *Tottenham Court*, also by Nabbes, prompts the outcry, "Yet more plots! sure the Parson of *Pancrace* hath beene here" (5.6).

There is sufficient historical evidence of the validity of these sentiments.[3] It is a frequent assertion among London historians that Old St. Pancras Church was the last church where Mass continued to be celebrated after the

---

3. There appears to have been real-life justification for the unfavorable light in which this church was viewed. According to Percy W. Lovell and William McB. Marcham, eds., *Old St. Pancras and Kentish Town*, p. 15, in 1629 John Elborowe, who was vicar of St. Pancras, had to be restrained from collecting too many tithes. In 1631, states Frederick Miller, *St. Pancras Past and Present* (London: Heywood, 1874), p. 20, Elborowe left to become vicar of Rainham, in Essex. He later had a post as rector of Wennington, also in Essex. Still, he retained the lease of the St. Pancras rectory until 1658.

The South East View of Pancrafs Church

Publifhed according to Act of Parliam.

Located in the countryside northwest of London, Old St. Pancras Church figures significantly in the merriment of *A Tale of a Tub* (Chatelain, c. 1750).

Reformation.[4] A manuscript (B5.53) in the Heal Collection at the Camden Public Library states that such services were conducted "by an old Incumbent, favoured for some particular reason by the Queen, and whom she would not permit to be disturbed."[5] The manuscript of John Norden's *Speculum Britanniae . . . Middlesex* (1592) furnishes some very interesting comments on the associations of this house of worship, "And although this place be as it were forsaken of all, and true men seldome frequent the same but upon devyne occasions, yet is it visyted and usually haunted of Roages, vagabondes, harlettes and theeves, who assemble not there to pray, but to wayte for praye, and manie fall into theire handes clothed, that are glad when they are escaped naked. Walke not there too late."[6]

Both the church and the general vicinity of St. Pancras figure significantly in *TT*. Several of its scenes occur in the parish countryside. The recusant associations of Old St. Pancras Church point up Jonson's awareness of contemporary local attitudes, thus weakening E. K. Chambers's conclusion that the play is set in the Marian era. Canon Hugh, the play's main intriguer, is in every way a "Pancridge Parson." Introduced as "*Vicar of* Pancrace" (persons, l.1), he reminds the audience of this several times in the play (1.1.8, 23). The wedding of John Clay and Audrey Turfe was to have taken place at Old St. Pancras Church (2.2.103–6). Hilts is sent there by Tub to inform Canon Hugh of the robbery trick's success in thwarting this union (2.4.23, 46). Soon after, Justice Preamble has Tub falsely arrested in order to further his own intents to escort Audrey "to *Pancridge*, to the Vicar" (2.6.38). Tub, however, soon gets free and speedily informs Audrey's father, Constable Turfe, of Preamble's plot (3.3.7–9). Turfe then hastens to Pancras Church, where he succeeds in preventing the justice from marrying Audrey (3.5.29). Bragging of his triumph, Turfe boasts, "I will ride / Above Prince *Arthur*," whereby the well-meaning but inept Council of Finsbury (q.v.) associates him with such worthies as the "*Pancridge* Earle" (3.6.4–6), a mock title used in City archery festivals, as H&S (9:293) have noted. In *DA* the scheming Meercraft introduces a fellow rogue as "a plain fellow" who "wi' not be sold for th'Earledome of *Pancridge*" (2.1.64). Upon another occasion Jonson sarcastically invokes this "honor." In *UV* 35, "To Inigo Marquess Would-be," he

4. The recusant associations of this church are upheld in C. H. Denyer, ed., *St. Pancras*, pp. 16–17, 48; as well as by Clinch, *Marylebone and St. Pancras*, p. 132; also Sir Walter Besant, *London North of the Thames*, p. 404; and most recently by K, p. 476.

5. Cited in Denyer, ed., *St. Pancras*, pp. 16–17.

6. As M. St. Clare Byrne, *Elizabethan Life in Town and Country*, 7th ed., rev. (London: University Paperbacks, 1961), pp. 118–19, has noted, this reference to the dangerous loiterers around the church occurs only in the manuscript of Norden's work, Harleian MS. 570, f. 27, in the British Museum.

advises his rival Inigo Jones, "Content thee to be Pancridge Earle ye whyle; /
An Earle of show" (ll. 20–21). Returning to *TT*, Canon Hugh, while
disguised as the robbery "victim," tells Constable Turfe to entrust a £100
bond to him in his true person, asking with grave irony, "Know you
Chanon *Hugh*, / The Vicar of *Pancrace*?" (4.1.81–82). Hugh then sends
the clerk Miles Metaphor off with a message to bring Audrey to Pancras
Church (ll. 100–102), but Tub later intercepts the pair and decides to
escort Audrey himself (4.5.47–49). Soon after, Lady Tub scoffs at Tub's
romantic interests by noting "Your mind runs much on *Pancridge*" (4.6.15)
after he mentioned it a moment ago (l. 13). Lady Tub and Dame Turfe then
decide to rejoin Constable Turfe at this church (ll. 18–20). Earlier, Tub's
servant Hilts wished to return home rather than travel on to Kentish Town
or Pancridge (4.2.3–5). When Clay is discovered in hiding, Lady Tub at
first cannot believe it, declaring, "*John Clay* at *Pancras*, is there to be
married" (4.6.77), restating it (l.89). Puppy also expresses this mistaken
view of Clay's whereabouts (ll. 102–3).

PANNIER ALLEY. A narrow City thoroughfare which runs north from
Paternoster Row to Newgate Street.

S (p. 388) provides a quotation and commentary which illustrate Jonson's allusion below. Apparently buff leather (the material for catchpoles'
jackets) was sold in this area. In Dekker and Webster's *Westward Ho* a
character remarks, "If I could meete one of these Varlets that wear Pannier-
ally on their baks (Serjeants) I would make them scud" (3.2.19–21). H&S
(10:181) give Stow's comments on its location (1:342), "an other passage
out of *pater-noster-row*, and is called of such a signe, Panyar Alley." This
locale was named after the messuage called the Pannyer or the Pannyer on
the Hoope.[7] According to W&C (3:23–24), it was once the standing place
for bakers with bread panniers.

In *BF* Quarlous denounces Winwife's propensity for widow-hunting and
its matrimonial results: "Tis a fine occupation thou'lt confine thy selfe to,
when thou ha'st got one, scrubbing a piece of Buffe, as if thou hadst the
perpetuity of *Pannyer-alley* to stinke in" (1.3.66–68).

PARIS GARDEN. A manor on the south bank of the Thames approximately opposite Blackfriars. Its name was transferred to the area directly
eastward, which was used for bearbaitings and some theatrical ventures (see
Bear Gardens).

Both S (p. 391) and H&S (10:642) devote considerable attention to the
original spelling and derivation of this name. S, following the practice of

7. H. E. Harben, *Dictionary of London*, p. 456.

previous authorities, erringly identifies the manorial grounds with the bear pits outside its bounds. He furnishes numerous citations reflecting the vulgarity and dissoluteness rampant in the area. H&S (11:366) note that according to *Satiromastix* (sig. G3ᵛ), Jonson played "Zulsiman" at a Paris Garden theater. The editors' comment about Henslowe owning property in Paris Garden (1:14) refers to the land to the east (as does the *Satiromastix* quote) which later became the Hope Theater site.

Much information on the boundaries and owners of the Paris Garden land is furnished in the London County Council's Survey of London volume on Bankside (pp. 94ff.). The first notable leaseholder was William Basely, who obtained the estate early in the reign of Henry VIII when it was in ruinous condition. Basely's "improvements" included turning the manor into a public gaming area, with "cardes, dyze, and tables" within.[8] Francis Langley, "a speculator of moderately wealthy means whose chief desire was to become even more wealthy," built the Swan Theater in Paris Garden in 1595. During the next few years Langley's continual neglect of his land-owning responsibilities was a major factor in the decline of this locale at the close of the sixteenth century.[9] The manor passed out of his hands in 1601 and did not regain prominence until 1632 when the manor house was probably the site of the brothel called Holland's Leaguer. Thus the literary allusions which associate Paris Garden with bearbaiting reflect the colloquial habit of "transference," rather than the occurrence of such activities upon the actual grounds of the manor (Roberts and Godfrey, pp. 66–67).

References to Paris Garden are plentiful in Jonson's works. In response to Captain Otter's defense of his drinking cups as famous "all over *England*, in *rerum natura*" (3.1.14–15), Mrs. Otter declares in *Epic*, "Fore me, I wil na-ture 'hem over to *Paris*-garden, and *na-ture* you thether too, if you pronounce 'hem againe (ll. 16–18). Soon after, she vows, "I'll commit you to the Master of the garden, if I heare but a syllable more" (ll. 29–30). Paris Garden is one of the noisy places to which Morose would commit himself if he were rid of Epicoene (4.4.15). In *MA* Urson declares his bears are "very sufficient Beares, as any are in the Ground, the *Parish-Garden*" (ll. 141–42). On the smells encountered by the "adventurers" in *Epig* 133, "On the Famous Voyage," Jonson avers, "The meate-boate of Beares colledge, *Paris-garden* / Stunke not so ill" (ll. 117–18). According to *Und* 43, "An Execration upon Vulcan," the Globe Theater (q.v.) fire signified to some people "a threatning to the beares; / And that accursed ground, the *Parish-Garden*" (ll. 146–47).

8. Sir Howard Roberts and Walter H. Godfrey, eds., *Bankside*, p. 96.
9. William Ingram, "'Neere the Play Howse': The Swan Theatre and Community Blight," *Renaissance Drama*, n.s. 4 (1971):64.

PENNY-RICH STREET. Most likely a corruption of Peneritch Street, no longer extant, which once ran southwest from Bucklersbury (q.v.) in the City.

As cited by H&S (10:565), Stow declares (1:260) that it was a "shorte lane" running to St. Sythe's Church. Although its course was near that of today's Pancras Lane, etymologists are now unwilling to accept "Peneritch" as a miswriting of "Pencritch," once believed by some to be a corruption of "Pancras."[10]

A pun on the literal suggestions of this street name is apparent in Jonson's sole reference to it. In *CHM* an offering is bestowed by one of Father Christmas's several sons, *"young* Little-worth," of whom it is said, *"in Penny-rich street he sleepeth"* (ll. 232–33).

PETTICOAT LANE. Known officially since about 1830 as Middlesex Street, which runs from Bishopsgate to Whitechapel High Street.

S (p. 407) provides citations which attest to its reputation as a haunt for women of ill fame and which illumine Jonson's reference to this district. Nashe, in his *Prognostication* (*Works*, 3:384), writes, "If the Beadelles of Bridewell [q.v.] be carefull this Summer, it may be hoped that Peticote lane may be lesse pestered with ill aires then it was woont; and the houses there so cleere clensed that honest women may dwell there without any dread of the whip and the carte." H&S (10:222) note how Stow gives no hint of its immoral associations (1:127), referring to it by its old name of Hog Lane and making only the innocuous observation that its course displays "a continuall building throughout, of Garden houses, and small Cottages."

In *DA* Iniquity, outlining a tour of infernal pleasures in London, suggests where some appropriate female companionship may be found: "We will survay the *Suburbs*, and make forth our sallyes, / Downe *Petticoat-lane*, and up the *Smock-allies* [q.v.]" (1.1.59–60).

PHILPOT LANE. A City thoroughfare running south from Fenchurch Street to Eastcheap (q.v.).

S (p. 191) and H&S (10:564) note that this street was named after Sir John Philpot, a onetime lord mayor and soldier-adventurer. Both these authorities avow their debt to Stow (1:203).

As his spelling makes apparent, Jonson plays upon the phonetic associations of this street name in his single reference therein. The narrator of

10. Eilert Ekwall, *Street-Names of the City of London* (Oxford: Clarendon Press, 1954), pp. 86–87, argues that even if "Pencritch" is the original form, it derived from "a surname taken from Penkridge in Staffordshire."

CHM remarks about one of the participants, "Kit Cobler *it is, I'me a Father of his, / and he dwells in the lane, call'd Fil-pot*" (ll. 204–5).

PHOENIX. A London drinking house the site of which is conjecturable.

S (p. 409) places the Phoenix in Lombard Street without taking other sites into consideration—chiefly on the basis of a quotation from Heywood, *1 Edward IV* (*Works*, 1:64). H&S (10:260) believe that Jonson had in mind a tavern near the Phoenix Theater in Drury Lane (see Cockpit) and point to the existence of a Phoenix Alley in this area at one time. W&C (3:81) state, however, that Phoenix Alley was built around 1637, when it was first mentioned in the rate books of the parish of St. Martin in the Fields. Toward the end of his life, John Taylor lived in a "Phoenix Alley," as evident from the title page of his *Journey into Wales* (1653).

In the stage prologue to *SN*, the author declares it not important to his scene "if *Dunstan* [see Devil Tavern], or the *Phoenix* best wine has" (l. 16). There is also the possibility that Jonson had in mind a special room in a tavern rather than the whole house. One of the rooms in the pre-Fire Talbot tavern in Ludgate was called the Phoenix.[11]

PICT HATCH. A rendezvous of thieves and prostitutes located behind a turning called Rotten Row on the east side of Goswell Road, opposite the Charterhouse wall. According to current topography, this site would be just south of the intersection of Goswell Road and Old Street.

S (p. 411) states that the term "Pict Hatch" was derived from the half-door, surmounted by spikes, often used in brothels. S also notes that authorities previously believed that Pict Hatch was located in equally notorious Turnbull Street (q.v.), not far away. In Middleton's *Black Book* (*Works*, 8:11), the Devil begins his peregrination at Pict Hatch, "which (as I may fitly name it) is the very skirts of all brothel-houses." H&S (9:351) offer only information about its location as given above, W&C (3:92) show that references in a grant of 1591 and a survey of 1649 have aided authorities in determining its precise site.

Some of the allusions in Wellbred's letter in *EMI* give rise to the elder Knowell's comments on its origin, "From the *Burdello* [see Stews], it might come as well, the *Spittle* [q.v.]: or *Pict-hatch*" (1.2.92–93). In *EMO* Shift is thus described in the list of characters: "*His profession is skeldring and odling* [begging and cheating], *his bank* Poules [see St. Paul's], *and his ware-house* Pict-hatch" (ll. 85–86). Later in this play Macilente denounces the boastful swaggerer Carlo, "Now the pox / Light on your *Pict-hatch* prowesse" (4.5.34–35). After Mammon eulogizes the restorative powers of his elixir in *Alch*, Surly remarks, "The decay'd *Vestall's* of *Pict-hatch* would thanke you, / That keepe the fire a-live, there" (2.1.62–63). One of the puppets in

11. *Notes and Queries*, 8th ser., 11 (1897):204.

BF insults Leatherhead, repeatedly calling him *"Goodman Hogrubber, o' Pict-Hatch"* (5.4.175–77). The title figure in *Epig* 12, "On Lieutenant Shift," is described as "not meanest among squires, / That haunt *Pict-hatch, Mersh-Lambeth* [see Lambeth], and *Whitefryers* [q.v.]" (ll. 1–2).

PIMLICO. A resort in Hoxton (see Hogsden) apparently quite popular in the early seventeenth century.

S (p. 412) furnishes several contemporary references to this spot, including a query from Dekker and Middleton's *The Roaring Girl*, "My Lord *Noland*, will you goe to Pimlico with us? we are making a boone voyage to that happy land of spice-cakes" (5.1.49–50). In Mayne's *The City-Match* is presented "a gentleman of valour, who has been / In Moorfields [q.v.] often: mary, it has been / To 'squire his sisters, and demolish custards / At Pimlico" (2.6). S also cites a 1598 pamphlet, *Newes from Hogsdon*, which declares, "Hey for old Ben Pimlicos nut-browne," and an encomium of 1609, *Pimlico; or, Runne Red-cap. Tis a mad world at Hogsdon.* H&S (10:109) note that the 1609 tract was reissued in facsimile by A. H. Bullen.

In the early twentieth century the approximate site of this tavern was marked by a "Pimlico Walk" which ran east from the corner of New North Road and St. John's Road to Hoxton Street. More recent urban development, however, has reduced Pimlico Walk to a very short thoroughfare called Pimlico Lane off the west of the southern portion of Hoxton Street.[12] The significance of this location is that it is but a short distance from the sites of the Theater, Curtain, and Fortune playhouses north of the City. This would certainly help explain the frequent references to the Pimlico tavern by the dramatists of Jonson's era.

In *Alch* Lovewit, upon his return, questions why his home has been invaded by a motley crowd who flocked "in threaves, these ten weeke, as to a second *Hogs-den* / In dayes of *Pimlico*, and *Eye-bright*!" (5.2.19–20). Earlier, a neighbor referred to his residence as "another *Pimlico*" (5.1.6). In *BF* Littlewit praises Win's holiday attire and challenges it to be outdone by "*Morefields, Pimlico* path, or the *Exchange* [q.v.], in a sommer evening" (1.2.6–7). Among the current social graces according to Wittipol in *DA* are the abilities to "coach it to *Pimlico*; daunce the *Saraband*" (4.4.164). The following two references are indexed by H&S under the subheading "Pimlico Fort" which they have located (10:242) according to a 1643 account of the Civil War defenses of London, as being directly south of Islington (q.v.). This classification appears questionable; present evidence suggests that the fort was constructed to meet the immediate dangers of the

12. Pimlico Lane appears on the current Ordinance Survey sheet 3382 SW. The accepted site of the Pimlico Tavern, given by K, p. 449, is approximately twenty inches away from that of the Theater on a scale of fifty inches to the mile.

Civil War.[13] The first quotation especially could just as easily refer to the tavern. Here Meercraft in *DA* boasts about how he will socially advance the youth Plutarchus, making him a "Captaine" who will parade around "and take in *Pimlico*, and kill the bush, / at every taverne" (3.3.170–71). In *Und* 44, "A speach according to Horace," the poet comments, "What a strong fort old *Pimblicoe* had bin! / How it held out! how (last) 'twas taken in" (ll. 21–22).

POPE'S HEAD ALLEY. A thoroughfare demolished in 1927-29, which in Jonson's time ran south from Cornhill (q.v.) to Lombard Street.

Both S (p. 418) and H&S (10:560; 11:77) note that Pope's Head Alley was then a center for booksellers and publishers. John Wolfe, who issued the first edition of Stow's *Survey*, had his shop there. Especially pertinent to Jonson's works is the fact that Nathaniel Butter, one of the popular newsmongers during the 1620s (targets of satire in *SN*), worked in Pope's Head Alley. His *Newes from most parts of Christendom* associates him with this locale, as H&S (2:172) have pointed out. Here too were published the topical ephemerae of Thomas Archer, also ridiculed in *SN*. W&C (3:105) refer to the *Calendar of State Papers, Domestic* (1619-23, p. 321) and (1623-25, p. 163) in citing a case where the publisher of an inflammatory pamphlet, "A Supplication of the Scottish Ministers," was sought in Pope's Head Alley. According to Lord Keeper Lincoln, the king was "very sensible of the wicked libel."

In *CHM* Jonson plays upon the literal denotations of this placename. The presenter of this piece declares, "I am old *Gregorie Christmas* still, and though I come out of *Popes-head-alley*, as good a Protestant, as any i' my Parish" (ll. 15–17). Because the speaker refers to "Christ-*mass*," rather than "Christ-*tide*," he does not exhibit the extreme Puritanism apparent in some other portions of this entertainment (see Curriers' Hall and Fish Street). Possibly Jonson employed this tactic to demonstrate comically the impropriety of overzealous attention to doctrine on festive occasions. In *Und* 43, "An Execration upon Vulcan," the poet alludes to the literary ventures associated with this area. Fitter than his own works for Vulcan's appetite are "Captaine *Pamp[h]lets* horse, and foot, that sallie / Upon th' Exchange [q.v.], still, out of Popes-head-Alley" (ll. 79–80).

PUDDING LANE. A narrow street running south from the west end of Eastcheap (q.v.) to Lower Thames Street.

13. London's Civil War fortifications are discussed in detail by Norman G. Brett-James, *The Growth of Stuart London*, pp. 268ff.; although no mention of a fort by this exact name is made, Brett-James's sources emphasize the multitude of London's defensive outposts and the haste with which they were set up.

For their comments, both S (p. 422) and H&S (10:563) rely on Stow (1:210–11), who writes that this thoroughfare got its name "because the Butchers of Eastcheape have their scalding House for Hogges there, and their puddings with other filth of Beastes, are voided downe that way to theyr dung boates on the Thames."

Jonson makes one mention of Pudding Lane. This reference does not play upon its etymology or historical background. Rather, Jonson uses this street's proximity to another London thoroughfare in emphasizing a familial relationship between two characters. In *CHM* Pudding Lane is mentioned as the dwelling place of Venus (ll. 118, 121), who in this work is characterized as a doting City mother. Her son Cupid, who is to act in *CHM*, is described (l. 119) as apprenticed to a maker of glass beads in Love Lane (q.v.), today known as Lovat Lane, which runs parallel to Pudding Lane two blocks westward. Again, this reveals Jonson's skillful use of London topography.

PUDDLE WHARF. A landing place on the north bank of the Thames. Its site today is represented by Puddledock, a street just east of Blackfriars Station.

S (p. 423) offers a choice of etymologies for this spot and several dramatic citations in which it is mentioned, often in connection with a romantic episode, e.g., *A Chaste Maid in Cheapside* (4.2) and *A Match at Midnight* (4.1). H&S (10:210) provide Stow's comments (2:13), "a water gate into the Thames, where horses use to be watered, & therfore being filed with their trampeling, and made puddle, like as also of one *Puddle* dwelling there: it is called Puddle Wharfe." W&C (3:129) point out that the noted Elizabethan correspondent Sir Dudley Carleton was living in this area in 1600. Also, Lady Arabella Stuart wrote to Sir Robert Cecil from Puddle Wharf requesting that her patent for the privilege of selling liquor licenses be soon granted.

In the puppet show in *BF* Leander is described as "a Diers sonne, about *Puddle-wharfe*" (5.3.123). In this burlesque of the Hero and Leander story, Puddle Wharf is the City equivalent of Abydos (5.4.119–20).

Q

QUEENHITHE. A landing place on the north bank of the Thames a little to the west of the present Southwark Bridge.

S (p. 425) points out that Queenhithe, once the chief landing place in London, had dwindled in importance by Tudor-Stuart times because the growing size of ships prohibited their passing beyond London Bridge. Stow (1:41) termed Queenhithe "the verie chiefe and principall watergate of this citie," but ended up admitting that by his time Billingsgate, below London Bridge, was much busier. H&S (10:275) refer the reader to an excerpt from *Westward for Smelts* (1620, sig. A3), which, like Jonson's citation below, bases a humorous quip on the fact that eel boats commonly moored at this dock. W&C (3:144) state that in the early seventeenth century Queenhithe was the headquarters of the watermen, who often met at an alehouse called the Red Knight.

In *SN* the news-hunter Fitton obtained his report about an "invisible *Eele*" built by the Dutch to destroy shipping at Dunkirk from "the *Eele*-boats here, that lye before *Queen-Hyth*" (3.2.84).

R

RAM ALLEY. A narrow passage, now called Hare Place, on the south side of Fleet Street (q.v.), near the Inns of Court (q.v.).

S (p. 426) points out that Ram Alley was named after a house with the name of the Star and Ram and was but seven feet wide. It ran down to a footway connecting the Inner Temple with Serjeants' Inn. S declares that it was chiefly occupied by "cooks, bawds, tobacco-sellers, and alehouse-keepers" and offers several dramatic references to support this. An early seventeenth-century play is entitled *Ram-Alley* and devoted mainly to the escapades of the gallants, usurers, and loose women who loitered there. H&S (10:269) state incorrectly that Ram Alley is presently known as Mitre Court. The latter is about thirty feet to the west of Hare Place, which, as stated above, occupies the site of Ram Alley.[1] Contributing to the boisterousness that must have been typical of this area was a custom observed by students at the Inns of Court. They created a lord of misrule who on Twelfth Night collected rents of five shillings from houses in Fleet Street and Ram Alley, as noted by W&C (3:147, who cite L'Estrange, *Reign of King Charles I*, p. 72). K (p. 494) furnishes a 1603 reference of interest not only to this thoroughfare but also to the location of the earlier Mitre Tavern (q.v.) in Fleet Street. Here it is mentioned "that there is a door leading out of Ram Alley to the tenement called the Miter in Fleet-streete, by which means thereof such persons as do frequent the house upon search made after them are conveyed out that way."

The usurer Penniboy Senior's residence in Ram Alley is the scene for act 2 of *SN*. Here Shunfield calls Lickfinger "mine old host of *Ram-Alley*" (2.4.35). Picklock the lawyer lives in this area too, for Penniboy Junior plans to eat "hard by, at *Picklocks* lodging. / Old *Lickfinger's* the Cooke, here in *Ram-Alley*" (2.5.112–13). Ram Alley would be an appropriate place for all these characters to live. Not only was it inhabited by disreputable persons, but it was also conveniently located for access to the Devil Tavern (q.v.), St. Paul's, and other "business" locales mentioned in this play.

RATCLIFFE. In Jonson's time a hamlet about a mile east of the City, close to the north bank of the Thames.

S (p. 427) notes that like most waterwise areas Ratcliffe had an unsavory reputation, and he cites Stephen Gosson (*School of Abuse*, p. 26) on the loose

---

1. *The Reference Atlas of Greater London*, 13th ed. (Edinburgh: Bartholomew, 1968), p. 8F, shows the proper relationship of Mitre Court to Hare Place.

women who "live a mile from the cittee, like Venus nunnes in a cloister of
Nuington, Ratliff, Islington [q.v.], Hogsdon [q.v.], or some such place."
H&S (10:34) point out only that Ratcliffe was "then an important place of
resort owing to the highway of the river." Typical of his practice, Stow
(2:71) confines his comments to facts concerning this area's growth and
appearance rather than the quality of its inhabitants, "There hath been of
late, in place of Elme trees many small tenements raysed, towards Radcliffe:
And Radcliffe itself hath beene also encreased in building eastward." There
also existed, according to Stow, "a continuall streete, or filthy straight
passage, with Alleyes of small tenements or cottages builded, inhabited by
saylors victualers, along by the river of Thames, almost to *Radcliff*, a good
mile from the Tower."

   In *Epic*, after Otter has been turned out of the house by his wife, he asks
Truewit to accompany him "downe to *Ratcliffe*, and havè a course yfaith"
(4.2.143–44). While planning their escape from Lovewit in *Alch*, Face
tells his fellow dupers "At night, Ile ship you both away to *Ratcliffe*, /
Where wee'll meet to morrow, and there wee'll share" (4.7.125–26). Later
Subtle decides to outfox Face and tells Doll that when they have boarded
their ship and are apparently headed "east-ward for *Ratcliffe*; we will turne
our course / To *Brainford* [q.v.], westward, if thou saist the word"
(5.4.76–77).

ROEHAMPTON. A district southwest of Putney on the south bank of
the Thames adjoined by Richmond Park and Wimbledon Common on the
west and south.

   H&S (11:97) state only that the Weston-Stuart marriage, praised by
Jonson below, took place at Roehampton Chapel on June 25, 1632. A local
historian notes that in 1626 King Charles granted Putney Park to Sir
Richard Weston, Lord High Treasurer, who built a summer residence at
Roehampton. Charles attended the marriage of Jerome, Sir Richard's son,
in the estate chapel, which had been consecrated by Archbishop Laud.[2]

   In *Und* 75, the "Epithalamium" for the marriage of Jerome Weston to
Frances, daughter of Esmé Stuart, Jonson writes that the road was lined
with coaches "all the way, / From *Greenwich* [q.v.], hither, to *Row-hampton*
gate" (ll. 11–12). The distance between the two is about ten miles, so this
comment is in accord with the poem's encomiastic nature.

RUMFORD (ROMFORD). An Essex village thirteen miles northeast
of St. Paul's, today a busy outlying part of the metropolis.

   S (p. 442) comments that Romford was a favorite place for summer

2. Rev. Henry Elkerton, *History of Roehampton Parish* (London: Patching, 1929), p. 4.

excursions and also the site of hog and cattle markets every Tuesday and Wednesday. Contemporary dramatic references often played upon the above associations. In Dekker and Middleton's *The Roaring Girl*, a gallant remarks, "The gruntling of five hundred hogs comming from *Rumford* market, cannot make a worse noyse than this canting language" (5.1.211–13). H&S (10:206) cite R. Brathwaite, *Times Curtaine Drawne* (1621, sig. K5ᵛ, "Here are no mincing *Dames* who long to goe / To Rumford, Hoggsden [q.v.], or to Pimlico [q.v.]." Both Hogsden and Pimlico were also common destinations for merrymakers.

Several of Jonson's characters talk of making excursions to Romford. In *NI* it is one of the several towns where the tailor Nick Stuffe and his wife display themselves in clothing made for their customers (4.3.70–72). For a full discussion of this habit, see the Hounslow entry. Captain Whit, one of the swaggerers in *BF*, promises Win and Dame Purecraft that if they will come with him, they will "ride to *Ware* [q.v.] and *Rumford* i' dy Coash, shee de Players, be in love vit'hem" (4.5.38–39).

S

ST. CLEMENT DANES. A church standing in the middle of the Strand (q.v.), just outside the western limits of the City.

S (p. 121) furnishes various etymological theories, along with some dramatic references attesting to the tendency for the parishioners of St. Clement's to be Inns of Court (q.v.) men, gallants, and noblemen. Few merchants, artisans, or laborers lived in this area. Local records show that among the late sixteenth-century residents of the parish were Lord Burghley, the earl of Leicester, the earl of Arundel, and the earl of Bedford.[1] K (p. 484) adds that the earl of Essex was another parishioner and that two of Burghley's sons were baptized in this church.

In *MA* the antimasquers from the breweries in the St. Katherine's district (q.v.) sing, *"Nor the Vintry Cranes* [see Three Cranes], / *Nor St. Clements Danes,* / *Nor the Devill* [q.v.] *can put us down-a"* (ll. 187–89). The mention of the Three Cranes in the Vintry and the Devil (two noted London taverns) along with the St. Katherine's brewery indicates that the first two locales are cited as examples of places where the ale and companionship fall short of the standards set by St. Katherine's. The inclusion of St. Clement Danes in a tavern list may be explained if one thinks of Jonson referring to the area covered by the parish rather than only the church. The boisterous quality of many residents of St. Clement's has been pointed out. Also pertinent is that by Jonson's time a maze of small courts and alleys had developed just off the north side of the church. Known as "Butchers' Row," this area had many taverns and resorts.

ST. GILES (CRIPPLEGATE); ST. GILES (IN THE FIELDS). Two churches dedicated to this saint, located just north of the City and on the westward road to Tyburn (q.v.) respectively.

S (p. 222) states that the church of St. Giles Cripplegate was first built in 1090. The present edifice dates in part from the fourteenth century.[2] Within was christened Nathan Field; John Foxe, Martin Frobisher, and

1. Isabel Greaves, "The Parish of St. Clement Danes: Churchwardens' Accounts, xxi–xxii Elizabeth," *Transactions of the London and Middlesex Archaeological Society*, n.s. 2 (1911–13):368.

2. K, pp. 123–25, states that although St. Giles Cripplegate was severely damaged by a blaze in 1545, it escaped destruction during the Great Fire. On August 24, 1940, it became the first City church hit in the Blitz and suffered severely from the ravages of later raids which left little more than the outer walls. Rebuilding has preserved its original appearance and saved many of its noted busts and memorials, while adding new windows at the east and west ends.

John Milton were buried there. The church of St. Giles in the Fields originated as a leper hospital in 1101. Its chapel later became the parish church for the countryside north of Charing Cross. In 1623 it was demolished and replaced seven years later. S (p. 223) furnishes several references to the bad reputation of the area which it served. Thomas Harman (*Caveat for Common Cursitors*, p. 87) was surprised that a rogue he was trailing fled south of the river. He had expected that his man had gone "into Holborn, or to St. Giles in the Field." One of the kidnappers in Barry's *Ram-Alley* orders that their victim be spirited away in a coach to St. Giles in the Fields (3.2). W&C (2:110) point out that the parish of St. Giles in the Fields was originally a separate village from the City and Westminster and was still considered such in Jonson's time. These authorities cite an act of 1605 for the paving of streets in "Drury Lane and the Town of St. Giles."

It seems logical to assume that Jonson had St. Giles in the Fields in mind when he wrote in *DA* of how Ambler consorted with a lady near Tyburn and gave her a pair of rose-trimmed shoes with garters. These, along with Ambler's clothes, were stolen by Pug, so that Ambler had to give the lady his own footwear and walk "in a rug, by her, barefoote, to Saint *Giles's*" (5.1.47). The church of St. Giles in the Fields was located along Ambler's walk back toward his master's house near Lincoln's Inn (q.v.). St. Giles Cripplegate, in contrast, would have been far out of his way. Without explanation, however, H&S (11:648) index this reference as "St. Giles Cripplegate." The latter does have some biographical ties with Jonson, for it was there that Mark Eccles discovered the baptism of "Joseph, the sone of Beniamyne Johnson," on December 9, 1599, and also where John Payne Collier found the notice of a marriage between "Beniamyne Johnson and Hester Hopkins" on July 27, 1623, both as noted by H&S (11:575).

ST. JAMES'S PARK. A royal property adjoining St. James's Palace, northwest of the built-up part of Westminster in Jonson's time.

S (p. 281) declares that the palace was formerly the site of a leper hospital until appropriated by Henry VIII, who walled in St. James's Park which contained over sixty acres. S, in remarking on the park's prominence by Jacobean times, refers to Peacham's verses prefixed to Coryat's *Crudities* (1611, 1:114). Here the notable sights of London include "Saint James his Ginny Hens, the Cassowarway moreover, / the Beaver i' the Parke." The "Cassowarway" is described in a note by Coryat as "an East Indian bird in the keeping of Mr. Walker, that will carry no coales, but eate them as whot [*sic*] as you will." These birds and animals were part of the extensive menagerie which James I located in the park.[3] K (p. 395) adds that this area was "improved" in a more orthodox fashion by Charles II, who employed

3. J. E. Egerton, "King James's Beasts," *History Today* 11 (1962):405–15, provides a fascinating and detailed account of this early zoo.

the noted landscape gardener Le Nôtre to replant and develop its gardens.

According to the Second Gypsie in *GM*, "*St. James'es, Greenewich* [q.v.], and *Tiballs* [see Theobald's]" (l. 95) are among the "finer walled places" where King James's game ought to be preserved.

ST. JOHN'S WOOD. Then a tract of forest about four miles northwest of the City, today an upper-class residential neighborhood.

S (p. 288) comments that the wood was used as a royal hunting ground after Henry VIII confiscated it in 1541 from the priors of the Hospital of St. John of Jerusalem.

In *TT* the servant Hilts sets the stage for his trumped-up story of a robbery with specific details of time and place, "This morning, at the corner of Saint *John's* wood, / Some mile o' this Towne, [we] were set upon" (2.2.86–87). Later Hilts laughs at his deception, "I follow Captaine *Thum's*? We rob'd in Saint *John's* wood? I' my tother hose!" (2.3.39–40). In *ML* Sir Moth Interest defends Dr. Rut, saying that he cured Needle, who "talk'd in's sleepe; would walke to Saint *John's* wood, / And *Waltham* Forrest [q.v.]" (5.8.13–14). A walk from this play's setting in the middle of the City to St. John's Wood, Waltham Forest, and back again would cover over twenty-five miles, a distance revealing the emptiness of Interest's vaunt. For a full discussion of the setting of this play, see the Waltham Forest entry.

ST. KATHERINE'S. Officially St. Katherine's by the Tower, a district on the north bank of the Thames extending from just east of the Tower of London to the neighborhood of Ratcliffe.

During the Middle Ages this area's most important institution was the Hospital of St. Katherine, founded in 1148 by Queen Matilda and modestly reconstituted by Queen Elizabeth to maintain a small body of clerics. Like other waterside and extra-judicial premises, this area had an unfavorable reputation. Dramatic references cited by S (p. 290) often display antipathy toward its many Flemish residents. In *Wealth and Health* (1554), Hance the Fleming is pictured as a drunkard living in St. Katherine's (l. 753), who ought to be expelled so that "English men shall live the better dayly" (ll. 761–62).[4] H&S (10:222–23) reinforce these attitudes with a citation from the "New and Choice Characters" added to the sixth impression of Overbury's *Wife* (1615, sig. K7^v), describing an inebriated Dutchman, "Let him come over never so leane, & plant him but one Moneth

---

4. *Wealth and Health*, ed. W. W. Greg (London: Malone Society, 1907). A similarly unflattering portrayal of Flemish behavior is contained in Ulpian Fulwell, *Like Will to Like*, ed. J. S. Farmer, Early English Dramatists, 1st ser. (London: Privately printed, 1906), pp. 21–26.

neere the Brew-houses in S. *Catherines*, and hee'll be puft up to your hand like a bloat Herring."

The above attitudes towards Flemish immigrants in St. Katherine's reflect feelings widespread in London beginning in the mid-sixteenth century. Throughout the Tudor period, fluctuations in the wool trade made London's attitude towards refugees from the Low Countries range from barely tolerant to violently derogatory. Conditions became especially bad during the sixties, when "Spanish meddling in the Netherlands further cut off vital export markets, and after 1567 accelerated the wave of Flemish and Walloon refugees expert at fashioning new and lighter cloths needed for a more diversified market."[5] Stow remarks (1:124) that the St. Katherine's district was "now of late yeres inclosed about, or pestered with small tenements, and homely cottages, having inhabitants, English and strangers, more in number then in some citie[s] in England." Stow also notes (2:143) that after the Dissolution the Hospital of St. Katherine took over the operation of the nearby Hospital of St. Mary which had been devoted to "men and women in the Citty of London, that were fallen into frensie or losse of their memory." This fact is especially pertinent to Jonson's St. Katherine's references in *EH* and *Alch* below.

Jonson's mentions of St. Katherine's stress its associations with St. Mary's mental hospital, its repute as a waterside drinking center, and the bad name of its Flemish residents. In *EH*, on first spying Winifred in the Thames, Slitgut cries out from his vantage point at Cuckold's Haven "A woman! yfaith, a woman, though it be almost at *S. Kath'rins*" (4.1.59–60). This was quite a feat, for St. Katherine's lies around a bend upriver at least two miles from Cuckold's Haven. Winifred is then rescued by a waiter, who comments that he was lucky to be passing by "to a house of my friends heere in *S. Kath'rines*" (ll. 85–86). She then tries to cover up her past inclinations toward adultery by entreating her rescuer to forget "what favour you doe me, or where such a one as I am bestowed" (ll. 103–4) and later pretends to have been at home the previous night (ll. 261–70). The landing of this wilful amnesiac and would-be strumpet at St. Katherine's is an apt bestowal indeed. During the tumultuous final act of *Alch*, Face declares that the neighbors who are thronging to Lovewit's house have all broken "out of S. KATHER'NES, where they use to keepe / The better sort of mad-folkes" (5.3.55–56). In *DA* Iniquity's tour of London promises a trip "To *Shoreditch* [q.v.]. *Whitechappel* [q.v.], and so to Saint *Katherines*, / To drinke with the *Dutch* there, and take forth their patternes" (1.1.61–62). One of the juicy tidbits offered by the newsgathering agency in *SN* is that "the perpetuall Motion, / Is here found out by an Alewife in Saint

5. David Bevington, *Tudor Drama and Politics* (Cambridge: Harvard University Press, 1968), p. 134.

Katherines, / At the signe o' the dancing Beares" (3.2.105–7). When Dame
Keepe insults Dame Polish in *ML*, the latter rebuffs her with "Dame *Keepe*
of *Katernes?* what? have you an oare / I' the Cockboat, 'cause you are a Saylors
wife?" (2.2.27–28). According to Jonson's stage directions, the "Presenters" of the antimasque portion of *MA* are from St. Katherine's (l. 3). Their
spokesman later tells a court groom that the antimasquers come from the
royal brewhouses in this area (ll. 71–72), information which is twice
reiterated (ll. 115–16, 174), as this introductory piece goes on to ridicule
some of the coarser tastes of the time.

ST. PAUL'S. The City's cathedral, situated on Ludgate Hill, at the west
end of Cheapside. In Jonson's time this church was a Gothic structure and
the second church to be built on this site.

S (pp. 395–98) furnishes general historical and literary background,
while H&S focus their commentary upon features of St. Paul's mentioned in
Jonson's works. One of the most prominent is its importance as a gossip
center and meeting place. H&S (9:444) refer to Francis Osborn (*Historical
Memoires on the Reigns of Queen Elizabeth and King James*, 1658, part 2, pp.
64–65), who emphasized that the middle aisle of Paul's was the most
fashionable spot for such matters. At the west end of this church were
posted bills, notes, and job offers. This is corroborated by passages from
B.R., *Greenes Newes both from Heaven and Hell* (1593, sig. C2ᵛ, and Dekker,
The Guls Horne Booke (*Non-Dramatic Works*, 2:235). The latter work is
famous for its detailed account of "How a Gallant should behave himself in
Powles walkes." Another work cited by H&S (9:445) is *The Meeting of
Gallants at an Ordinarie; or, The Walkes in Powles* (1604, sig. B2). The
editors also note a passage from Middleton's *Black Book* (Works, 8:8–9)
about how heavy-footed country people have worn off the brasses in the
walks. In *The House of Correction* (1619, sig. D2ᵛ) occurs the suggestion
that women of ill fame solicited business within St. Paul's. The choir was
dominated by the massive tomb of Lord Chancellor Sir Christopher Hatton
(d. 1591). H&S (9:459) note that Dekker (*Guls Horne Booke*, p. 236)
urged country visitors not to miss seeing Hatton's tomb. John Earle's
verdict in *Micro-cosmographie* (p. 73) on St. Paul's as a source of news, "the
generall Mint of all famous lies," is noted by H&S (10:262) in connection
with *SN*. In 10:265, a quotation from "The News-Monger" in B. Rich,
My Ladies Looking Glasse (1606, p. 52), is provided. One of the favorite
haunts of job hunters in Paul's was "Duke Humphrey's Walk" near the
supposed monument to Humphrey, Duke of Gloucester. H&S (10:280)
remind readers that this monument was actually in memory of Sir John
Beauchamp, pointing to Stow's awareness (1:335) of this mix-up.

Many fascinating sidelights in the history of this notable church are

North side of the exterior of Old St. Paul's. The steeple, which burned down after being struck by lightning in 1561, was never replaced (Wenceslaus Hollar, 1656).

furnished by K (pp. 433ff.). In 1411 a proclamation was made against wrestling within the sanctuary; offenders were fined and imprisoned for forty days. The first state lotteries were held at the west door of St. Paul's in 1569. Forty thousand lots at ten shillings each were offered. The prizes were plate, and the proceeds were to be used for "repairing the havens of the kingdom." The variety of activities occurring here was the dramatist's delight and the bane of clergymen such as Bishop Braybroke. He denounced those who "expose their wares as it were in a public market, buy and sell without reverence for the holy place. Others too by the instigation of the Devil do not scruple with stones and arrows to bring down birds, pigeons and jackdaws which nestle in the walls and crevices of the building; others play at ball . . . breaking the beautiful and costly windows."

Jonson's works illustrate many of the features of this church discussed above. In *EMI* Captain Bobadil is introduced as a *"Paules-man"* (persons, ll. 24–25), and *EMO*'s shoddy rogue Shift is described as having Paul's as his bank (persons, l. 86). In the latter play, Sordido, emphasizing his reluctance to market his corn until his warehouse is full, declares, "Till then, / Ech corne I send shall be as big as *Paules*" (1.3.100–101). The action of the play moves closer to this institution with Sogliardo's promise to meet his friends "at the *Heralds* office" (2.3.286). St. Paul's itself is first mentioned as a meeting place by Deliro (2.6.91–92). Later Fungoso comments that Sogliardo is to be found "at the *Heralds* office, yonder by *Paules*" (2.6.134–35), reiterated by Carlo (3.2.24–25). According to S (p. 151), this office was located in Derby House, about two hundred yards south of the cathedral. The choric figure Cordatus strips away much of this play's Italianate quality when he asks the audience to assume that the stage represents the west end of the middle aisle of Paul's (2.6.183–84), where Shift conducts his "business affairs" (ll. 191–93). The first six scenes of act 3 are set there, and the audience is constantly kept aware of this location (3.1.6,19; 3.2.26). The characters' movements within the church are also clearly described, as in Brisk's request to Macilente and Deliro: "Come, let's walke in *Mediterraneo*" (3.3.1). Carlo's description of Shift acts as another signpost: "I doe usher in the most strange peece of militarie profession, that ever was discover'd in *Insula Paulina*" (3.5.31–32). He "comes every morning to emptie his lungs in *Paules* here: and offers up some five, or sixe *Hecatomb's* of faces, and sighes, and away againe" (ll. 36–38). Later Shift asserts that if he denied putting up some bills promoting his skill in the art of tobacco-smoking, "I were worthie to be banisht the middle I'le, for ever" (3.6.130–31). Macilente shows no awe for the majesty of Chancellor Hatton's tomb (3.9.23). St. Paul's is once more mentioned as a meeting spot near the close of *EMO* (5.6.15–16). In *Epic* the tower of St. Paul's is singled out as a "braver height" from which Morose may jump and permanently escape his "wife" (2.2.24–25). Face threatens Doll in *Alch*, "I will, / Since thou hast mov'd me . . . / Write thee up bawd, in *Paules*" (1.1.91–93). At the start of *BF*, the self-satisfied clerk Littlewit describes himself as "one o' the pretty wits o' *Pauls*" (1.1.11–12). In *SN* Paul's is one of the four "Cardinall Quarters" yielding news to the Staple (1.2.59–60). The news-gatherer from Paul's is one Master Ambler of the "middle Ile" (1.2.68–70), a fact which is repeated (1.4.15; 1.5.110). Both clerks who assist the chief newsmen are also associated with St. Paul's. One is "a decay'd *Stationer*" who is "true *Paules* bred, / I'th the *Church-yard*" (1.5.120, 122–23). This, of course, refers to the many booksellers and pamphleteers who vended their wares in the churchyard at the east end of St. Paul's. The other side is a barber "at the *West-dore*, / O'th' other side" (ll. 123–24). Later it is agreed that a newsmonger who cannot satisfy his readers' tastes plies "a hungry trade. . . . Much like *D[uke] Humphries*" (3.3.51). Also in *SN* one manifestation of Penniboy the Usurer's unbalanced behavior is his committing a pair of dogs to prison in a pair of packing cases "the one of which, he calls his *Lollard's* tower" (5.3.41). The Lollards' Tower, writes S (p. 312), was in the southwest corner of the cathedral and used as the Bishop of London's prison.

There are also numerous references to St. Paul's in Jonson's masques and poems. In *TV* the masquers Eyes, Ears, and Nose complain that Time did not fulfill its promises to them, among which was the freedom to have "censur'd the Counsell, ere they censure us," emphasizing that "we doe it in *Pauls*" (ll. 210–11). To the *Olla Podrida* concocted by the antimasquers of *NT*, "Grave Mr. *Ambler*, Newes-master of *Poules*" (l. 295), contributes a capon. In *Epig* 75, "On Lippe, the Teacher," the poet effectively criticizes ministers who histrionically denounce players, "Though LIPPE, at PAULS, ranne from his text away, / T[o] inveigh 'gainst playes: what did he then but play?" (ll. 3–4). Among the affectations of "English Monsieur," *Epig* 88, is "the new *french*-taylors motion, monthly made, / Daily to turne in PAULS, and helpe the trade" (ll. 15–16). In his "Character" of Thomas Coryat, *UV* 11, prefaced to the first edition of Coryat's *Crudities* (1611), Jonson comments, "The greatest *Politick* that advances into *Paules* he will quit, to go talke with the *Grecian* [madman] that begs there; such is his humility" (ll. 42–44). Jonson also states in the "Characterisme Acrostich" accompanying the "Character" that through his far-reaching discourse Coryat "dares more then *Paules Church-yard* durst do" (l. 85). Finally, in the "Execration upon Vulcan," *Und* 43, the author believes that among the literature suited to Vulcan's appetite are "the weekly Corrants, with *Pauls* Seale" (l. 81). Jonson also exclaims, "Pox on your flameship, *Vulcan;* if it be / To all as fatall as 't hath beene to me, / And to *Pauls-Steeple*" (ll. 191–93). Here one is reminded of the destruction of this steeple by lightning and fire in 1561.[6] H&S (11:80–81) furnish Stow's description (1:331–32) of the event. They also note (10:222) that this circumstance made the following boast by Iniquity to Pug in *DA* a practical impossibility, "I will fetch thee a leape / From the top of *Pauls*-steeple, to the Standard in *Cheepe*" (1.1.55–56). Even if the steeple remained, this still would have been quite a feat because the distance between the steeple and the Standard in Cheapside was just under a quarter of a mile.

ST. SEPULCHRE OR ST. PULCHRE. Officially the Church of the Holy Sepulchre without Newgate, located on the north side of Newgate Street. In Jonson's time it stood opposite Newgate Prison (q.v.).

S (p. 461) provides some citations illustrating his statement that one of this church's notable features was its set of bells. In addition, after 1605 a death bell was rung and the services of a bellman (who visited the condemned nearby) were furnished. H&S (11:32) quote F. P. Wilson, *The Plague in Shakespeare's London* (p. 96), "A pathetic letter written from Newgate on 25 July [1603] by a Roman Catholic gentleman informs us that the bells of St. Sepulchre's never stopped tolling by day or night." Stow (2:28) points out that these bells were acquired during the Dissolution from the nearby priory church of St. Bartholomew.

An interesting aspect of St. Sepulchre's "connections" with Newgate is discussed by K (p. 153). This is the tradition that there once was a tunnel leading from the church across the road to Newgate, from where condemned men were brought to receive the last sacraments. The passage was reputedly blocked up in 1879. The parish which St. Sepulchre served was one of the most congested and noisome in London. A 1560 plague tract declared, "The most corrupt and pestering is S. Poulkars parish, by reason of many fruiterers, pore people and stinking lanes as Turnagaine, Secolayne [see Seacoal Lane], and other such places."[7]

In *Epic* Truewit remarks about Captain Otter's impressive collection of weapons, "You would think hee meant to murder all Saint PULCHRES

6. As K, p. 433, has illustrated, the height of the remaining tower portion was still lofty enough to inspire such adventurous deeds as the ascent of Banks's horse in 1600. Thirty years later, Sir Thomas Gardiner, Recorder of London, wrote in a petition to Charles I, "My youngest daughter . . . without my consent or knowledge, shee mounted upp to Topp of Powles, the nearer to Heaven, for to shewe God there howe wise she was in her Actions, and there she was married unto Sir Henry Maynewaringe, and yet she was not there taken up into heaven, but came down again upon Earth, here further to trouble mee." (also cited by K, above).

7. Dr. John Jones, *Dyall of Agues* (1560); cited by Norman G. Brett-James, *The Growth of Stuart London*, p. 249. Adding to this parish's disrepute is a note in Bullen's edition of Middleton, 8:25, that St. Sepulchre's churchyard was the usual burial spot for criminals executed at Tyburn.

parish" (4.5.115–17). H&S (10:39) conjecture that perhaps Morose's house was located there. As a recent editor of this play has pointed out, however, its action appears to be circumscribed within the newly fashionable area near the Strand (q.v.) west of this parish.[8] A more pertinent motive for Jonson's mention of this particular parish is its crowded and rambunctious nature, as pointed out above. In *DA* a jailor comments on the smoke cloud which Pug leaves behind in his escape from Newgate, "Such an infernall stincke, and steame behinde, / You cannot see St. *Pulchars Steeple*, yet" (5.8.132–33). Finally, Jonson exclaims about the dangers facing the "adventurers" in *Epig* 133, "On the Famous Voyage," "Cannot the *Plague*-bill keepe you backe? nor bells / Of loud SEPULCHRES with their hourely knells" (ll. 173–74).

ST. THOMAS A WATERING. A small stream on the Old Kent Road at the second milestone southeast of London. It got its name from its prominence along the route of Canterbury pilgrims.

S (p. 512) points out that because it was the regular place of execution for criminals in the county of Surrey, it became, like its northern counterpart Tyburn (q.v.), a common allusion in grim jokes. H&S (10:303–4) provide similar comments and references from Tudor drama. W&C (3:375) note that among the important persons hanged at St. Thomas a Watering in Jonson's era were John Henry (or Penry), author of several Marprelate tracts (1593); and Franklin, one of the agents implicated in the Overbury murder (1615).

Jonson's single reference to St. Thomas a Watering shows his awareness of its punitive associations. In *NI* the Host winds up a discourse on current degeneracy by stating that students of the "seven liberall deadly sciences / Of Pagery, or rather Paganisme," may "come to read a lecture / Upon *Aquinas* at *S. Thomas* a Waterings" (1.3.82–83, 86–87).

SCALDING ALLEY. A no longer extant City thoroughfare which ran north from Poultry, past St. Michael's Church.

Both S (p. 454) and H&S (10:564) rely on Stow for their brief comments. Stow remarks (1:186) that poulterers used to scald their fowls there and that they "are but lately departed from thence into other streets."

A member of the procession in *CHM* is *"an honest Cooks wife, / and comes out of Scalding-Alley"* (ll. 208–9).

---

8. Ben Jonson, *Epicoene*, ed. L. A. Beaurline (Lincoln: University of Nebraska Press, 1966), p. xvii. Another view is provided by Ralph Cohen, "London and the Techniques of Setting in Ben Jonson's Comedies," dissertation, Duke University, 1973, pp. 212–14, who contends that Morose's residence is located within the walls, close to the river, and southeast of Bow Church.

SEACOAL LANE. A narrow avenue, presently known as Old Seacoal Lane, running from Farringdon Street to Fleet Lane.[9]

In Jonson's time the Fleet Ditch (q.v.) occupied the site of Farringdon Street and had a landing place at the foot of Seacoal Lane. According to S (p. 459), this thoroughfare got its name from boats discharging loads of seaborne coal at this spot and was chiefly occupied by cookshops, chandlers' stores, and alehouses. Stow (2:38) identifies Seacoal Lane with one "Limeburners Lane," but Kingsford (2:362) cites a 1308 document which proves them separate routes.

Abel Drugger, *Alch*, boasts that his only hangover was cured by a "good old woman" who dwelt in this street (3.4.118–19). Seacoal Lane was in the midst of the sort of neighborhood where one could expect to find such medical practitioners. A 1560 tract terms this thoroughfare one of the many "stinking lanes" inhabited by "fruiterers" and "pore people" which made up the chronically disease-ridden parish of St. Sepulchre (q.v.).[10]

SHADWELL. A parish about two miles east of the City wall on the north bank of the Thames between Wapping and Limehouse.

S (p. 463) states that this locale had a bad reputation in Jacobean times and cites a passage from Webster (*Cure for a Cuckold*, 2.3.127–30) where its popularity among women of easy virtue is implied. Maintaining his practice of not mentioning the racier aspects of London life, Stow (2:71) says that there were many small tenements in this region on the road to Ratcliffe.

In *ML* Dame Polish remonstrates with Nurse Keepe for interrupting her, "Dame *Keepe* of *Katernes*? [St. Katherines, another waterside area with a bad reputation] what? have you an oare / I' the Cockboat, 'cause you are a Saylors wife? / And come from *Shadwell*?" (2.2.27–29). In another situation this mention of Shadwell could be a perfectly innocent reference to its nautical associations. However, this particular context makes it apparent that Jonson intended to emphasize the seamier connotations of this locale.

SHOREDITCH. A London parish lying just northeast of the City, between City Road on the west and Bethnal Green on the east.

S (p. 465) points out that because Shoreditch High Street was part of the old Roman road to the north, many inns were located there. Both the

9. Old Seacoal Lane once ran as far north as Snow Hill. During the nineteenth century this portion was swept away for the extension of the London, Dover, and Chatham Railway to Holborn Viaduct. Old Seacoal Lane should not be confused with a newer thoroughfare called simply "Seacoal Lane" which today follows a curving course northwest from Ludgate Hill to Fleet Lane.

10. Dr. John Jones, *Dyall of Agues* (1560); cited by Brett-James, *The Growth of Stuart London*, p. 249.

Theater and Curtain playhouses were located in Shoreditch, gaining for it much the same notoriety as Bankside (q.v.). In Middleton's *Inner Temple Masque* (*Works*: 7), Dr. Almanac says to Shrove-Tuesday, "'Tis in your charge to pull down bawdy houses, / To set your tribe a-work, cause spoil in Shoreditch" (ll. 171–72). H&S (9:293) explain the origin of the mock title, "Duke of Shoreditch," which Jonson uses for satiric purposes. H&S also (p. 384) cite a passage from Nashe (*Pierce Pennilesse; Works*, 1:217), which includes Shoreditch women among the city's "uncleane sisters." They also disavow (10:328), as did Stow, the popular etymology which linked this area with the death of Jane Shore.

Jonson's earliest professional years are associated with Shoreditch. Just to the north lay Hoxton Fields, where he dueled with Gabriel Spencer in 1598. At this time, as H&S (11:575) have mentioned, Jonson was writing for the Curtain Theater. The playwright uses the unappealing reputation of the Shoreditch neighborhood to enrich both the realism and the satire in his characterizations. The former technique is evident in *DA*, where a trip "to *Shoreditch, Whitechappell* [q.v.], and so to Saint *Katherines* [q.v.], / To drinke with the *Dutch* there, and take forth their patternes" (1.1.61–62) is highly appropriate to the personalities of the intending travelers because they are a pair of devils. In *EMI* Shoreditch is mentioned for the purpose of satire. In this play Captain Bobadil boasts how swordsmen have accosted him in "divers skirts i' the towne, as *Turne-bull* [q.v.], *White-chappell*, and *Shoreditch*" (4.7.44–45). He could not have chosen a worse trio of resorts in his attempt to convince his hearers of his military expertise and refined tastes. A second instance when a reference to Shoreditch produces a satiric effect is in *TT*. Here Constable Turfe boasts about outwitting Justice Preamble and declares, "I will ride; / Above Prince *Arthur*." A well-meaning but unsophisticated neighbor adds, "Or our *Shore-ditch* Duke" (3.6.4–5). Turfe's friend, impressed with the pomp attending the winners of local archery contests who received such titles, was earnestly trying to praise the constable. Readers familiar with Jonson's habit of using this and other mock titles to satirize sham and pretence (see Pancras) will have little difficulty in noting how an unflattering truth is couched in an apparent compliment. This fake title is also used in *DA*, but with open sarcasm. In this play Wittipol taunts Fitzdottrel as he goes off to meet the latter's wife, "Wee'll see her, Sir, at home, and leave you here, / To be made *Duke o' Shore-ditch* with a project" (4.7.64–65).

SILVER STREET. A thoroughfare which until the late 1960s ran from Wood Street in the City, just south of London Wall, west to Falcon Square. Its site is now occupied by a telephone exchange.

Both S (p. 469) and H&S (10:280) rely on Stow for much of their information. Stow remarks (1:299), "Downe lower in Woodstreete is Silver streete (I thinke of silver smithes dwelling there) in which bee divers fayre houses." H&S also cite a comment by Samuel Rowlands utilizing the literal associations of this street name. In *The Melancholie Knight* (1615, sig. B2), Rowlands says of wealthy friends, "For they and I, I know shall never meete / In Golding lane, nor yet in Silver streete."

In Jonson's *Epic* Otter comments on his wife's appearance, "All her teeth were made i' the Blacke-*Friers*: both her eye-brows i' the *Strand*, and her haire in *Silver-street*" (4.2.92–94). As H&S (10:33) have briefly noted, this remark also puns on the literal meaning of these street names. Besides stating that his wife's teeth were black with decay, Otter informs us that her eyebrows were coarse and her hair steel-gray. During the third intermeane of *SN* the Gossips call Penniboy Senior *"A notable tough Rascall! . . . right City-bred! In* Silver-*streete, the* Region *of* money, *a good seat for a Usurer*" (ll. 1–4).[11]

SIX CLERKS' OFFICE. A Chancery office, located before its abolition in 1842 on the west side of Chancery Lane, just south of Carey Street.

H&S (11:80) note that according to the diary of Sir Simonds D'Ewes (Harleian MS. 646, f. 63a), the Six Clerks' Office burned down on December 20, 1621. The site of the original structure is directly across from the Public Records Office.

In the "Execration upon Vulcan," *Und* 43, the poet comments upon his inability to act against this malefactor who "didst invade part of the Common-wealth, / In those Records, which were all Chronicle[r]s gone, / Will be remembered by *Six Clerkes*, to one" (ll. 170–72).

SMITHFIELD. In Jonson's time, a triangular open space of five to six acres just northwest of the City. It is reduced today to a grassy plot roughly encircled by the Central Markets, St. Bartholomew's Hospital (q.v.), and St. Bartholomew's Church.

Throughout London's history Smithfield has been the site of an unequalled range of human activities. Many of these are mentioned in Elizabethan literature, as S (pp. 471–72) has noted. Smithfield was perhaps best known as the site of Bartholomew Fair (q.v.). From early medieval times until 1855 a horse, sheep, and cattle market was also regularly held in this area. The tricks of Smithfield horse dealers were

11. Ralph Cohen, "London and the Techniques of Setting in Ben Jonson's Comedies," p. 304, states that because act 2, scene 5 is set as Penniboy Senior's residence in Ram Alley (q.v.) off Fleet Street, the Silver Street reference is an error on Jonson's part. However, the Gossips may well be discussing Penniboy's origins and background rather than his present lodging.

recounted by Dekker (*Lanthorne and Candle-light; Non-Dramatic Works*, 3:272). Donald Lupton, another of Jonson's contemporaries, summed up an all-too-common situation with "He that lights upon a Horse in this place, from an old Horsecourser, sound in both wind and limbe, may light of an honest Wife in the Stews [q.v.]."[12] Executions for the county of Middlesex were carried out at Smithfield before the gallows were moved to Tyburn during the reign of Henry IV. Trials by combat also took place here. H&S limit their information on Smithfield to details mentioned by Jonson. They quote (10:193) a previous editor, F. Cunningham, "Smithfield (more particularly Cow lane) was the recognized place for coachmakers." On the southern outskirts of Smithfield, remote from the bustle of activity, was Pie Corner, named after a prominent tavern sign featuring a magpie. As H&S (10:184) have stated, its chief attractions were cook shops. Like "Duke Humphrey's Tomb" in St. Paul's Cathedral, Pie Corner was a favorite loitering place for the indigent. H&S (10:55) cite Jack Dawe, *Vox Graculi* (1623, sig. C4), wherein are mentioned "such as walke snuffing up and downe in *Winter* Evenings through *Pie-corner*, yet have not one crowne to replenish their pasternes." The area near the horse market at Smithfield was known as Ruffians' Hall, where, according to Fuller (*Worthies*, 2:347), "such men met casually and otherwise, to try Masteries with sword and buckler" (cited by H&S, 9:648).

Several other types of activities that occurred in Smithfield are noted by Stow. In 1391 there was staged "a play by the Parish Clearkes of London at the Skinners well besides Smithfield: which continued three dayes togither" (1:93). Stow himself (1:74) remembers seeing scholars at Smithfield dispute "upon a banke boorded about under a tree . . . and in the end the best apposers and answerers had rewards." Finally (1:245), Smithfield was the usual site for tourneys, jousts, "or otherwise to shew activities before the king and states of the Realme." Edmund Howes, in his continuation of Stow's *Annales* (1631), describes some improvements made in 1615: "They also made strong rayles round about Smithfield, and sequestered the middle part of the said Smithfield, into a verie faire and civill Walke, and rayled it round" (pp. 1023–24).

Jonson makes notable use of Smithfield as the chief setting in *BF*. The wide range of activities and motifs abounding in the play parallels the above array of associations which Smithfield had acquired by Jonson's time. In the induction the author pokes fun at himself when he allows the Stage-keeper to criticize his efforts, "You were e'en as good goe to *Virginia*, for any thing there is of *Smith-field*" (ll. 10–11). The Stage-keeper then stresses that the play will not look back to "the sword and buckler-age of *Smithfield*" (ll. 116–17). He warns of the play's frank language which "savours of

12. Donald Lupton, *London and the Countrey Carbonadoed*, pp. 36–37.

Smithfield, the Booth, and the Pig-broath" (l. 151) and that the Hope Theater (q.v.), where this play was first presented, is "as durty as *Smithfield*, and as stinking every whit" (ll. 159–60). In the play itself the gingerbread seller Joan Trash asserts that she is as honest in her trade "as any woman in *Smithfield*" (2.2.26). Justice Overdo addresses the fair people as "you sonnes and daughters of Smithfield" (2.6.68). Rabbi Busy warns his entourage, "Look not toward them, harken not: the place is *Smithfield*, or the field of Smiths, the Grove of Hobbi-horses and trinkets" (3.2.39–41). Waspe tries to warn Cokes against wasting his money on foolish trifles by reminding him where he is (3.4.25). Later, Rabbi Busy declares, "Thou art the seate of the Beast, O *Smithfield*, and I will leave thee" (3.6.44–45). After seeing Grace, Quarlous wishes to "carry her, yet, ere she went out of *Smithfield*" (3.2.141–42). After the theft of his hat and cloak, Cokes views himself as a new type of Smithfield martyr (4.2.72–73): There is also a mock-heroic touch to Captain Whit's avowal to Ursula that he is "the patientsh man i' the world, or in all *Smithfield*" (4.4.220–21). Winwife and Quarlous allude strikingly to one of the trades mentioned earlier when they comment that Ursula, an "inspir'd vessel of Kitchin-stuffe," would "make excellent geere for the Coach-makers, here in Smithfield, to anoynt wheeles and axell-trees with" (2.5.80–82). Ursula is also taunted by Punque-Alice as "Thou Sow of *Smithfield*" (4.5.75). Earlier, Knockem the horse-dealer had jokingly called her "the good race-*Bawd* o' Smithfield" (2.5.172). Before the puppet show, Leatherhead observes that if their audience is not pleased, "all the dirt in *Smithfield* . . . will be throwne at our Banner" (5.1.3–5). Before exposing the "enormities" of the fair people, Justice Overdo declaims, "Looke upon mee, O *London!* and see mee, O *Smithfield*" (5.6.33–34). Jonson singles out a special part of Smithfield when he has Littlewit advise his wife Win to make sure that her longing to eat pig seizes upon her "i' the heart o' the *Fayre*, not at *Pye-Corner*" (1.5.155). This last-named spot is also mentioned in *Alch* when Face reminds Subtle of their first meeting, as the destitute Subtle was loitering near "*pie-corner*, / Taking your meale of steeme in, from cookes stalls" (1.1.25–26). Ruffians' Hall is cited in *EH*. The City goldsmith Touchstone, on seeing his profligate apprentice Quicksilver arrayed like a gallant, tries to uncloak him, saying, "You shall give up your cloake tho you be no Alderman. Heyday, Ruffins hall. Sword, pumps, heers a Racket indeed" (1.1.17–19). In *Volp* Sir Politik's attempt to hide beneath a large tortoise shell is termed "a rare motion, to be seene in *Fleet-street!* [q.v.] / . . . or *Smithfield*, in the faire" (5.4.77–78). Finally, in *TT* the servant Hannibal Puppy comically misinterprets a reference to "discourse" and exclaims, "What's that, a Horse? Can 'scourse nought but a Horse? / I neere read o' hun, and that in *Smith-veld*" (1.2.35–36).

SMOCK ALLEY. A no-longer-extant thoroughfare on the site of today's Artillery Passage and the eastern part of Artillery Lane.[13] This is in the vicinity of Petticoat Lane (q.v.), just east of the City.

S (p. 472) comments that houses of ill repute stood in Smock Alley, but he provides only Jonson's citation as evidence. H&S (10:222) say only that Smock Alley was "off Petticoat Lane."

Jonson displays both his associative wit and his topographical knowledge of London in a passage from *DA* where Iniquity promises Pug that on their tour of the city, "We will survay the *Suburbs*, and make forth our sallyes, / Downe *Petticoate-lane*, and up the *Smock-allies*" (1.1.59–60).

SPICERY. A household office connected with the Palace of Whitehall (q.v.).

H&S (10:564) say only that it was "a department of the royal household managed by a Clerk of the Spicery." W&C (3:531–32) locate the Spicery at Whitehall, enhancing our appreciation of the Jonsonian quotation below. According to a mid-sixteenth-century plan re-engraved by George Vertue about 1738, the Spicery was one of a group of buildings surrounding the Woodyard (q.v.) between Whitehall and the Thames. Its position today would be just east of Great Scotland Yard.

In *CHM* one of the masquers needs a clove to stick in his orange, prompting the suggestion, "Why, let one go to the Spicery" (l. 156). Jonson's masques were usually presented at the Banqueting House in Whitehall; thus this advice is appropriate to the occasion.

SPITTLE. Either any hospital or specifically the Hospital of St. Mary, founded in 1471 on what is now the south side of Spital Square, just east of the north end of Bishopsgate Street.

S (p. 483) points out that this entire district was known as the "Spittle" and had a bad reputation for harboring prostitutes and thieves. S cites Nashe, *Pierce Penilesse* (*Works*, 1:217), where the author hands over to the Devil "our uncleane sisters in *Shorditch* [q.v.], the *Spittle, Southwarke, Westminster* [q.v.], & *Turnbull streete* [q.v.]." In Davenport's *A New Trick to Cheat the Divell*, Slightall orders his servant to find him a "good lusty Lasse" by searching out "all the Allyes, Spittle, or Pickt-hatch [q.v.]" (1.2). H&S (9:350–51) gloss the place in only its general sense, terming it "a hospital, especially for foul diseases." They discuss (10:345) the "Spital Sermons" regularly preached in the churchyard of St. Mary Spitalfields, near the old hospital, and also cite (11:72) Stow's description (1:167) of these events.

In *EMI* the elder Knowell says of Wellbred's letter, "From the *Burdello*

13. F. H. W. Sheppard, ed., *Spitalfields and Mile End New Town*, Survey of London, 27 (London: Athlone Press, 1957), p. 226.

[see Stews], it might come as well; The *Spittle*: or *Pict-hatch*" (1.2.92–93). In *EH* Quicksilver's repentant song closes, "*So shall you thrive by little and little, / Scape* Tiborne [q.v.], Counters [q.v.], *& the* Spitle" (5.5.121–22). The reference in *Alch* (1.4.23) to a "spittle" is not capitalized, thus making it unclear whether Jonson had any particular institution in mind. Also somewhat vague is the reference to "a Spittle" in *NI* (1.5.35). The contexts of the first two citations above, however, suggest that Jonson was referring to the notorious Spital Square area. The same is true in *Und* 42, "An Elegie," where Jonson mocks poets who write madrigals commending "the French-hood and Scarlet gowne / The Lady Mayresse pass'd in through the Towne, / Unto the Spittle Sermon" (ll. 69–71).

STAINES. A village in Surrey on the north bank of the Thames nineteen miles west of London by road.

As S (p. 485) has observed, nearly opposite Staines on the south bank of the river is Runneymede, where the Magna Carta was signed. Staines was a favorite destination for excursions from London, as evident in Dekker and Middleton's *The Roaring Girl* when the gallant Laxton asks Moll to go with him "honestly to *Brainford* [q.v.], *Staines*, or *Ware* [q.v.]" (2.1.249–50). Staines forms the basis for some bawdy wordplay in another Middleton play, *A Fair Quarrel*. Here Chough says that he could have had a whore "at Maidenhead in Berkshire: and did I come by Maidenhead, to go out by Staines?" (5.1.182–83).

In *EMO* Shift boasts of his prowess in taking tobacco. He vows he will teach Sogliardo to become so adept at discharging his "whiffe" that he may "take his horse, drinke his three cups of *Canarie*, and expose one at *Hounslow* [q.v.], a second at *Stanes*, and a third at *Bagshot*" (3.6.147–49). This tobacco-spouting journey covers over thirty miles southwest from London; the distances involved expose Shift's propensity towards exaggeration.

STAR CHAMBER. A room in Westminster Palace used by the monarch's council when sitting as a court of justice.

S (p. 486) furnishes the traditional etymology, that this room originally had gold stars on the ceiling. He also points out that this court proceeded without any attention to the rules of common law and could inflict any penalty short of death. Both Kingsford (2:377) and K (p. 582) cite evidence which adds to our information on the origin of its name. K comments, "Its name originated with the Jewish starrs, or bonds, at a time when they were kept there by the early Plantagenets" and that the ceiling was so decorated later. Shakespeare's *Merry Wives of Windsor* opens as Justice Shallow threatens to make "a Star Chamber matter" out of a petty quarrel.

W&C (3:303) declare that the Star Chamber's most famous case dealt with William Prynne, who in Charles I's reign wrote several virulent pamphlets attacking royal absolutism and Arminianism. In 1633 he published *Histriomastrix*, an attack on the stage—during the time when Queen Henrietta Maria fancied herself an actress. As J. L. Davis writes, "He had both ears clipped on the pillory, was degraded by Oxford and Lincoln's Inn, suffered disbarrment, was fined £5000, had his books and papers sold, and was sentenced to life imprisonment."[14]

In *EMO* would-be gentlemen are advised by Carlo Buffone, "Speake nothing humbly, never discourse under a nobleman, though you ne're saw him but riding to the *Starre-chamber*, it's all one (3.4.104–7). In *NI* as the protagonist Beaufort strives to clear up the network of plots which has accumulated, he asserts, "There is a royall Court o'the *Star-chamber*, / Will scatter all these mists, disperse these vapours" (5.5.43–44). Later, the Host jokingly reminds him of this threat (l. 112). Similarly, in *ML* the devious lawyer Practise tries to dissuade Compass from bold action, saying, "Sir, you forget / There is a Court above, o' the *Starre-Chamber*, / To punish Routs and Riots" (3.4.32–34). In this same play there is a reference to "one that hath lost his eares, by a just sentence / O' the *Starre-Chamber*, a right valiant Knave" (3.6.139–40). H&S (10:354) point out that this was probably Alexander Gill the younger, who was pardoned from this punishment in 1630. Prynne, who earlier scholars thought was the subject of this allusion, did not lose his ears until the year after *ML* was on stage. In *UV* 39 Jonson asks what it will take to stop Gill's unfounded denunciations, "Shall no *Star-Chamber* Peers, / Pillory nor Whip, nor want of Ears . . . Keep in thy barking Wit?" (ll. 3–4, 8). Critics of Jonson's work are also mentioned in *Epig* 54, "On Chev'ril," where the poet writes, "CHEV'RIL cryes out, my verses libells are; / And threatens the *starre-chamber*, and the barre" (ll. 1–2). Finally, in *Epig* 92, "The New Crie," Jonson describes the discretion of subtle men-about-town by saying they may be trusted to "keepe a *starre*-chamber sentence close, twelve dayes" (l. 19).

STAR TAVERN. A drinking house probably located in Coleman Street (q.v.).

This was a common London tavern name, and S (p. 486) gives special attention to a Star near the north end of Bread Street. He also mentions the existence of one in Coleman Street. Although H&S (9:381) note Matthew's affected manner in discussing this spot in *EMI*, they say nothing about its location. Other authorities for this period of London history cite the above

14. Joe Lee Davis, *The Sons of Ben* (Detroit: Wayne State University Press, 1967), p. 38. Later, Prynne turned into "an unsparing critic of the Independents, the Army, and Cromwell and was to play a major role in effecting the restoration of Charles II, whose admirer and pensioner he ultimately became" (pp. 38–39).

locales, as well as Star inns and taverns in Fish Street Hill, Fenchurch Street, and elsewhere.[15]

In *EMI* Matthew, with a pretension of rakish flair, calls on Bobadil as a witness to the originality of his verses, "He saw me write them, at the—(poxe on it) the starre, yonder" (4.2.68–69). In the Quarto (3.4.94–95), this reference is to the Mitre (q.v.). Jonson's alterations from Quarto to Folio consistently limit the play's geographic references to an area of only a few blocks within the City. The Star Tavern which best fits these conditions is the Star in Coleman Street, where Justice Clement's house was located. The nearest Mitre Tavern was in Cheapside, a little too far south of this play's normal range of references. Also, it is logical to assume that in the Quarto, where he had no concern for topographical unity, Jonson had in mind one of the more prominent Mitre Taverns. These were located in lower Bread Street and in Fleet Street, even farther from the neighborhood later stressed in the Folio.

STEWS. Generally, a set of brothels. More specifically, in pre-Fire London, this term denoted a collection of such houses in the vicinity of Bankside (q.v.).

As late as Elizabethan times, this property, long held by the bishops of Winchester, was the site of several fish ponds, or "stews." This etymology, put forth as early as 1655 in Fuller's *Church History* (3:203), has been accepted by recent scholars.[16] H&S (11:79) refer the reader to Stow (2:54–55) for an extensive account of the relations between this district and the local authorities. Recent study of records has disclosed some interesting facts about certain establishments in the "Stews" locale. The Cardinal's Hat, listed by Stow as a "stewhouse," is now believed to have been a prominent inn. John Taylor, *The True Cause of the Watermen's Suit* (1613?), mentions having supped with "the players" at the Cardinal's Hat. In 1617 Edward Alleyn's diary notes that he dined there with the vestrymen of St. Saviour's parish. Current authorities suggest that Stow, whose personal acquaintance with this district was minimal, probably included

---

15. Kenneth Rogers, *Signs and Taverns round about Old London Bridge*, pp. 88, 129. In addition, Star Taverns in Bishopsgate Street, Bloomsbury, and Cheapside are cited in T. C. Dale, "A List of the Taverns in London and Its Suburbs in 1641, Held by Members of the Vintners' Company" (London, 1932). This is the Guildhall Library's typed copy of P.R.O. E 179/251/22.

16. C. L. Kingsford, "London Topographical Gleanings," *London Topographical Record* 13 (1923):53–54, believes that the original reference of the "Stews" in Southwark was to the fish ponds there and that "Stewes side" was the name for the row of houses backing on to the ponds of the Pike Garden. Kingsford cites as additional evidence the continued ownership of property in this area by London fishmongers between 1362 and 1533.

the Cardinal's Hat as a house of ill-repute because of its Bankside location.[17]

Jonson, discussing the Puritan reaction to the burning of the Globe Theater (q.v.) in the "Execration upon Vulcan," *Und* 43, declares, "The Brethren, they straight nois'd it out for Newes, / T'was verily some Relique of the Stewes" (ll. 139–40).

STRAND. A major London thoroughfare running from Temple Bar (q.v.) west to Charing Cross. It originated as the road between London and Westminster.

During Elizabethan times the residences on its south side were inhabited by various nobles, who came into possession of these erstwhile London seats of important ecclesiasts. S (p. 489) gives numerous dramatic citations showing that in early Stuart times the Strand was regarded as the most fashionable district in which to reside or display oneself. The ideals of this elite are well represented by Celestina in Shirley's *The Lady of Pleasure*, "I live i' the Strand, whither few ladies come / To live, and purchase, more than fame . . . I'll have / My house the academy of wits . . . my balcony shall be the courtier's idol" (1.2). In Middleton's *A Chaste Maid in Cheapside* the newly rich Mistris Allwit boasts, "Let's let out lodgings then, / And take a house in the Strand" (5.1.157–58). H&S (10:11) cite A. Wilson, *The History of Britain* (1653, p. 146), who maintains, "*Drury-lane* (the *Covent-Garden* being then an inclosed field) and . . . the *Strand* were the places where most of the *Gentry* lived."

More relevant that Stow's account of its notable buildings (2:91–95) is the information about the Strand's notable residents in Elizabethan and Jacobean times furnished by K (pp. 477–82). Sir Walter Raleigh lived in Durham House from 1584 until James's accession, and, when ordered to leave, he became indignant. Lady Raleigh, however, called it "a rotten house." Next on the east, between George Court and Durham Street, the New Exchange (q.v.) opened in 1609. Arundel House nearby was restored in 1608 to the Howard family. Thomas Howard, second earl of Arundel, was a good friend of Francis Bacon, Sir Robert Cotton, and thus probably of Jonson. In 1619/20 Bacon celebrated his sixtieth birthday at York House in the Strand, an occasion which Jonson commemorated in *Und* 51. London's most significant expansion during this period occurred in the area immediately northwest of the Strand. Howes, in his continuation of Stow's *Annales* (1631, p. 1021), remarked on the number of "new buildings, on the west end of the City, namely the two new streets neere Charing Crosse,

---

17. Roberts and Godfrey, eds., *Bankside*, pp. 62–63; also named are some of the lessees of the Cardinal's Hat, including one proprietor who issued a trade token near the middle of the seventeenth century.

Guildhall Library

Evidence of the popularity of *The Alchemist* is apparent
in this tobacconist's label featuring Abel Drugger,
the gullible tobacco-shop owner in the play.

and the Strand, aunciently called Saint Martines Lane, and Drury lane, and
the innumerable new buildings there adjacent."

Jonson's references to the Strand show that life in this part of London was
seldom dull. The Strand ran through the center of the area dominated by the
Inns of Court (q.v.), and thus it was thronged with witty gallants,
nouveau-riche social climbers, and opportunists of every sort—exactly the
persons Jonson often satirized. In *Epic* LaFoole lodges in the Strand
(1.3.35) and boasts of its prestige (1.4.8). According to Captain Otter in
the same play (4.2.92–94), his wife's eyebrows were made in the Strand,
while her teeth came from Blackfriars (q.v.) and her hair from Silver Street
(q.v.). As H&S (10:33) have pointed out, Otter's assertion plays on the
literal meanings of these placenames. "The Strand" would suggest that her
eyebrows were coarse. In *DA*, while outlining a tour of London, Iniquity

declares that in the Strand one can see lawyers clinging to clients "like Ivie to Oake; so Velvet to Leather" (1.1.75). The Strand was the only practical pedestrian route from the law courts in Westminster to the City. In one of Jonson's addresses written for King James's 1604 coronation procession through London (see also Fenchurch Street and Temple Bar), the Strand was the scene for a device signifying a rainbow, along with the sun, moon, and the Pleiades (H&S, 7:106–9). The speaker, Electra, was presented "hanging in the ayre, in figure of a Comet" (ll. 696–97); she confidently foresaw a reign free from "all tumult, faction, and harsh discord" (l. 752). The Watermen's closing song in the *EB* expresses the hope "that still theire come gossips, the best in the land, / to make the Blacke Fryars compare with the Strande" (ll. 285–86). A less sanguine view of the Strand is contained in the "Epistle to Sir Edward Sackville," *Und* 13, which warns of professional borrowers who "turne Pyrats here at Land, / Ha' their *Bermudas* [q.v.], and their streights [q.v.] i'th *Strand*" (ll. 81–82).

STRATFORD ATTE BOW. An Essex village in Jonson's day, some three and one-half miles east of St. Paul's and one mile east of Mile End (q.v.).[18]

S (pp. 489–90) supplies dramatic evidence of this area's popularity with Londoners as a destination for outings and the site of a yearly Goose Fair (q.v.). Both S and H&S (11:28) refer to Will Kempe (*Nine daies wonder*, 1600, ed. Dyce, p. 4), who said he went to Stratford because "many holde, that Mile-end is no walke without a recreation at Stratford Bow with Creame and Cakes." The Goose Fair was held each Whitsun week on Thursday. The anonymous *Penniles Parliament* orders that would-be merrymakers "should suit yourselves handsomely against goose-feast; and if you meet not a fair lass betwixt St. Paul's and Stratford that day, we will bestow a new suit of satin upon you, so you will bear all the charges."[19]

Jonson wittily displays his familiarity with Chaucer in *NI* when he has Latimer and Beaufort declare that Fly speaks "a little taynted, fly-blowne *Latin*, / After the Schoole. Of *Stratford* o' the Bow. / For *Lillies Latine*, is to him unknow" (2.4.22–24). In *Epig* 129, "To Mime," Jonson portrays his rival Inigo Jones as addicted to the petty social pleasures of the period. According to Jonson, "There's no journey set, or thought upon, / To *Braynford* [q.v.], *Hackney* [q.v.], *Bow*, but thou mak'st one" (ll. 3–4).

18. W&C, 3:326–27, point out that this village is now known simply as "Bow" and that the "Stratford" depicted on many London maps is properly Stratford Langthorn, located about a mile east of Stratford atte Bow.

19. *The Penniles Parliament of Threed-bare Poets* (1608), in *The Harleian Miscellany*, 1:186.

STREIGHTS. A triangle of alleys and courts at the east end of the Strand (q.v.) just east of the church of St. Clement Danes.

S (p. 488) points out that these byways were frequented by thieves and other disreputable folk, but he provides only a vague suggestion as to the Streights' location in London. H&S (10:195), like W&C (3:328), are mistaken in their placement of these thoroughfares. They locate the Streights at the *west* end of the Strand, in the same region as the "Bermudas" (q.v.), between the bottom of St. Martin's Lane, Chandos Street, and Bedford Street, near today's Trafalgar Square.

Several local historians concerned primarily with the region around St. Clement Danes have successfully pinpointed the exact site of the "Streights." In *Some Account of the Parish of St. Clement Danes* (London: Diprose and Bateman, 1866, 1:115–16), John Diprose writes, "Fifty years ago there was a block of houses eastward of St. Clement Danes. . . . The passage between the ancient block and the southern side of the Strand, immediately to the west of Temple Bar, was so narrow that the cant name of the place in Addison's time was 'The Pass' or the 'Streights of St. Clement.'" This location is corroborated by other authorities, who furnish full details concerning the living conditions in and ultimate fate of this area.[20] The Streights are mentioned, although not by this cant name, by Stow (2:91), who remarks, "On the north side or right hand, some small distance without Temple barre . . . stretcheth one large middle row or troupe of small tenementes, partly opening to the south, partly towardes the north, up west to a stone crosse, now headles, over against the Strand."

The disrepute of this neighborhood is illustrated in *BF*, where Justice Overdo warns, "Looke into any Angle o' the towne (the Streights, or the *Bermuda's*) where the quarelling lesson is read, and how doe they entertaine the time, but with bottle-ale, and tabacco?" (2.6.76–79). In the "Epistle to Sir Edward Sackville," *Und* 13, Jonson warns against professional borrowers who "turne Pyrats here at Land, / Ha' their *Bermudas*, and their streights i'th *Strand*" (ll. 81–82). Jonson's apparent care in mentioning each of these places individually seems to be further testimony that they were separate. The epithet "angle o' the towne," used by Justice Overdo, would be an especially appropriate way of describing the Streights because of their geographic shape.

SURGEONS' HALL. The headquarters of the Barber-Surgeons' Company, located in Monkswell Square, then near the west side of Cripplegate (q.v.).

20. E. B. Chancellor, *Annals of the Strand* (London: Chapman & Hall, 1912), pp. 69–70, also precisely locates the area. Sir Walter Besant and G. E. Mitton, *The Strand District* (London: Black, 1903), pp. 93–94, 99, mention the noxious conditions which led to the removal of this tenement block early in the nineteenth century.

Here, writes S (p. 46), corpses, especially those of criminals, were brought for dissection. Both S and H&S (11:62) cite Webster, *Duchess of Malfi*, where a character threatens to "flea off his skin, to cover one of the Anatomies, this rogue hath set i'th'cold yonder, in Barber-Chyrurgeons hall" (5.2.76–77). In Rowley's *Alls Lost by Lust* a character asks, "Were you never / At Barbar Surgeons hall to see a dissection?" (2.6.155–56).

In his "Ode to James, Earle of Desmond," *Und* 25, Jonson declares, "O vertues fall, / When her dead essence (like the Anatomie / In Surgeons hall) / Is but a Statists theame, to read Phlebotomie" (ll. 36–39).

SWAN TAVERN. A common name for a London drinking house; Swan Taverns in the Old Fish Street (q.v.) and Charing Cross areas are relevant to Jonsonian studies.

S (p. 494) provides dramatic references to Swan taverns in Newgate, Old Fish Street, and Dowgate. H&S (10:211) write inaccurately concerning the Swan Tavern mentioned by Jonson in *BF* below, "The site is marked by Old Swan Lane and the Swan Stairs just west of London Bridge." The Swan Stairs was a landing place used by persons going downriver who were reluctant to "shoot the bridge" at London Bridge (q.v.). They re-embarked below this hazard at Billingsgate (q.v.). The Swan Stairs stood just west of today's Fishmongers' Hall in Upper Thames Street near the thoroughfare of Old Swan Lane.[21] Kenneth Rogers, however, has shown that these stairs were named after a brewery called the Old Swan which once stood nearby.[22] Jonson's reference below was most probably to one of several Swan Taverns in Old Fish Street, the precise locations of which Rogers has also succeeded in determining. Its full name was the Swan on the Hoope, and it stood near Bread Street Hill, almost half a mile west of the area put forth by H&S.[23] The Swan in Old Fish Street is also mentioned in a list of the taverns held by members of the Vintners' Company in 1639.

A careful reading of the last act in *BF* shows that Jonson provides a sufficient number of topographical references for following the movements of the puppet show characters. According to Littlewit's preview, Hero, a "wench o' the *Banke-side* [q.v.]" (5.3.124), crosses northward and lands at Trig Stairs (q.v.) in her journey to Old Fish Street (l. 125). Leander, who lives at nearby Puddle Wharf (q.v.), sees Hero disembark. Later, during the puppet show itself, Leander "*gets on all his best clothes; and will after to the Swan*" (5.4.156). A short time later Cupid makes Hero fall in love with Leander while in one of its rooms called the Conney (ll. 199–206). Thus the site of the Swan Tavern proposed by H&S above is geographically

21. Leopold Wagner, *London Inns and Taverns*, p. 98.
22. Kenneth Rogers, *Signs and Taverns round about Old London Bridge*, p. 32.
23. Kenneth Rogers, "On Some Issuers of Seventeenth-Century London Tokens," p. 87. For full information concerning the Vintners' list mentioned above, see n. 15.

unsuited to its location in the play. An association between Jonson and a Swan Tavern in Charing Cross was made by Aubrey, whose notes, cited by H&S (1:180), record that Jonson was pleased by the canary wine served there. It is accepted that in his later years Jonson resided in Westminster. The location of this Swan Tavern (in the northeast part of Westminster) would have been quite convenient for the poet.

T

TEMPLE BAR. A marker denoting the limits of City jurisdiction at the west end of Fleet Street (q.v.).

S (p. 505) notes that Temple Bar first consisted of a set of posts and a chain, which by Jonson's time had developed into a timber house with a narrow gateway. H&S (10:386–87) provide information on the City entertainments of 1604 discussed below. Christopher Wren's Temple Bar marker, which replaced the Tudor structure described above, still exists, although far from its original site. Today this Palladian gateway, deemed a traffic hazard in 1878, is in Theobald's Park, Hertfordshire. Richard D. Altick described it as "partly boarded up and hedged about with barbed wire: a depressing sight."[1]

Temple Bar, Fenchurch Street (q.v.), and the Strand (q.v.) were the sites along the route of King James's official coronation progress for which Jonson wrote welcoming speeches. (Dekker and Middleton composed others, delivered at different City locations.) Jonson's Temple Bar address (H&S, 7:95–104) was presented at an arch representing a Temple of Janus containing a tableau with numerous allegorical figures, Irene (Peace) being the principal one. The greetings to James were delivered by the Flamen Martialis and the Genius Urbis, who stood in the center of the arch.

TEMPLE CHURCH. The official church for the law students of the Middle and Inner Temples (see Inns of Court). It stands south of Fleet Street (q.v.), just west of Bouverie Street.

Construction of this church was begun in 1185 by the Knights Templar in imitation of the Church of the Holy Sepulchre in Jerusalem, making it one of the four remaining specimens of the "round church" style in England.[2] By Jonson's time this church was the legal profession's equivalent of the Exchange (q.v.) or St. Paul's (q.v.) for news gathering and appointment making. Both S (p. 504) and H&S (10:85) cite a passage from Middleton (*Father Hubburd's Tales; Works,* 8:67) showing this practice, "For advice 'twixt him and us, he had made choice of a lawyer, a mercer, and a merchant, to whom he was much beholding, who that morning were appointed to meet in the Temple church." W&C (3:351) remind us that three of Jonson's close friends—James Selden, Richard Martin, and James Howell—are buried in Temple Church.

1. Richard D. Altick, *To Be in England* (New York: Norton, 1969), p. 269.
2. According to the most recent guides to these respective towns, the remaining "round" churches are at Cambridge, Northampton, and the Essex village of Little Maplestead.

In *Alch* an appointment is arranged at Temple Church between Face and Surly (2.3.288–90). Soon after, Face exults, "The *Temple*-church, there have I cast mine angle" (2.4.17). When Surly does not appear, Face remarks disconsolately, "I ha' walk'd the round [interior of the nave], / Till now, and no such thing" (3.3.2–3). Temple Church is farther from the Blackfriars headquarters of Face and Subtle than St. Paul's, but it was probably chosen as a meeting place by Face because its more sophisticated clientele might be more impressive to such a "tough customer" as Surly and also because there was less chance for one of Face's roguish colleagues to recognize him there.

THAMES. London's river, which rises in Gloucestershire, joins with the Thame near Dorchester in Oxfordshire, and reaches the Nore (a point on the North Sea estuary) forty-seven miles below London Bridge.[3]

As S (p. 507) and most London historians point out, the river was navigable for large ships up to London Bridge in Jonson's day. Even though the city's sewage polluted the Thames, it was still clear, the home of salmon and swans, and the bathtub of London. Although poets were given to idealizing the Thames, it was often held in low esteem by other commentators. The German traveler Paul Hentzner complained that clothes washed in Thames water never lost the smell of mud and slime, and the Venetian diplomat Horatio Busino denounced its "turbid and stinking waters" where "the odor remains even in clean linen."[4] These adverse qualities did not seem to affect the Thames's original inhabitants. W&C (3:365) state that William Harrison in his *Description of England* praised the quality of Thames salmon and said that sturgeon taken in the vicinity of London Bridge graced the tables of the lord mayor and the monarch.

The epilogue "To the Queen" in *EMO* draws a parallel between the pollution of Dowgate Torrent (q.v.) negated by the amplitude of the Thames and the way the audience's low passions are overwhelmed by Queen Elizabeth's perfections (ll. 8–13). Slitgut, the butcher's apprentice in *EH*, comments from his vantage point at Cuckold's Haven (q.v.) on the weather following the abortive Virginia voyage of Sir Petronel Flash and his cohorts, "Saint *Luke* blesse me, that I be not blowne into the *Thames* as I clime, with this furious Tempest. . . . Lord! what a coyle the *Thames* keepes," and "What pranckes the rude *Thames* playes" (4.1.9–11, 13, 20–21). On

---

3. The Nore is a sandbank three miles north of Sheerness; however, this term is often used (as by S and W&C) to denote a part of the North Sea as well. See the *Survey Gazeteer of the British Isles* (Edinburgh: Bartholomew, 1932), p. 512.

4. R. J. Mitchell and M. D. R. Leys, *A History of London Life* (London: Longmans, 1958), pp. 130–31, cite the *Calendar of State Papers, Venetian, 1617–1619* (for Busino) and W. B. Rye, ed., *England as Seen by Foreigners* (for Hentzner).

spying Winifred in the water, he cries out, "Alas, how busie the rude *Thames* is about her" (ll. 64–65). Sir Petronel ends up "washt in the *Thames*" (l. 174), complaining how "greedy *Thams*" consumed his money (l. 196), while "Thames, *and Tempest*" also ruined his follower Quicksilver (5.5.71). In *Epic* Truewit wonders why Morose does not choose drowning as a method of suicide, "the *Thames* being so neere" (2.2.20–21). Also in *Epic* Sir John Daw, in discussing female promiscuity, asks, "Is the *Thames* the lesse for the *dyers* water, mistris?" (4.3.34–35). During one of his drinking bouts in this play, Captain Otter shouts, "Sound *Tritons* o' the *Thames. Nunc est bibendum, nunc pede libero*" (4.2.68–69). In the puppet show climaxing *BF*, the Thames represents the Hellespont (5.3.122). Leander vows to swim across at night (5.4.302–4) and asks Hero to set a candle in her window to guide him (ll. 307–9). In *TT* To-pan the tinker brags that his ancestors came "over the *Thames*, at a low-water marke" before any bridges were built on it (1.3.57–59). In *MB* (H&S, 7:190), the Thames was played by the choreographer, Thomas Giles. The masque featured him "leaning upon his Urne (that flow'd with water,) and crown'd with flowers: with a blue cloth of *Silver* robe about him" (ll. 294–96). With the command, "Rise aged *Thames*," (l. 300) Vulturnus entrusts the nymphs in this masque into his custody. A more detailed personification of the Thames is the description of a speaker adorning one of several arches erected for King James's official coronation procession in 1604, for which Jonson, Dekker, and Middleton wrote welcoming addresses. One of Jonson's speeches was delivered at an arch representing "Londinium" erected in Fenchurch Street (q.v.), (H&S, 7:83–94). "TAMESIS" was part of the tableau: "Under-neath these, in an Aback thrust out before the rest, lay TAMESIS, The river, as running along the side of the citie; in a skin-coate made like flesh, naked, and blue. His mantle of sea-greene or water colour, thin, and bolne out like a sayle; bracelets about his wrests, of willow and sedge, a crowne of sedge and reede upon his head, mixt with water-lillies; alluding to VIRGILS description of *Tyber*" (ll. 99–107). In *EB* Jonson uses the river's permanency to heighten a comment made by one of the Gossips. It is remarked that a child similar to the one just christened (a son of Sir William Cavendish) will not be seen "while wee know the Thames, / Unles't bee a James" (ll. 298–99). In *For* 6, "To the Same [Celia]," the poet vows to give his lady kisses equal to "all the grasse that *Rumney* yeelds, / Or the sands in *Chelsey* [q.v.] fields, / Or the drops in silver *Thames*" (ll. 13–15). In *Und* 39, "An Elegie," the poet uses an allusion to the Thames to illustrate a lady's unwillingness to dispense her favors, "Sooner that Rivers would run back, or Thames / With ribs of Ice in June would bind his streames" (ll. 29–30). In *Und* 75, "An Epithalamium," for the Weston-Stuart marriage, the Thames is mentioned as part of the joyous surroundings of the nuptial pair, "Harke how the Bells upon the waters play / Their Sister-tunes, from *Thames* his either side" (ll. 33–34). Jonson effectively utilizes the Thames's associations with swans in two poems honoring contemporary writers. Throughout *UV* 6, an ode to the Welsh poet Hugh Holland who contributed an encomium to Shakespeare's First Folio, the identification of Holland with a black swan is maintained. Jonson asserts, "A gentler Bird, then this, / Did never dint the breast of *Tamisis*" (ll. 7–8). He praises Holland's previous poetic flights, asking that he not stop "Till thou at *Tames* alight, / From whose prowde bosome, thou began'st thy flight. / *Thames*, prowde of thee, and of his Fate / In entertaining late / The choise of *Europes* pride" (ll. 79–83). Near this poem's close, Jonson declares that Holland as the black swan ought to be enshrined in Leda's place "Or *Tames* be rap't from us / To dimme and drowne / In heav'n the Signe of old *Eridanus*" (ll. 107–9). Upon a more familiar occasion, *UV* 26, Jonson immortalizes Shakespeare, "Sweet Swan of *Avon!* what a sight it were / To see thee in our waters yet appeare, / And make those flights upon the bankes of *Thames*, / That so did take *Eliza*, and our *James*" (ll. 71–74). Finally, Jonson uses the fact that the Thames was often polluted by floodwaters when he lashes out against Inigo Jones in *UV* 35, "To Inigo Marquess Would be." Here Jones is ridiculed as a "canvas tyrant" whose grandiose scenic efforts in *MBl* are equated with "Dowgate Torrent [q.v.] falling into Thames" (l. 16).

THAMES STREET. A City thoroughfare running along the north bank of the river from Blackfriars east to the Tower of London.

S (p. 508) gives a number of dramatic situations revealing the crowded and often dangerous conditions prevailing in this street because of the many carts bringing merchandise from ships to warehouses. H&S (9:371) refer to Henry Machyn's *Diary* (p. 296), "The xxvj day of November [1562] at nyght was slayne a carter by a Frenche-man, because that the carter cold [not give] hym rome for presse of cartes that was ther that tyme." The variety of industries in Thames Street, as noted by Stow (1:213), added to the confusion and bustle common to the area during Jonson's time. Stow terms the north end of the London Bridge area which included part of Thames Street "Stockefishmonger Row" after earlier pointing out (p. 81) that the brewers also tended to "remaine near to the friendly water of Thames." In addition, he asserts (1:136) that on the north side of Thames street were "many fayre houses large for stowage, builded for Marchants."

Wellbred, *EMI*, tries to boost Edward Knowell's confidence by commenting that if Old Knowell can outwit them, "Would we were eene prest, to make porters of; and serve out the remnant of our daies, in *Thames*-street, or at *Custome*-house key [q.v.], in a civill warre, against the car-men" (3.2.67–70).

THEOBALD'S. A village in southeast Hertfordshire about thirteen miles north of London near the town of Cheshunt.

S (pp. 510–11) points out that Lord Burghley built a beautiful palace in this vicinity. At this estate his son, Robert Cecil, entertained King James on his arrival in England. In 1607 James "persuaded" Cecil to exchange his property at Theobald's for Hatfield House. Both places became favorite summer retreats for the Jacobean nobility. In 1878 Temple Bar (q.v.) was re-erected on the grounds at Theobald's after it was removed from the Strand to make room for traffic.[5]

In 1606 Jonson wrote an entertainment honoring the visit of King James and the king of Denmark to the Theobald's estate. This production (H&S, 7:148–50) must have been popular with King James, for a year later Jonson was again called upon to write the text for a royal entertainment there. This piece celebrated (H&S, 7:154–58) the above trade between the king and Sir Robert Cecil. Many years later, Theobald's, along with St. James's Park and Greenwich, is praised in *GM* as one of "the finer walled places . . . Where the akorns [are], plumpe as chiballs [shallots]" (ll. 95, 97).

THREADNEEDLE STREET. A City thoroughfare running from the intersection where stand the Bank of England and the Mansion House eastward to Bishopsgate.

S (p. 514) describes this street as it may have looked in Jonson's day when it held many taverns, as well as the Hospital of St. Anthony, the Royal Exchange (q.v.), and Merchant Taylors' Hall (q.v.). H&S (10:565) note that Stow (1:175) calls it "Three needle streete." W&C (3:376) furnish a colorful account by Sir John Hawkins in the eighteenth century, "In that space near the Royal Exchange and Threadneedle Street, the number of taverns was not so few as twenty; on the side of the Bank there stood four; and at one of them, the Crown, it was not unusual to draw a butt of mountain, containing a hundred and twenty gallons, in gills, in a morning."

In some of his works Jonson utilizes the convivial associations of Threadneedle Street. In *ML* Sir Moth Interest remembers that he once met the woman who supposedly buried a fortune in Lady Loadstone's well "at Merchants-Taylors-hall, at dinner, / In *Thred-needle* street" (5.7.86–87). One of the many examples of wordplay based on topographical references in *CHM* deals with "*our jolly* Wassell." This figure is portrayed by a girl named Nell, who "*workes by the Ell*" and "*dwells in Thred-needle-street too*" (ll. 228–29). This is an appropriate address for such an efficient seamstress; in England the ell, a unit of length chiefly used to measure cloth, amounted to forty-five inches, as opposed to only twenty-eight in Holland.

5. Richard D. Altick, *To Be in England*, p. 269.

THREE CRANES IN THE VINTRY. A tavern which stood in Upper Thames Street just below where Southwark Bridge is now located.

S (p. 514) provides some literary evidence of its somewhat shady reputation. Dekker (*The Belman of London; Non-Dramatic Works*, 3:310) declares, "You shal find whole congregations of them [thieves and whoremasters] at *Saint Quintens, The three-Cranes* in the *Vintry.*" H&S (10:20–21) furnish Stow's explanation of its name. Stow (1:239) points out the "three strong Cranes of Timber placed on the Vintrie wharfe by the Thames side, to crane up wines there." This landing place was long the center of the wine trade and was often used by prominent City and royal officials. Mentions of such embarcations are made in Machyn's *Diary* (p. 25) and by W&C (3:377). This tavern was visited by Pepys and some of his relatives on January 23, 1662, upon which occasion he complained about being seated in "such a narrow dogghole" of a dining room.

In *MA* the antimasquers from the brewhouses of St. Katherine's (q.v.) boast of their beer, *"Nor the Vintry Cranes, / Nor St. Clements Danes* [q.v.], / *Nor the Devill* [q.v.] *can put us down-a"* (ll. 187–89). In *Epic* Morose describes the fate of unthrifty gallants. Hounded by creditors, such unfortunates "shall go to the Cranes, or the Beare at the *Bridge*-foot [q.v.], and be drunk in feare" (2.5.114–15). Littlewit, *BF*, boasts of his own ingenuity, "A poxe o' these pretenders to wit! your *Three Cranes, Miter* [q.v.], and *Mermaid* [q.v.] men" (1.1.33–34). In *DA* Iniquity outlines a pleasure tour of London to Pug, "From thence shoot the *Bridge*, childe, to the Cranes i' the *Vintry*, / And see, there the gimblets, how they make their entry" (1.1.70–71). Because it was possible to "shoot" the piers of London Bridge only if one was traveling downriver, Iniquity's proposal at first sounds ridiculous, as the Three Cranes was located upriver from this bridge. However, when it is remembered that the speaker is a devil, we see how this trip might be arranged. See the St. Paul's entry for a similar topographically-oriented joke involving the steeple of this church.

TOTNAM (TOTTENHAM HIGH CROSS). A village approximately six miles north of St. Paul's on the Great North Road.

This town's outstanding feature, according to S (p. 518), was an ancient cross on its green. Most of the dramatic references to this village mention this landmark; in *The Merry Devil of Edmonton* Fabell declares, "Ile make my spirits dance such nightly Jigs / Along the way twixt this and Totnam crosse, The Carriers Jades shall cast their heavie packs" (1.3.134–36). Tottenham High Cross has often been confused with Tottenham Court (q.v.), the setting for several scenes in Jonson's *TT*. The latter was a manor house situated across the road from a popular drinking and dancing resort easily reached by Londoners out for an afternoon walk. Florence Snell, in the Yale edition of *TT*, several times confuses the outlying village with the suburban manor and tavern.[6] H&S mislead readers by indexing Jonson's reference to "Totnam" in *BF* together with a mention of "Totnam" from *DA*. The problem is that the *BF* reference is clearly to Tottenham Court while that in *DA* refers to Tottenham High Cross. Nowhere do these editors point out that, although the spellings of both citations are alike, they refer to two different locales.[7]

DA contains what appears to be a clear reference to Tottenham High Cross. Here Satan dispels any of Pug's illusions about his own diabolical prowess by declaring that he is capable only of such petty tricks as "the crossing of a Mercat-woman's Mare / 'Twixt this, and *Totnam*" (1.1.10–11). These details imply a social and economic context more appropriate to the village of Tottenham High Cross than to the manor house and tavern at Tottenham Court.

TOTTEN (TOTTENHAM) COURT. A manor located in the southern portion of the parish, later the borough, of St. Pancras. Beginning in the early seventeenth century this name also designated a popular place of entertainment opposite the manor house at the southern end of the Hampstead Road, two and one-half miles from St. Paul's.

S (p. 519) cites some literary references to the pleasures which Londoners found at the resort near the manor house. In 1633 Thomas Nabbes used it as the setting for most of a play titled appropriately enough, *Tottenham Court*. Later, a character from Nabbes's *The Bride* (1638) referred to a "hide-bound student that . . . wencheth at *Tottenham court* for stewed prunes and cheesecakes" (2.4). George Wither remarked in *Britain's Remembrancer* (1628, 1:sig. L^v, "And *Hogsdone* [q.v.], *Islington* [q.v.], and *Tothnam-Court*, / For Cakes and Creame, had then no small resort." The parish books of the church of St. Giles in the Fields record the following entries, often cited by historians of this locale:

1644—Rec^d of three poore men, for drinking on the Sabbath daie at Tottenham-court—4*s*.

1645—Rec^d of Mr. Bringhurst, constable, which he had of Mrs. Stacye's maid and others, for drinking at Tottenhall Court on the Sabbath daie, xij*d* a piece—3*s*.

6. *A Tale of a Tub*, ed. Florence Snell (New Haven: Yale University Press, 1915). In furnishing historical background on Tottenham Court in her introduction to this play, Miss Snell confuses Tottenham High Cross with Tottenham Court, thus rendering many of her critical conclusions invalid. For example, she cites a ballad which she calls "The Tournament of Tottenham Court" as relevant to the play. Its correct title, however, is "The Tournament of Tottenham," and it deals with the village of Tottenham High Cross. Also, her conclusion that it is a burlesque of a medieval poem because it was first printed in 1631 is incorrect. It is accepted today as a genuine product of the fifteenth century.

7. H&S, 10:180, gloss the reference to "Totnam" in *BF* with some lines from the prologue to Nabbes's *Tottenham Court*, which suggests that H&S were aware that the *BF*

The significance of the Tottenham Court area is that Jonson used the manor house as the home of a leading character in *TT*, a play that has received relatively little critical study. In 1569 the manor was leased to Queen Elizabeth in the name of Robert Dudley. The queen then appointed Alexander Glover, an Exchequer clerk, to the office of "heard under Her Majesty," with custody of the house and grounds at Tottenham Court.[8] On this property were pastured the sheep and cattle of the royal household. Around 1592, Daniel Clarke, who served as master cook to Queen Elizabeth and King James for twenty-nine years, took over the tenancy.[9] A crown survey of 1591 furnishes much information about the size and plan of the manor house.[10] Londoners were familiar with this area chiefly because of the aforementioned resort, also known as Tottenham Court, which lay on the west side of the Hampstead Road directly across from the manor house.[11] By the mid-eighteenth century the resort was known as the Adam and Eve Tavern, which led to its confusion with the Adam and Eve Tavern in Pancras Road, about a mile away.[12]

The audience of *TT* is constantly reminded that the play's protagonist, Tripoly Tub, is the master at Tottenham Court (persons, l. 2; 1.1.9–10; 1.4.23–24; 2.3.64–65; 2.4.67; 5.2.19; 5.10.10; epilogue, l. 1). Tub,

---

quote pertained to that resort area. In their notes to *DA*, 10:220, H&S do not mention this placename.

8. Lovell and Marcham, eds., *Old St. Pancras and Kentish Town*, p. 14.

9. Lovell and Marcham, *Old St. Pancras*, p. 14. Clarke died in 1626, leaving his daughter and her husband, Daniel Bateman, to manage the property. A possible Jonsonian connection with Tottenham Court is the fact that Jonson dedicated a copy of the 1616 Folio to "my worthy and deserving Brother, Mr. Alexander Glover." H&S, 11:303–4, state that Glover was an Exchequer clerk, who in 1618 was granted the office of gamekeeper in Lambeth Marsh for life. They also cite other details concerning his career, none of which are connected with the Tottenham Court region. The full dedication is reprinted in H&S, 8:666.

10. Walter H. Godfrey and William McB. Marcham, eds., *Tottenham Court Road and Vicinity*, Survey of London, 21 (London: London County Council, 1949), pp. 120–21. The surveyor, William Necton, described it as "a very slender building of timber and brick" which "hath beene of a larger building than now it is." A royal survey made in 1649 adds more details: the house stands within a moat and has a gatehouse with a chamber and two closets over the gate. The visitor crosses a courtyard to reach the main hall. A parlor, a staircase, one large chamber with an inner room, seven other rooms, and a pair of back stairs are also cited. Outbuildings, orchards, and a garden complete this catalogue. All evidence indicates that the manor house was pulled down before 1745. Sir Walter Besant, *London North of the Thames*, p. 388, adds the fact that in 1649 the manorial lands covered two hundred and forty acres.

11. Godfrey and Marcham, *Tottenham Court Road*, p. 122.

12. Warwick Wroth, *The London Pleasure Gardens of the Eighteenth Century*, p. 127; the tavern was located just west of Old St. Pancras Church. Like many others in this period, this establishment also had tea gardens.

along with his mother, "Lady *Tub* of *Totten-Court*" (1.1.14–15), inherited the estate "to revell, and keepe open house in" (l. 15). He is termed "the young worship of *Totten-Court*" (l. 29) and "worshipfull *Tripoly*, / The Squire of *Totten*" (ll. 52–53). Tub calls himself "Squire *Tub* of *Totten*" (5.2.17, 50). Late in the play Lady Tub decides to "leave the way to *Totten*" (4.5.21) during an afternoon walk. Tub states that In-and-In Medlay's masque will be staged "in *Tubs*-Hall, / At *Totten-Court*, my Ladie Mothers house" (5.2.51–52) and gives orders for Medlay and "the other wise Masters" to be welcomed there (ll. 62–64). Tub boasts that this presentation "shall make the name of *Totten-Court* immortall" (5.6.26), and bursts out later, "'Tis merry in *Tottenham* Hall, when beards wag all" (5.9.12). Lady Tub, having welcomed the guests, remarks, "Now doth *Totten-Hall* / Shew like a Court: and hence shall first be call'd so" (5.10.1–2). The location of Tottenham Court is pertinent to the content of this play in several ways. It lies in an area familiar to City dwellers but also close to more provincial and semirural areas such as Kentish Town (q.v.), Marylebone (q.v.), and Paddington (q.v.), which figure in the play. Also, the play's character types—presumptuous petty officials, unsophisticated bumpkins, and nouveau-riche landowners—all could be found in a survey of this area in the early seventeenth century. Jonson's *BF* reference to "Totnam," mentioned in the preceding entry, contains a punning allusion to Tottenham Court. In this play Quarlous is concerned over the "reform" of his fellow gallant Winwife. He asks Winwife to "come about againe. Because she is in possibility to be your daughter in law, and may aske you blessing hereafter, when she courts it to *Totnam* to eat creame" (1.3.59–61). Cakes and cream were among the favorite fare offered at resorts such as Tottenham Court.

TOWER OF LONDON. The city's ancient fortress, located at the southeast corner of the city wall half a mile below London Bridge.

S (pp. 519–21) provides several literary mentions of the Tower pertinent to Jonson's references below. Among these is Dekker's sketch in the *Guls Horne Booke* (*Non-Dramatic Works*, 2:225) of "a country gentleman, that brings his wife up to learne the fashion, see the Tombs at Westminster, the Lyons in the Tower, or to take physicke." Another quotation furnished by S illustrates the potency of the Tower cannon. In Davenport's *A New Tricke to Cheat the Divell*, Changeable says to his wife, "I never heare thy tongue in this high key, / But I still thinke of the Tower Ordnance" (2.1). H&S (9:385–86) note that until 1632 couples could be married at once in the Tower because its precincts were extraparochial. H&S (p. 700) also point out the topical accuracy of Jonson's *Volp* reference to the Tower lions below by noting that according to Stow's *Annales* (1615, pp. 844, 857), the Tower lions whelped on August 5, 1604, and again on February 26, 1604/5. In addition, H&S (2:91) point out an actual parallel to the situation referred to in *Alch* below, the case of the alchemist de Lanney who completed his "career" within the Tower confines.

Stow's comments on the Tower (1:59) are an excellent summary of all its past uses: "This Tower is a Citadell, to defend or commaund the Citie, a royall place for assemblies, and treaties. A Prison of estate, for the most daungerous offenders: the onely place of coynage for all England at this time: the armorie for warlike provision: the Treasurie of the ornaments and Jewels of the crowne, and generall conserver of the most Recordes of the kings Courts of justice at Westminster." K (p. 540) reminds us that the visit of James and the entire court to the Tower in 1604 to watch a battle between a lion, a lioness, and a cock reveals that the taste for such "sports" was not limited to patrons of the Bankside (q.v.).

In the Folio text of *EMI* the Tower replaces the "Friery" as the site of Wellbred and Bridget's wedding (4.8.65). Jonson deftly utilizes wordplay in their avowal, "We must get our fortunes committed to some larger prison, say; and, then the tower, I know no better aire: nor where the libertie of the house may doe us more present service" (ll. 67–70). As mentioned above, the Tower was one of the City "liberties" where municipal ordinances were not enforceable. The Tower lions are mentioned several times by Jonson. In *Volp* the news of a recent whelping at the Tower is regarded by Sir Politik as a major event (2.1.34–35). In *CR* Mercury succinctly expresses his familiarity with current gossip, "I have seene the Lyons" (5.4.112–13). In *MA* Notch uses his acquaintance with this aspect of the Tower to enter the court buttery, "I ha' seene the Lyons ere now, and he that hath seene them, may see the King" (ll. 8–9). In *Alch* Subtle states the consequences if his roguish crew is apprehended, "If the house / Should chance to be suspected, all would out, / And we be lock'd up, in the tower, for ever" (4.7.79–81). In *Und* 44, "A speach according to Horace," Jonson states that the city has enough ammunition stored in the Tower to wake the Spanish Ambassador Gondomar if he were asleep (ll. 3–5). The Tower artillery is again mentioned in *Und* 67, where the poet urges the public to celebrate Queen Henrietta Maria's birthday "though the thriftie Tower / And Gunnes there, spare to poure / Their noises forth in Thunder" (ll. 7–9). Jonson also offers King Charles a loud birthday greeting in *Und* 72, as he commands the guns, "Speake it, thou *Towre*, / Unto the *Ships*" (ll. 1–2). Tower Wharf, the river frontage where the Tower guns were mounted, appears in several Jonsonian references. In *EMO* Puntarvolo sets the condition, "That upon my returne, and landing on the Tower-wharfe . . . I am to receive five for one, according to the . . . summes put forth" (4.3.44–47). In *Epic* Truewit tells how he will vex Morose, "I would make a false almanack; get it printed: and then ha' him drawne out on a coronation day to the *tower*-wharfe, and kill him with the noise of the ordinance" (1.2.13–16). Later in this play Tower Wharf is mentioned by Morose himself as one of the places where he would do "superogatorie penance" if rid of his "wife" (4.4.14). Finally, the Tower is indirectly cited in *DA* when mention is made of the "Mint" (3.5.3).

TRIG STAIRS. A landing place on the north bank of the Thames at the bottom of Trig Lane, which runs from Upper Thames Street to the river.

It is from Trig Stairs that the hilarious river chase sequence in Middleton's *A Chaste Maid in Cheapside* (4.2.6ff.) begins. H&S (10:210) comment only that these stairs were located "in Queenhithe Ward next to Puddle Wharf [q.v.]." This is somewhat misleading, for Trig Lane is about a quarter-mile east of Puddle Wharf, and is separated from the latter by Wheatsheaf Wharf and Paul's Pier Wharf. W&C (3:407) informs us that by the late nineteenth century the stairs had disappeared and the placename retained by Trig Wharf.

According to Littlewit's synopsis of the puppet show in *BF*, Leander will fall in love with Hero when he sees her land at Trig Stairs (5.3.125–26), which indeed he does (5.4.143–44, 147–48).

TRIPOLY TAVERN. An establishment whose existence is still a matter for conjecture.

H&S (9:276) believe that certain lines from a poem praising the Pimlico Tavern (q.v.) in Hoxton refer to a drinking spot by the above name, "*Tripoly* from the *Turke* was taken, / But *Tripoly* is againe forsaken; / What newes from *Tripoly*? Would you know? / *Christians flye thence to Pimlico*" (sig. D3ᵛ). These editors also note that "A ballad of *Tripoli*" was entered in the Stationers' Register on June 19, 1587.

In Jonson's *TT* (persons, 1.2; 1.1.10, 29) one of the chief characters is named Squire Tripoly Tub. H&S have thus attempted to find a topical reason for this nomenclature. Because Squire Tub is a convivial, easy-going fellow, such an etymology would be appropriate.

TURNBULL (TURNMILL) STREET. A thoroughfare which today runs south from Clerkenwell Green to Cowcross Street, near Farringdon Station.

According to S (p. 533), it was "the most disreputable street in London" during the late sixteenth century. Ample literary evidence is offered attesting to this claim, including Falstaff's comment on Justice Shallow in *2 Henry IV*, "This same starved Justice hath done nothing but boast to me of the wildness of his youth and the feats he hath done about Turnbull Street"

(3.2.326–29). A vivid account of conditions in this area is furnished by a character in Beaumont and Fletcher's *The Scornful Lady*, who declares, "Here has beene such a hurry, such a din, such dismall drinking, swearing, and whoring, 'thas almost made me mad: We have al liv'd in a continuall *Turneball-streete*" (3.2.143–45). H&S (9:384) term this street "a noted haunt of prostitutes," citing Nashe's reference in *Pierce Penilesse* (*Works*, 1:217) to "our uncleane sisters in *Shorditch* [q.v.], the *Spittle* [q.v.], *Southwarke, Westminster* [q.v.], & *Turnbull streete*."

In *EMI* Bobadil tells of how those trying to test his swordsmanship have challenged him "as I have walkt alone, in divers skirts i' the towne, as *Turne-bull, White-chapell* [q.v.], *Shore-ditch*" (4.7.43–45). This would-be military hero is thus made ridiculous by associating himself with such disreputable areas. In "The Persons that Play" (l. 19) preceding *BF*, Dan Jordon Knockem is described as "*A Horse-courser, and ranger o' Turnbull.*" Knockem's occupation, reiterated later (2.3.33), suggests a homophonic pun appropriate to the associations of this locale. Also, his job is in keeping with the fact that horse dealing was a prominent feature of Bartholomew Fair (q.v.). In this play Ursula inveighs against Knockem, "You are one of those horsleaches, that gave out I was dead, in Turne-bull streete, on a surfet of botle ale, and tripes?" (2.3.13–15). According to Ursula, Punk-Alice is also from this area (4.5.61) and later in this scene, Alice is taunted with the cry, "Thou tripe of *Turnebull!*" (l. 76).

TUTTLE (TOTHILL) FIELDS. A tract of open land in Westminster, ranging from Tothill Street to as far south as today's Vauxhall Bridge Road.

S (p. 535) declares that until the end of the seventeenth century this region was a dueling site, and he gives passages from several Tudor-Stuart plays to support this. Here also troops and archers trained, and a yearly fair was held starting in 1542 for nearly three hundred years. H&S (10:281) term Tothill Fields the Westminster equivalent of the City's Smithfield (q.v.) and Moorfields (q.v.). W&C (3:387) state that Tothill Fields was also the place where punishments for witchcraft and necromancy were carried out.

These associations with the occult help explain the comment made by Gossip Mirth in *SN*. She feels that a more interesting news item than any of Jonson's offerings is "*who conjur'd in* Tutle-fields, *and how many*" (third intermeane, ll. 28–29).

TUTTLE (TOTHILL) STREET. A thoroughfare extending from the front of Westminster Abbey west to Broadway.

W&C (3:388) point out that in the seventeenth century this street was lined with mansions and gardens. Some of the notable residents of Tothill Street in early Stuart times were Lord Gray of Wilton and Sir George Carew. The actor Thomas Betterton was born in this street in 1635, and in 1665 Sir Henry Herbert had his office as master of the revels at Lincoln House in Tothill Street.

Tothill Street's reputation as an aristocratic residential area clarifies Jonson's reference to it in *SN*. In this play some of the tidbits offered by Gossip Tatle include *"all the newes of Tutle-street, and both the* Alm'ries [q.v.]" (third intermeane, ll. 20–21). Also, Jonson, in a letter to the earl of Newcastle, cited by H&S (1:214), recalls a dream in which he found his cellar all ploughed up as if by moles and thus "sent presently into Tuttle-street, for the Kings most Excellent Mole-chatcher to releive mee, & hunt them."

TYBURN. The former site of the Middlesex gallows, near today's Speaker's Corner in Hyde Park at the junction of Oxford Street and Edgware Road.

Drawing its name from its proximity to one of the many streams that ran from the hills north of London to the Thames, Tyburn was a village by approximately 1400. Its grisly associations, illustrated by S (p. 536), made it one of the earliest London places to be mentioned regularly in drama. References to Tyburn are found in *Hickscorner, Magnificence,* and *Impatient Poverty*. H&S (10:303) cite W&C (3:413) for some very precise details on the site of the "triple tree" in Connaught Place or at 49 Connaught Square. W&C (p. 415) also note that among the executions at Tyburn during Jonson's lifetime were those of Dr. Lopez (1587), Robert Southwell (1595), a "Mrs. Turner" implicated in the Overbury murder (1615), and Buckingham's assassin Felton (1628).

Typical of an author concerned with folly and its results, Jonson makes many references to Tyburn. In *TT* Turfe at a critical moment wishes he were "hang'd up at *Tiburne*" (2.2.100), while Metaphor promises to keep his master's trust, "or let me be truss'd up at *Tiburne* shortly" (2.6.52). *EH* contains several references, beginning with Touchstone's reply to Quicksilver's iteration of "Eastward Hoe": "Sir, Eastward Hoe will make you go Westward ho; I will no longer dishonest my house . . . with your licence" (2.1.120–22). As H&S (9:654) have noted, this allusion is to the journey of the condemned from the City to Tyburn. The same grisly prediction of the possible fate of this youth is made later by Touchstone again in his warning that none of Quicksilver's fair-weather friends will support him, "They'le look out at a window, as thou rid'st in triumph to *Tiborne*, and crye, yonder goes honest *Franke*, mad *Quicksilver*" (4.2.297–99). Quicksilver's song at the end of this play admonishes apprentices on the proper way to live, *"So shall you thrive by little and little, / Scape* Tiborne, Counters [q.v.], *& the* Spitle [q.v.]" (5.5.121–22). Tyburn also figures importantly in *DA*. Near the start of the play, Iniquity tells Pug of the circumstances pertaining to his day on earth, "There is a handsome Cut-purse hang'd at *Tiborne*, / Whose spirit departed, you may enter his body" (1.1.140–41). Later, Jonson's topographical artistry is evident in the aptness of Anbler's ill-fated outdoor assignation with a lady of pleasure "hard by the place toward *Tyborne"* (5.1.28). Pug suffers a more serious misfortune. Accused of being a roguish imposter, he is committed to Newgate Prison (q.v.) until his case may come up a month later at the sessions. Iniquity informs Pug of the waiting period, warning him that he must spend the interim as a filthy, ragged, louse-ridden wretch who curses his impending doom at the gallows, "damn me, renounce me, and all the fine phrases; That bring, unto *Tiborne*, the plentifull gazes"(5.6.27–28). The Great Devil then enters and reprimands Pug for the dishonor he has done to the devilish profession, especially his inability to "save a body, that he tooke / From *Tyborne*, but it must come thither againe" (ll.71–72). To avoid more embarrassment, Pug's infernal comrades carry him off. The Newgate-Tyburn episode not only reveals Pug's ineptitude but also implies that his intended victims, who freely philander, cheat, and misrepresent themselves are the play's true demons. A final mention of Tyburn is in *NI*, where the Host warns that those who follow the "seven liberall deadly sciences / Of Pagery, or rather Paganisme," may in time "take a degree at *Tiburne"* (1.3.82–83, 85).

U

UXBRIDGE. A market town in Middlesex sixteen miles from London.

The rights to hold an annual fair and a weekly market were granted to Uxbridge, an important corn-milling center, in 1294. S (p. 540) notes that these fairs were held on March 25 and September 29.

In *EMO* Shift hangs up a bill in St. Paul's advertising his skill at teaching young gentlemen the art of using tobacco. This gallant boasts that his student will be able to inhale a whiff *"here at* London, *and evaporate at* Uxbridge, *or farder, if it please him"* (3.3.58–59). Uxbridge was prominent enough in Jonson's time for most audiences to be aware of the distance involved in this avowal and to realize its speciousness. In *BF* Waspe tells where he has vainly searched for Cokes, "I ha' beene at the *Eagle*, and the blacke *Wolfe*, and the *Bull* with the five legges, and two pizzles; (hee was a Calfe at *Uxbridge Fayre*, two yeeres agone)" (5.4.83–86). Waspe's reference to Uxbridge Fair is in keeping with his background. Near the start of the play (1.1.4) the audience is informed that his master, Bartholomew Cokes, is from Harrow, a village about six miles from Uxbridge.

V

VERGE. A Westminster area within which people were safe from arrest.[1]

S (p. 546) states that the Verge extended southwest from Charing Cross, taking in Whitehall and St. James's Park, and he terms it "a favorite resort of insolvent debtors and members of the criminal classes." H&S (9:466) comment only, "The Verge extended for twelve miles round the King's place of residence, wherever he happened to be." This appears to have been an early, generalized definition of this term, contained in the *New English Dictionary* (12:126), where a meaning closer to the one suggested by Jonson's citations also appears, "in the eighteenth century commonly the precincts of Whitehall as a place of sanctuary."

In *EMO* Carlo says, "O, I cannot abide these limmes of sattin, or rather *Sathan* indeed, that'll walke . . . all day in a melancholy shop . . . readie to swallow up as manie poore unthrifts, as come within the verge" (4.4.14–18). In *CR* Maria, an inquisitive court lady, declares, "There should not a *Nymph*, or a widdow be got with childe i' the verge, but I would guesse . . . who was the right father" (4.1.149–51). In *LR* Robin Goodfellow tells of the difficulties of entering the masque area, "'Twas well there was not a sow in the verge, I had beene eaten up else" (ll. 77–78). In *ML* Chaire entreats Dame Polish to "keepe these women-matters, / Smock-secrets to our selves, in our owne verge" (4.7.40–41). Here this term is used figuratively, but a knowledge of its literal meaning adds to the pretensions of the women.

---

1. W&C, 3:432, provide a detailed description of the extent and boundaries of the Verge as set forth in Trusler's *London Adviser and Guide* (1790).

WALTHAM FOREST. A wooded area thirteen miles north of London, just across the county border in Hertfordshire.

S (p. 555) furnishes some historical background and also notes that the hilarious nocturnal escapades in *The Merry Devil of Edmonton* occur within its boundaries. H&S (10:360) gloss the Waltham Forest reference by stating merely "Epping Forest." This is misleading; Epping Forest is a relic of the once extensive forest of Waltham, located in what used to be its southeast corner.[1]

In *ML* Sir Moth Interest praises Dr. Rut's cure of Needle, who was given to talking and walking in his sleep "to Saint *John's* wood [q.v.], and *Waltham* Forrest" (5.8.13–14). Lady Loadstone's house, where this play's action occurs, is located near the center of the City. The parish church (see the Exchanges entry) stands "behind the old Exchange" (4.6.10–11, 23–27). A walk from this region to St. John's Wood, Waltham Forest, and back again would cover well over twenty-five miles, quite a ramble even for a "humours" character with a propensity for perambulation.

WAPPING. A district on the Thames's north bank east of the Tower, today situated directly south of the London docks.

As S (p. 556) has illustrated, Wapping was frequently mentioned in literature because it was the execution spot for pirates and other nautical criminals. During the early seventeenth century, the Wapping locale became distasteful for another reason. An alum factory and some brewhouses were erected there and stood until 1628 when the many complaints about these encroachments led to their removal. H&S (9:667) quote Stow (2:70–71), "Wapping in the Woze [ooze], the usuall place of execution for hanging of Pirates & sea Rovers, at the low water marke there to remaine, till three tides had overflowed them." These editors also note Kingsford's citation (2:67) from Samuel Rowland's *Knave of Hearts* (1612, epilogue, sig. F4ᵛ) on the punitive associations of this locale.

In *EH* Slitgut, from a high riverside vantage point, directs the audience's attention to Quicksilver's rescue from his calamitous voyage, "See, see, see! I hold my life, there's some other a taking up at *Wapping*, now" (4.1.112–13). Jonson thus successfully employs a bit of irony when he has Quicksilver saved at a place noted for its executions. This respite is only

1. Corporation of London, *City of London—Open Spaces* (1971), pamphlet available from the City Information Centre, St. Paul's Churchyard, E. C. 4.

temporary, however, and when the unlucky adventurer is about to be committed to prison, he reminds the audience of his prior proximity to the Wapping gallows, "Would it had beene my fortune, to have beene trust up at *Wapping*, rather than ever ha' come here" (4.2.181–82). In *MA* the brewery folk, presenters of the antimasque, sing, *"The Wives of* Wapping, / *They trudge to our tapping, / And still our Ale desire"* (ll. 202–4). This reference to Wapping is quite in keeping with the tone of this antimasque which stresses the coarseness and vulgarity of both the presenters and their ideals.

WARE. A well-known coaching and market town in Hertfordshire twenty-four miles north of London on the Great North Road.

As S (p. 557) and other historians of London have pointed out, Ware was noted for its "Great Bed" which measured ten feet nine inches square with a canopy seven and one-half feet off the ground. In Jonson's day this domestic wonder stood in Ware's Saracen's Head Inn; today it reposes in London's Victoria and Albert Museum. Jonson's mention of the Great Bed below is but one of several dramatic references to it. Dekker and Middleton's *Northward Ho* opens at the Saracen's Head and concludes with a character remarking, *"Come, weele dare, / Our wives to combate ith' great bed in Ware"* (5.1.516–17). Along with Brentford (see Brainford), Ware was probably the most notorious London-area rendezvous for assignations in Jonson's time. This is repeatedly stressed in some of Middleton's plays. In *A Chaste Maid in Cheapside* Sir Oliver commands, "Saddle the white mare: I'll take a whore along, and ride to Ware" (3.3.109–10). In Dekker and Middleton's *The Roaring Girl* the amorous gallant Laxton asks the heroine to accompany him "honestly to *Brainford, Staines* [q.v.], or *Ware*" (2.2.249–50).

For the most part, Jonson utilizes Ware's erotic notoriety for the purposes of character enrichment and satire. In *Epic* Mrs. Otter angrily recounts how London life has threatened her wardrobe, "A fourth time, as I was taking coach to goe to *Ware*, to meet a friend, it dash'd me a new sute all over . . . with a brewers horse" (3.2.72–75). A Jacobean listener would have been more interested in Mrs. Otter's unconscious self-association with this questionable resort than in the accident which was the main point of her comments. Near the close of this play, Sir John Daw and Sir Amorous La Foole, in a fit of mutual amity, remark that they have been "in the great bed at *Ware* together in our time" (5.1.64). In *BF* Captain Whit tries to seduce Win and Dame Purecraft by promising that they "will ride to *Ware* and *Rumford* [q.v.] i' dy Coash, shee de Players, be in love vit 'hem" (4.5.38–39). In *DA*, however, a reference to Ware is made only to emphasize distance. Here the jailers remark about the noxious smoke which accompanies Pug's escape from Newgate [q.v.], "They smell't as farre as *Ware*, as the wind lies" (5.8.134).

WATER WORK. One of several enterprises commenced during Jonson's lifetime for providing Londoners with water.

S (p. 558) notes only the engine invented by the entrepreneur Bevis Bulmer, which pumped from a site by Broken Wharf on the north bank of the Thames starting in 1594–95. This provided prosperous Londoners in the neighborhood of Cheapside and St. Paul's with piped-in river water. H&S (10:70–71) quote Stow (1598 ed., p. 18), who discusses Bulmer's project, as well as an earlier one, "*Thames* water conveyed into mens houses by pypes of lead from a most artificiall forcier standing neare unto *London* bridge and made by *Peter Moris Dutchman* in the year 1582 for service of the Citie, on the East part thereof." H&S (10:97) do not provide any information on Sir Hugh Myddelton's monumental New River enterprise, other than the dates of its commencement and completion, April 21, 1609, and September 29, 1613, respectively. Myddelton's project conveyed spring water thirty-eight miles in wooden pipes from near Amwell, Hertfordshire, to the north London suburb of Islington.

In *Alch* Mammon's vow that he will munificently give away his elixir to all in the metropolis is deflatingly interrupted by Surly's analogy, "As he that built the water-worke, do's with water?" (2.1.76). Surly's comment is an effective rejoinder to Mammon; Bulmer certainly was not bestowing his services free of charge to the wealthy burghers of London. Later in the same play, Face discovers that one of Drugger's sicknesses resulted from grief, "for being sess'd at eighteene pence, / For the water-worke" (3.4.123–24). This refers to the municipal charges levied on London residents to help finance the cost of Myddelton's effort, to which he contributed much of his own capital.[2]

WESTMINSTER. The administrative and royal seat adjoining the City on the west. In the sixteenth century Westminster was still separate from the City, and its near-rural boundaries stretched from Temple Bar to Kensington and from the Thames to Marylebone Park. In Jonson's work, however, "Westminster" usually refers to only the area in the vicinity of Westminster Abbey.

S (p. 560) states that the sanctuary privileges afforded by the abbey and the court (see Verge) contributed to make this district a haunt of disreputable persons. Also associated with this area was Long Meg of Westminster, a

---

2. Clunn, *The Face of London*, pp. 173–74, notes that when lack of funds halted progress at Enfield, King James agreed to pay half the remaining expense in return for half the profit, which ensured the completion of the project and the salvation of Myddelton's fortune. A reminder of this enterprise and of London living conditions in Jonson's time may be seen at the Museum of Welsh Antiquities in Bangor, where Myddelton's countrymen have preserved a section of the conduit which once served London from the New River project. A statue of Myddelton stands on Islington Green. Since 1946 the New River has ended at the Stoke Newington waterworks in Green Lanes and is now only twenty-four miles long.

"roaring-girl" whose pranks and accomplishments were celebrated by several late Elizabethan writers. In *Pierce Penilesse* (*Works*, 1:216) Nashe lamented, "*Westminster, Westminster,* much maydenhead hast thou to answere for at the day of Judgement." H&S (11:571), commenting on Jonson's relations with this area, explain why there is no notice of the poet's birth in the two Westminster parishes then extant. His Westminster connections began when his widowed mother married a bricklayer who lived in Hartshorn Lane, a thoroughfare near Charing Cross. H&S believe that Jonson left Westminster in about 1588 to learn the trade of bricklaying. They also provide a description (11:576) of Jonson's last residence, also in Westminster. According to abbey records, these lodgings were composed of four rooms on the ground, first, and second floors, topped by garrets. The building itself stood between St. Margaret's Church and Henry VII's Chapel and was owned by the dean and chapter of Westminster. H&S declares (1:98n.) that it is impossible to determine the exact date of Jonson's removal from the City to Westminster in his last years, although when interrogated in October 1628 about the Buckingham murder, he is associated with this locale.

In *Epic* Morose drives everyone away, calling them "you sonnes of noise and tumult, begot on an ill *May*-day, or when the Galley-foist is a-floate to *Westminster*" (4.2.125–26). In *SN* Gossip Tatle boasts that some of the best sources of juicy news are "*the conduicts in* Westminster" (third intermeane, l. 20). The colorful Long Meg of Westminster is comically portrayed in the antimasque of *FI* (ll. 401, 422), another sign of Jonson's familiarity with the popular associations of this district.

WESTMINSTER ABBEY. Officially the Abbey of St. Peter, founded in its present form by Edward the Confessor.[3] Except for the towers added at the west end around 1700, the abbey's external appearance has remained much the same since the building of Henry VII's chapel in 1502.

S (p. 561) furnishes some interesting details about the abbey tombs and monuments pertinent to Jonson's allusion in *BF* below. In *The Worth of a Peny* (1664, p. 20), Henry Peacham comments, "For a penny you may hear a most eloquent Oration upon our English Kings and Queens, if keeping your hands off, you will seriously listen to *David Owen,* who keeps the Monuments in *Westminster*." Donne refers to "the man that keepes the Abbey tombes, / And for his price doth with who ever comes, / Of all our

3. According to K, p. 563, one account ascribes the Abbey's original founding to Sebert, king of the West Saxons, c. 616. More reliable is a charter of 785 from Offa, King of Mercia, confirming lands and privileges here to a church of St. Peter. Nothing now remains of Edward's church above ground, but archaeological evidence below the present floor level shows that his abbey was virtually the same length as today's church.

Harries, and our Edwards talke" (*Satyre* IV, ll. 75–77). W&C (3:466ff.) inform the reader about the burial places of several notable persons associated with Jonson's career and works. Among them are the poet's royal patron, King James, who lies in the vault below Henry VII's chapel, and the legendary virago Long Meg of Westminster (q.v.), who is said to lie in the south cloister beneath a large uninscribed blue stone.

Jonson was buried in the north aisle of the nave, although there is a tablet honoring him in the "Poets' Corner" (eastern side of the south transcept). Added information about his burial is provided by H&S (1:117–18, 179–80). The unobtrusiveness of his marker kept it from being the sort of tourist sight singled out by a "*Master* of the *Monuments.*" This title, used in *BF* to refer to one of the puppet-show promoters (5.3.2), is defended as an abbey reference by H&S (10:208). Mention of another abbey area, the Sanctuaries, is made in *SN*. During the third intermeane the gossips chatter about all the places in Westminster which they consider sources of juicy news. Among these are "*the two* Sanctuaries" (ll.21–22).

WESTMINSTER HALL. The great hall of the Palace of Westminster, originally built by William Rufus and altered to its present basic form by Richard II about 1397.

The Courts of Common Law were held in Westminster Hall from the reign of Henry III until the late eighteenth century. Among the great state trials which took place there were those of Sir Thomas More, Anne Boleyn, the earl of Strafford, and Charles I. S (pp. 561–62) furnishes many examples of the hall being mentioned as either a "synonym for the Law" or as one of the noisiest spots in London. Stow (1:199) provides readers with an anecdote revealing that Westminster Hall's legal associations did not prevent roguish deeds from happening there, "I have read of a Countrey man, that then having lost his hood in Westminster hall, found the same in Cornehill [q.v.] hanged out to be solde." W&C (3:484) point out that part of the hall was taken up by booksellers, seamstresses, toy vendors, and dealers in small wares, features which surely must have added to its noisiness.

Keeping Westminster Hall's reputation for clamor in mind, Morose's comment in *Epic* is very appropriate. In order to be rid of his "wife," Morose vows he would do "superogatorie penance, in a bellfry, at *Westminster* hall, i' the cock-pit [q.v.], at the fall of a stagge" (4.4.12–14). During Nightingale's monitory song about pickpockets in *BF*, mention is made of Westminster Hall as one of the places where this crime has been perpetrated (3.5.89). According to Iniquity in *DA*, one of London's special sights is how lawyers leave Westminster Hall clinging to their clients "like Ivie to Oake; so Velvet to Leather" (1.1.75). In *SN* it is revealed that

Westminster Hall, the great hall of the Palace of Westminster and the scene of many important state trials. Jonson lived quite near during his last years (Wenceslaus Hollar, 1647).

Westminster Hall is one of the four "Cardinall Quarters" from which news is to be gathered (1.2.59–60) and also that the Westminster emissary's post is "undispos'd of yet" (l. 74). A short time later, however, a clerk reveals that Pecunia's presence has been discovered by the new *Emissary Westminster*" (1.4.7–8). This information is later conveyed to Penniboy Junior (1.5.82–83). Soon after this, the audience learns that the post of Emissary Westminster is held by a lawyer (ll. 99–101) named Picklock (l. 111). Picklock then boasts that he knows how to cant "in all the languages in *Westminster-Hall*" (4.4.103) and backs up his contention with several examples. The hall is mentioned as a symbol of permanence in *ML* where Dame Polish praises the shrewd lawyer Practise as "a neat young man," who is "like to be some body, if the Hall stand!" (2.3.45–47). Finally, in *Und* 33, "An Epigram to the Counsellour," Jonson declares that his recent acquaintance with an honest lawyer has made him disbelieve that "the great Hall at *Westminster* [is], the field / Where mutuall frauds are fought" (ll. 3–4). Jonson himself was at least once a part of the scene at Westminster Hall, for in 1599, according to H&S(11:572), he was prosecuted there for a debt owed to one Robert Browne.

WESTMINSTER SCHOOL. A noted public school located in the Dean's Yard of Westminster Abbey.

S (p. 563) points out that besides Jonson this school's eminent alumni included his literary "sons" Field, Randolph, and Mayne. The playwright Nicholas Udall was the master at Westminster from 1553 to 1556. Around 1570 a group of boy actors was organized there to play at the court and elsewhere. H&S (10:281–82) note that the acting skill of Westminster's students apparently prompted "raids" of its talent. There was a complaint recorded in the Star Chamber (q.v.) against Nathaniel Gyles, master of the Children of the Chapel Royal, that he appropriated Westminster students and apprentices for work with his own boys' company. The success of the Westminster boys' training is mentioned in Judge Bulstrode Whitelock's tribute to the eminent master Richard Mulcaster, as cited by H&S, "Yeerly he presented sum playes to the Court, in whiche his scolers were only actors, and I among them; and by that means taught them good behaviour and audacitye."

Concerning the "prophane Poet," whose work they are judging, the gossips in *SN* comment *"that he kept schole upo' the* Stage, *could conjure there, above the* Schole *of* Westminster, *and* Doctor Lamb *too"* (first intermeane, ll. 50–51). As H&S point out in a fascinating note (10:267), John Lamb was a noted astrologer who enjoyed court favor but was feared and hated by the masses. See the Windmill entry for details about his death at the hands of a City mob. Later in *SN* Gossip Tatle refers to "a limbe o' the schoole" who told of Lamb forgetting to put away his conjuring book (third intermeane, ll. 34–36). During the induction to *ML* the Boy completes a line of Latin for Damplay, saying "I understand that, sin' I learned *Terence*, i' the third forme at *Westminster*" (ll. 46–47). Jonson would have been quite familiar with the Westminster curriculum, having attended Westminster himself for a time. An incident like that of the Star Chamber case mentioned in the preceding paragraph may have prompted the complaint about current schoolmasters made by Gossip Censure in *SN*, "*They make all their schollers* Play-boyes! *Is't not a fine sight, to see all our children made* Enterluders?" (third intermeane, ll. 46–47).

WHITECHAPEL. In Jonson's time a parish in the eastern outskirts of London, today a crowded neighborhood in the East End.

According to S (p. 564), the Whitechapel Road, newly paved in 1572, was lined with butchers' and shoemakers' shops. The district had a reputation as the haunt of thieves and prostitutes, a point reinforced by H&S (10:222). As usual, Stow (2:72) does not mention Whitechapel's social conditions, complaining only of the "filthy Cottages" and "other purprestures, inclosures, and Laystalles" which extended beyond Aldgate "even up to White chappel church: and almost halfe a mile beyond it, into the common field." Whitechapel also contained an inn-yard theater, the Boar's Head, recently termed "no less than the third house at the end of Elizabeth's reign—in importance probably, in legality certainly."[4]

Whitechapel is cited in *EMI* as one of the places where swordsmen have often accosted Captain Bobadil (4.7.44). His frequenting of such an area, along with the other disreputable districts mentioned in this passage, helps deflate his continual pretensions to chivalric excellence. Whitechapel is also an appropriate highlight of the London tour proposed by the devil Iniquity to Pug in *DA* (1.1.61).

WHITEFRIARS. A district lying between Fleet Street and the Thames, just west of the City, bounded on the west by the Inner Temple and on the east by Whitefriars Street.

As S (p. 564) has pointed out, this area was formerly devoted to a Carmelite monastery founded in 1241. During the Dissolution all of its buildings were pulled down except for the refectory. By the end of Elizabeth's reign, the large private residences which had replaced the monastic edifices were divided into tenements. The privileges of sanctuary which had lingered with this locale lured fugitives, debtors, and prostitutes to Whitefriars until these rights were abolished in 1697. Dramatic refer-

4. Herbert Berry, "The Boar's Head Again," in David Galloway, ed., *The Elizabethan Theatre—3* (Hamden, Conn.: Archon Books, 1973), p. 33.

ences to this district's notoriety are common. In Middleton's *Black Book* (*Works*, 8:30), the narrator mentions "the dice running as false as the drabs in Whitefriars," and in Dekker and Webster's *Westward Ho* Birdlime says that the usual nightly companion of a student is "his Nun [whore] in white Fryers" (2.2.193–94). H&S (9:208) remind us that the Children of the Queen's Revels, who performed several of Jonson's plays, were known as the Children of Whitefriars when they performed at an indoor theater in this area. Their playhouse was the old refectory hall of the monastery, which was modified in 1606 by Thomas Woodford and Michael Drayton, using the Second Blackfriars playhouse (q.v.) as a model. The boys' companies of the King's Revels (1608–9) and the Queen's Revels (1609–13), plus the Lady Elizabeth's Men (1613–14) all acted at the Whitefriars Theater. Its brief career apparently ended after 1613, but the nearby Salisbury Court playhouse, commencing operations in 1629, kept this district associated with the theater for many years longer.[5]

According to a fellow lodger in the Counter (q.v.), Sir Petronel Flash in *EH* is no scholar, "but he will speake verie well, and discourse admirably of running Horses, and *White-Friers*, and against Baudes" (5.5.23–25). When Sir Politic tries to defend Peregrine as "of our nation" in *Volp*, Lady Would-be responds with "I, your *white-Friers* nation?" (4.2.51). In *Epig* 12, "On Lieutenant Shift," the title figure is described as "not meanest among squires / That haunt *Pict-hatch* [q.v.], *Mersh-Lambeth* [see Lambeth], and *White-fryers*" (ll. 1–2). The prologue to *Epic* promises something for all tastes, including "some for your men, and daughters of *white-Friars*" (l. 24). This play, as noted by H&S (9:208), was acted at the Whitefriars Playhouse in late 1609 or early 1610. As in other Jonsonian dramas, the location of the theater where the play was first staged was not far from the London neighborhood represented within the play itself.

WHITEHALL. A onetime royal palace in Westminster. Situated on the northwest bank of the Thames, its precincts extended from where Westminster Bridge now stands to north of Scotland Yard and west to St. James's Park.

S (p. 565) provides an account of Whitehall's history in Tudor-Stuart times, beginning when Henry VIII acquired this onetime town house of the archbishops of York in 1530. Among his improvements were a bowling alley, tennis courts, and a set of sumptuous gates. Elizabeth enhanced Whitehall with several banqueting houses, the most important of which was erected in 1581. Under James I regular use was made of a cockpit on the grounds, which in 1629–30 was remodeled by Inigo Jones (see

5. Alfred Harbage, *Annals of English Drama*, p. 305; also Bentley, *The Jacobean and Caroline Stage*, 6:115–17.

Cockpit). James pulled down Elizabeth's latest banqueting house in 1605; its successor burned in 1618. H&S (11:80) point out that a brief account of the fire and the losses incurred is furnished by Thomas Parker (Cotton MS. Tit. B viii, f. 376). Another Stuart addition was a new wine cellar, also built under Jones's direction. According to details provided by H&S (11:86–87), it featured a "vaulted undercroft five bays long and two wide, with vaulting ribs of cut-brickwork."

A vivid description of the banqueting house built in 1581 was set down by a visitor named von Wedel. He termed it "a high and spacious house with many windows, and inside full of seats and benches one above the other, so that many people may be seated there. The ceiling is hung with leaves and thick bushes. When foreign gentlemen are present the queen orders all sorts of amusements to be arranged here, while above in the bushes the birds sing beautifully."[6] In contrast, Howes in his continuation of Stow's *Annales* (1615, p. 892), called it "old, rotten, sleight." Concerning James's first banqueting house, Sir Dudley Carleton wrote that the monarch could "scarce see by reason of certaine pillars wh^{ch} are sett up before the windowes, and he is nothing pleased wth his Ld Architect for that device."[7] After this edifice burned down in 1618, Jones had plans and cost estimates for its successor ready within three months. Even though masques were staged there as early as 1621, the final painting and gilding was not completed until 1635. The total bill submitted in 1633 amounted to £14,940.[8]

Jonson's plays, masques, and poems contain numerous references to various features of Whitehall Palace. *Epic* contains a reminder of the less aesthetic tastes of Stuart aristocrats when Captain Otter reminds his wife that before their marriage she was rarely looked upon by persons of quality, "but on the Easter, or Whitson-holy-daies? and then out at the banquetting-house windore, when NED WHITING, or GEORGE STONE [famous bears], were at the stake?" (3.1.47–50). The instant popularity of *BF* is apparent in the fact, pointed out by H&S (2:131), that its premiere performance at the Hope Theater (q.v.) on Bankside was followed on the very next day with a show at Whitehall. The various banqueting houses at Whitehall, beginning with the structure erected in 1581, were the normal sites for the presentation of Jonson's masques. In a few instances there are explicit references to this setting made in the texts. In *MA* the antimasquers

6. Montague H. Cox and G. T. Forrest, eds., *The Parish of St. Margaret, Westminster, Part 2*, Survey of London, 13 (London: London County Council, 1930), p. 118. The editors quote from *Transactions of the Royal Historical Society*, 2d ser., 9 (1895):236.

7. Cox and Forrest, *Parish of St. Margaret*, p. 119; the letter, dated September 16, 1607, is from the *State Papers Domestic, 1603–10*, p. 370.

8. Cox and Forrest, *Parish of St. Margaret*, p. 121, print these costs from P. R. O. E 351 / 3391.

arrive on stage by way of the Whitehall Buttery Hatch (ll. 2, 23–24). *TV* has in its first setting a backdrop featuring "a prospective of Whitehall." This latter detail is provided by H&S (2:321), who obtain it from the office book of Sir Henry Herbert, master of the revels. The proximity of the banqueting house to the domestic service areas of Whitehall Palace adds to the appropriateness of the antimasque portion of *NT*, which features an outspoken *"Master-Cooke"* and his associates. Part 6 of *Und 2*, "A Celebration of Charis," shows Jonson using a Whitehall setting as the basis for a graceful compliment, "You were more the eye, and talke / Of the Court to-day, then all / Else that glister'd in *White-hall*" (ll. 14–16). In *Und 43*, "An Execration upon Vulcan," the poet warns of this deity's malevolent power, "Nay, let *White-Hall* with Revels have to doe, / Though but in daunces, it shall know his power" (ll. 156–57). As mentioned above, the banqueting house in Whitehall was in 1618 the scene for some of Vulcan's pyrotechnics. Finally, *Und 48*, "The Dedication of the Kings new [wine] Cellar: To Bacchus," shows Jonson writing an occasional poem honoring a portion of Whitehall Palace in which he took a special interest.

WINDMILL. A City tavern at the corner of Lothbury and Old Jewry (q.v.).

Stow (1:278) provides a detailed account of this no-longer-extant tavern's long history. In summary, Stow declares, "It is now a Taverne, and hath to signe a Windmill. And thus much for this house, sometimes the Jewes Synagogue, since a house of Fryers, then a Noble mans house . . . now a Wine Taverne." H&S (9:350) call readers' attention to a woodcut of the Windmill in *The Notorious Life and Ignominious Death of John Lambe, otherwise called Doctor Lambe* (1628). The picture shows this controversial figure attacked by a City mob in front of this tavern, where he took refuge for a time until thrust out by the vintner.

In *EMI* Wellbred's letter is signed, "From the wind-mill" (1.2.91), and this tavern is the scene of act 3, scenes 1-2 and act 4, scene 5. Brainworm also mentions this setting for the meeting of Wellbred and Young Knowell (3.2.43–44). Later Brainworm gets himself invited to a drinking session at the Windmill with Justice Clement's clerk Formall (4.6.77–79). Brainworm afterwards boasts how he had the unlucky Formall "bestow the grist o'me, at the wind-mil, to hear some martial discourse" (4.8.52–53). Near the close of the play Brainworm informs all that Wellbred and Bridget are married "and by this time are readie to bespeake their wedding supper at the wind-mill" (5.3.94–95). The couple's choice of dining places fits in extremely well with the very specific and restricted range of geographical references in most of this play. Coleman Street (q.v.), a short thorough-fare in which Justice Clement resides, runs into Lothbury at a point almost opposite to where the Windmill stood. In the Quarto text the "Meeremaid" is twice mentioned in contexts later occupied by the "Windmill" (4.1.73; 5.3.192). None of the Mermaid Taverns (q.v.) of the period fits in the locale of the Folio as well as does the Windmill.

WINDSOR. A town twenty-two miles southwest of London and across the Thames from Eton College.

S (p. 568) writes that since the time of Henry I (1100–35) Windsor has been an important residence of English rulers. Much of the present castle was built by Edward IV in the later part of the fifteenth century. Henry VIII added several buildings; Elizabeth constructed its terraces. The castle grounds are surrounded by the Little Park; beyond lies Windsor Forest, scene of the hilarious denouement of *The Merry Wives of Windsor*. One of the backdrops in Carew's masque *Coelum Britannium* is a prospect of Windsor Castle, and in Mayne's *The City-Match* (3.1), a character refers to this royal residence as a popular Caroline tourist attraction.

One of the three places where Jonson's masque *GM* was presented was at Windsor Castle, and in the Windsor production the "wenches" referred to in the versions presented at Burley and Belvoir become locally individualized as "*Prue* o' the parke," "*ffrancis* o' the Castle," "longe *Meg* of *Eaton*," and "*Christian* o' *Dorney*" (ll. 781–85).

WOODYARD. A stretch of ground between the north end of White-hall Palace (q.v.) and the Thames.

H&S (9:473) note that it was also known as the Tilt Yard or Scotland Yard. The present-day thoroughfare of Great Scotland Yard marks the Woodyard's approximate site. W&C (3:531–32) refer to it as an "outlying portion" of Whitehall Palace. They point out that in Vertue's re-engraving of a Tudor plan of London, the Woodyard is "surrounded by buildings— the Small Beer Buttery, the Great Bakehouse, the Queen's Bakehouse, the Charcoal House, the Spicery [q.v.], the Cyder House, etc."

The Woodyard is twice mentioned by Jonson, both times in works that are set in the Whitehall area. In *EMO* after Puntarvolo entrusts his dog to an unwilling groom in act 5, scene 1, he is told not much later that his pet "lies giving up the ghost in the wood-yard" (5.3.56–57). Details of the setting are furnished by Brisk, who declares that the dog is "in the court" (5.2.8) and by Shift's comment at the opening of scene 3, "I am come to the court." In *LR*, which was presented at Whitehall, Robin Goodfellow makes his entry into the masquing area "over the wall, and in by the wood-yard, so to the tarras" (ll. 73–74).

WOOLSACK TAVERN. A London drinking establishment whose site has not yet been precisely determined.

S (p. 571) mentions Woolsack Taverns outside Aldgate on the eastern edge of the City and in Ivy Lane. No evidence is furnished for the former locale. Regarding the latter, a character remarks in Dekker's *Shoemakers' Holiday*, "A messe of shoomakers meate at the wooll sack in Ivie lane" (4.4.153–54). H&S (10:112) also cite this Dekker quotation but say nothing about a Woolsack in Aldgate. W&C (3:532) state that the Woolsack in Aldgate was famous for its pies and note a reference in Machyn's *Diary* to its "goodman" being carried to the Tower on July 20, 1555. Without giving any specific evidence, W&C declare that it is this Woolsack in Aldgate which Jonson probably had in mind below. However, a study of the context of both Jonsonian references points strongly to several other possible locations, discussed below.

Subtle, in *Alch*, gives Dapper the "orders" of the Queen of Faery, "Her grace would ha' you eate no more *Wool-sack* pies, / Nor *Dagger* [q.v.] frume'ty" (5.4.41–42). In *DA* Iniquity mentions that cheating apprentices and their accomplices tend to spend their ill-gotten gains "in pies, at the *Dagger*, and the *Wool-sacke*" (1.1.66). Recent scholarship has located Dagger-Woolsack combinations in Foster Lane, in Cheapside (near Bow Lane), and in the southern part of Friday Street, which would explain why Jonson linked the two spots in his dramas.[9]

WOOLSTAPLES, LONG AND ROUND. Places in Westminster where wool was registered for export and the necessary duty paid. They stood roughly north of New Palace Yard, where Bridge Street now runs.

H&S (10:281) furnish the specific locations of both these edifices. Referring to Kingsford (2:375), they point out that the Long Woolstaple extended from the south end of Chanon Row to King Street. The Round Woolstaple stood at a right angle to it on approximately the site of today's Parliament Street.

Some good sources of news, according to Gossip Tatle in *SN*, are *"long, and round* Wool-staple" (third intermeane, l. 22). As with the rest of the places mentioned in this discussion of sources for juicy anecdotes, the Woolstaples fit into a locale that would have been quite familiar to Jonson because he was by then probably living in the Westminster (q.v.) area which was his final place of residence.

WOOLWICH. A town on the south bank of the Thames about eight miles east of London.

H&S (9:700) furnish a pertinent notice from Howes's continuation of Stow's *Annales* (1615, p. 880) for the year 1606: "The 19 of Jan. a great Porpus was taken alive at Westham, in a small creeke a mile, & a halfe within the land, and presented to *Francses Gofton*, Esquire, cheefe auditor of

9. Kenneth Rogers, *Old Cheapside and Poultry*, pp. 48–51.

ye Imprests, and within few dayes after, a very great Whale came up within 8. mile of London whose bought [shoulder] was seene divers times above water, and Judged to exceede the length of the longest ship in the river, and when she tasted the fresh water and sented the land she returned into the Sea." Another "monster" seen on the exact site of Jonson's reference below some twenty years later also was described in the *Annales* (1631, p. 1043a): "Sunday the 13 of August 1627, a great fish called a Grampas [another term for the small 'killer whale'], of ten yards long, about five foote high, and of like breadth, was taken neere *Woolwich*, eight myles from London, where beeing seene above water, was shot with musquets, and drawne into a small docke where for three dayes space, many thousands came from all parts to see it."

In *Volp* Peregrine's news from England includes the fact that on the date of his departure from London seven weeks before, "There was a whale discover'd, in the river, / As high as *Woolwich*" (2.1.46–47). H&S (2:49n.) use the former Stow citation above for dating the first performance of *Volp* in March 1606. They contend that it would be "quite in the manner of Jonson's realism" to identify the time of the action within the play with the actual date of performance.

Bibliography

The Ape-Gentle-woman: or, the Character of an Exchange-wench. London: Pye, 1675.

Barry, Lord David. *Ram-Alley*. In *A Select Collection of Old English Plays*. Edited by R. Dodsley and W. C. Hazlitt. Vol. 10. London: Reeves and Turner, 1874.

Beaumont, Francis, and John Fletcher. *Dramatic Works*. Edited by Fredson Bowers. 2 vols. to date. Cambridge: Cambridge University Press, 1966–.

————. *Wit at Several Weapons*. In *Works*, edited by A. Glover and A. R. Waller. Vol. 9. Cambridge: University Press, 1905–12. (Not yet contained in the Bowers edition.)

The Birth of Merlin. In *The Shakespeare Apocrypha*, edited by C. F. Tucker Brooke. Oxford: Clarendon Press, 1908.

Bradford, John. *Writings*. Edited by Aubrey Townsend. 2 vols. Cambridge: Parker Society, 1848.

Brathwaite, Richard. *Barnabae Itinerarium, or Barnabee's Journal*. 7th ed. London: Harding, 1818.

Brome, Richard. *Dramatic Works*. Edited by R. Shepherd. 3 vols. London: John Pearson, 1873.

Calendar of State Papers, Domestic Series. Volumes *1547–80, 1601–3, 1603–10, 1619–23*, and *1623–25*. Edited by Robert Lemon and M. A. E. Green. London: Longman, Brown, Green, Longman, and Roberts, 1856–59.

Chapman, George. *Sir Gyles Goosecap, Knight*. Edited by J. S. Farmer. Tudor Facsimile Texts, 91. London: Privately printed, 1912.

Collections III: A Calendar of Dramatic Records in the Books of the Livery Companies of London. Edited by Jean Robertson and D. J. Gordon. Oxford: Malone Society, 1954.

Cooke, J. *Greene's Tu Quoque*. In *A Select Collection of Old English Plays*, edited by R. Dodsley and W. C. Hazlitt. Vol. 11. London: Reeves and Turner, 1874.

Coryat, Thomas. *Coryat's Crudities*. 2 vols. Glasgow: MacLehose, 1905.

————. *Thomas Coriate, Traveler for the English Wits: Greeting. From the Court of the Great Mogul*. 1616. Facsimile. London, 1810?.

Dale, Thomas Cyril. "A List of the Taverns in London and Its Suburbs in 1641, Held by Members of the Vintners' Company." From P. R. O. E 179/251/22: the poll tax return. London: Guildhall Library, 1932.

D'Avenant, Sir William. *Dramatic Works*. Edited by James Maidment and W. H. Logan. 5 vols. Edinburgh: Paterson, 1872–74.

Davenport, Robert. *Works*. In *A Collection of Old English Plays, New Series*, edited by A. H. Bullen. Vol. 3. London: Hansard Publishing Union, 1890.

Dekker, Thomas. *Dramatic Works*. Edited by Fredson Bowers. 4 vols. Cambridge: Cambridge University Press, 1953–61.

————. *Non-Dramatic Works*. Edited by A. R. Grosart. 5 vols. 1884–86. Reprint. London: Russell & Russell, 1963.

Donne, John. *Satires, Epigrams, and Verse Letters*. Edited by W. Milgate. Oxford: Clarendon Press, 1967.

Dryden, John. *Dramatic Works*. Edited by Montague Summers. 6 vols. London: Nonesuch Press, 1932.

Earle, John. *Micro-cosmosmographie*. In *English Reprints*, edited by Edward Arber. Vol. 12. London: Alexander Murray, 1868.

Fennor, William. *The Compter's Commonwealth*. In *The Elizabethan Underworld*, edited by A. V. Judges. 1930. Reprint. London: Routledge & Kegan Paul, 1965.

Field, Nathan. *Plays*. Edited by William Peery. Austin: University of Texas Press, 1950.

Fulwell, Ulpian. *Like Will to Like*. In *Dramatic Writings*, edited by J. S. Farmer. Early English Dramatists, 1st Series. London: Privately printed, 1906.

Gascoigne, George. *Complete Works*. Edited by J. W. Cunliffe. 2 vols. Cambridge: Cambridge University Press, 1910.

Glapthorne, Henry. *Plays and Poems*. Edited by R. Shepherd. 2 vols. London: John Pearson, 1874.

Gosson, Stephen. *The School of Abuse*. Edited by J. P. Collier. New Shakespeare Society, 2. London: New Shakespeare Society, 1841.

Hall, Joseph. *The Discovery of a New World*. Translated by John Healey, edited by Huntingdon Brown. Cambridge: Harvard University Press, 1937.

Harman, Thomas. *A Caveat for Common Cursitors*. In *The Elizabethan Underworld*, edited by A. V. Judges. 1930. Reprint. London: Routledge & Kegan Paul, 1965.

Haughton, William. *Englishmen for My Money*. Edited by A. C. Baugh. Philadelphia: University of Pennsylvania Press, 1917.

Hickscorner. In *Six Anonymous Plays*, edited by J. S. Farmer. Early English Dramatists, 1st Series. London: Privately printed, 1905.

Jonson, Benjamin. *Works*. Edited by C. H. Herford and Percy and Evelyn Simpson. 11 vols. Oxford: Clarendon Press, 1925–52.

————. *The Alchemist*. Edited by F. H. Mares. The Revels Plays. Cambridge: Harvard University Press, 1967.

————. *Eastward Ho*. Edited by C. G. Petter. The New Mermaids. London: Benn, 1973.

————. *Epicoene*. Edited by L. A. Beaurline. Regents Renaissance Drama Series. Lincoln: University of Nebraska Press, 1966.

————. *A Tale of a Tub*. Edited by Florence Snell. New Haven: Yale University Press, 1915.

Killigrew, Thomas. *The Parson's Wedding*. In *A Select Collection of Old English Plays*, edited by R. Dodsley and W. C. Hazlitt, vol. 14. London: Reeves and Turner, 1876.

The London Prodigal. In *The Shakespeare Apocrypha*, edited by C. F. Tucker Brooke. Oxford: Clarendon Press, 1908.

Lupton, Donald. *London and the Countrey Carbonadoed and Quartred into Severall Characters*. London: N. Okes, 1632.

Machyn, Henry. *Diary of Henry Machyn Citizen and Merchant-Taylor of London from A. D. 1550 to A. D. 1563*. Edited by John Gough Nichols. Camden Society, 42. London: Camden Society, 1848.

Maroccus Extaticus. Edited by F. E. Rimbault. Percy Society, 9. London: T. Richards, 1843.

Marston, John. *The Malcontent*. Edited by M. L. Wine. Regents Renaissance Drama Series. Lincoln: University of Nebraska Press, 1964.

Massinger, Philip. *The City Madam*. Edited by Cyrus Hoy. Regents Renaissance Drama Series. Lincoln: University of Nebraska Press, 1964.

Mayne, Jasper. *The City-Match*. In *A Select Collection of Old English Plays*, edited by R. Dodsley and W. C. Hazlitt. Vol. 12. London: Reeves and Turner, 1874.

The Merry Devil of Edmonton. Edited by W. A. Abrams. Durham, N.C.: Duke University Press, 1942.

Middleton, Thomas. *Works*. Edited by A. H. Bullen. 8 vols. London: John C. Nimmo, 1885–86.

Nabbes, Thomas. *Works*. In *A Collection of Old English Plays, New Series*, edited by A. H. Bullen. Vols. 1-2. London: Wyman & Sons, 1887.

Nashe, Thomas. *Works*. Edited by R. B. McKerrow, with supplemental notes and corrections by F. P. Wilson. 5 vols. Oxford: Blackwell, 1958.

Nichols, John. *The Progresses and Public Processions of Queen Elizabeth*. 3 vols. London: John Nichols and Son, 1823.

_____. *The Progresses, Processions, and Magnificent Festivities, of King James the First*. 4 vols. London: John Nichols, 1828.

Nobody and Somebody. Edited by J. S. Farmer. Tudor Facsimile Texts, 78. London: Privately printed, 1911.

Norden, John. *Speculum Britanniae, the First Parte: An historicall, and Chorographicall Discription of Middlesex*. London: Norden, 1593.

_____. Manuscript (1592) of the above. Harleian MS. 570 (British Museum).

Parkes, W. *The Curtaine-Drawer of the World*. In *Occasional Issues of Unique or Very Rare Books*, edited by Alexander Grosart. Vol. 3. Manchester: Charles Simms, 1876.

Peacham, Henry. *The Worth of a Peny*. London: Griffin, 1664.

The Penniles Parliament of Threed-Bare Poets: Or, All Mirthe and Wittie Conceits. In *The Harleian Miscellany*, edited by William Oldys and Thomas Park. Vol. 1. London: John White, 1808.

Pepys, Samuel. *Diary*. Edited by Robert Latham and William Matthews. 6 vols. to date. London: G. Bell and Sons, 1970–.

Pimlyco, or Runne Redcap. In *Ancient Drolleries*, preface by A. H. Bullen. Oxford: Printed for private circulation, 1891.

Rowley, William. *Alls Lost by Lust* and *A Shoemaker, a Gentleman*. Edited by Charles W. Stork. University of Pennsylvania Series in Philology and Literature, 13. Philadelphia: John C. Winston for the University of Pennsylvania, 1910.

_____. *A Match at Midnight*. In *A Select Collection of Old English Plays*, edited by R. Dodsley and W. C. Hazlitt. Vol. 13. London: Reeves and Turner, 1876.

_____. *A New Wonder: A Woman Never Vexed*. In *A Select Collection of Old*

English Plays, edited by R. Dodsley and W. C. Hazlitt. Vol. 12. London: Reeves and Turner, 1874.

Rye, W. B., ed. *England as Seen by Foreigners in the Days of Queen Elizabeth and James the First*. London: J. R. Smith, 1865.

St. Hillaries Teares Shed upon All Professions from the Judge to the Petty Fogger Written by One of His Secretaries That Had Nothing Else to Doe. London: 1642.

Shakespeare, William. *Complete Works*. Edited by G. B. Harrison. 3d ed. New York: Harcourt, Brace, & World, 1968.

Shirley, James. *Dramatic Works and Poems*. Edited by Alexander Dyce. 6 vols. London: John Murray, 1833.

Skelton, John. *Complete Poems*. Edited by Philip Henderson. 3d ed. London: Dent, 1959.

Stow, John. *The Annales, or Generall Chronicle of England, Begun First by Maister John Stow, and after Him Continued and Augmented with Matters Forrayne and Domestique, Auncient and Moderne, unto the Ende of This Present Yeere 1614, by Edmund Howes, Gentleman*. London: Thomas Adams, 1615.

Stow, John. *Annales . . . Continued . . . by Edmund Howes*. London: Meighen, 1631.

_____. *A Survey of London* (1603). Edited by C. L. Kingsford. 2 vols. Oxford: Clarendon Press, 1908.

_____. *A Survey of the Cities of London and Westminster, Corrected, Improved, and Very Much Enlarged by John Strype*. 2 vols. London: Churchill, 1720.

Taylor, John. *Works*. Spenser Society, 2–4, 7, 14, 19, and 21. London: Spenser Society, 1868–77.

Thomas Lord Cromwell. In *The Shakespeare Apocrypha*, edited by C. F. Tucker Brooke. Oxford: Clarendon Press, 1908.

Wealth and Health. Edited by W. W. Greg. London: Malone Society, 1907.

Webster, John. *Complete Works*. Edited by F. L. Lucas. 4 vols. London: Chatto & Windus, 1927.

Wilson, Robert. *The Three Lords and the Three Ladies of London*. In *A Select Collection of Old English Plays*, edited by R. Dodsley and W. C. Hazlitt. Vol. 6. London: Reeves and Turner, 1874.

Wither, George. *Britain's Remembrancer*. Spenser Society, 28–29. London: Spenser Society, 1880.

Wright, James. *Historia Histrionica*. Introductory notes by P. Davison. New York: Johnson Reprint Corporation, 1972.

SECONDARY SOURCES

Akrigg, G. P. V. *Jacobean Pageant*. Cambridge: Harvard University Press, 1962.

Allen, Thomas. *The History and Antiquities of the Cities of London, Westminster, and Southwark*. 2nd ed. 4 vols. London: Virtue, 1839.

Altick, Richard D. *To Be in England*. New York: Norton, 1969.

"At the Sign of the Marygold." Edinburgh: R. & R. Clark, n.d. Reprint of article in *Three Banks Review*, September 1969.

Baines, F. E., ed. *Records of the Manor, Parish, and Borough of Hampstead*. London: Clay, 1890.

Barish, Jonas A., ed. *Ben Jonson: A Collection of Critical Essays*. Englewood Cliffs, N.J.: Prentice-Hall, 1963.

Barratt, Thomas G. *The Annals of Hampstead*. 3 vols. London: Black, 1912.

Baskerville, C. R. *English Elements in Jonson's Early Comedy*. Austin: University of Texas Press, 1911.

Bebbington, Gillian. *London Street Names*. London: Batsford, 1972.

Bentley, Gerald E. *The Jacobean and Caroline Stage*. 7 vols. Oxford: Clarendon Press, 1941–68.

Bergeron, David M. *English Civic Pageantry 1558–1642*. Columbia: University of South Carolina Press, 1971.

_____. "Harrison, Jonson, and Dekker: The Magnificent Entertainment for King James (1604)." *Journal of the Warburg and Courtauld Institutes* 31 (1968):445–48.

_____. "Jack Straw in Drama and Pageant." *Guildhall Miscellany* 2, no. 10 (1968):459–63.

Berry, Herbert. "The Boar's Head Again." In *The Elizabethan Theatre–3*, edited by David Galloway. Hamden, Conn.: Archon Books, 1973.

Besant, Sir Walter. *London North of the Thames*. London: Black, 1911.

_____, and G. E. Mitton. *The Strand District*. London: Black, 1903.

Bevington, David. *Tudor Drama and Politics*. Cambridge: Harvard University Press, 1968.

Bolitho, Hector, and Derek Peel. *Without the City Wall: An Adventure in London Street-Names, North of the River*. London: John Murray, 1952.

Brett-James, Norman G. *The Growth of Stuart London*. London: George Allen & Unwin, 1935.

Brewer, J. Norris. *London and Middlesex*. 4 vols. London: J. Harris et al., 1816.

Brock, D. Heyward, and James M. Welsh. *Ben Jonson: A Quatercentenary Bibliography, 1947–1972*. Metuchen, N.J.: Scarecrow Press, 1974.

Bryant, J. A., Jr. *The Compassionate Satirist*. Athens: University of Georgia Press, 1973.

Byrne, Muriel St. Clair. *Elizabethan Life in Town and Country*. 7th ed., rev. London: Methuen, University Paperbacks, 1961.

Champion, Larry S. *Ben Jonson's "Dotages."* Lexington: University of Kentucky Press, 1967.

Chancellor, E. B. *The Annals of the Strand*. London: Chapman & Hall, 1912.

_____. *The Pleasure Haunts of London during Four Centuries*. London: Constable, 1925.

Clinch, George. *Marylebone and St. Pancras*. London: Truslove & Shirley, 1890.

Clode, C. M. *The Early History of the Guild of Merchant Taylors*. 2 vols. London: Harrison, 1888.

Clunn, Harold P. *The Face of London*. Rev. by E. R. Wethersett. London: Spring Books, 1970.

Coghill, Nevill. "The Basis of Shakespearean Comedy." *Essays and Studies by Members of the English Association* n.s. 3 (1950): 1–28.

Cohen, Ralph. "London and the Techniques of Setting in Ben Jonson's Comedies." Dissertation, Duke University, 1973.

Corporation of London. *City Churches*. London: The Corporation, 1971.

_____. *Guildhall*. London: The Corporation, 1971.

_____. *City of London—Open Spaces*. London: The Corporation, 1971.

Coull, Thomas. *The History and Traditions of Islington*. London: Miles, 1864.

Cox, Montague H., and G. T. Forrest, eds. *The Parish of St. Margaret, Westminster, Part 2*. Survey of London, vol. 13. London: London County Council, 1930.

_____, eds. *The Parish of St. Margaret, Westminster, Part 3*. Survey of London, vol. 14. London: London County Council, 1931.

Darlington, Ida, and James Howgego. *Printed Maps of London, 1553–1850*. London: Philip, 1964.

Davis, Joe Lee. *The Sons of Ben*. Detroit: Wayne State University Press, 1967.

Denyer, C. H., ed. *St. Pancras through the Centuries*. London: LePlay House, 1935.

Diprose, John. *Some Account of the Parish of St. Clement Danes*. 2 vols. London: Diprose & Bateman, 1866.

Eccles, Mark. "Jonson's Marriage." *Review of English Studies* 12 (July 1936):257–72.

Egerton, J. E. "King James's Beasts." *History Today* 11 (1962): 405–15.

Ekwall, Eilert. *Concise Oxford Dictionary of English Place-Names*. 4th ed. Oxford: Clarendon Press, 1960.

_____. *Street-Names of the City of London*. Oxford: Clarendon Press, 1954.

Elkerton, Rev. Henry. *History of Roehampton Parish*. London: Patching, 1929.

Elliott, William. *Some Account of Kentish Town*. London: Bennett, 1821.

Esdaile, Katherine A. "Ben Jonson and the Devil Tavern." *Essays and Studies by Members of the English Association* 29 (1943):93–100.

Feldman, Abraham. "Playwrights and Pike-Trailers." *Notes and Queries* 198 (1953):184–87.

Finkelpearl, Philip. *John Marston of the Middle Temple*. Cambridge: Harvard University Press, 1969.

Foster, Frank M. "Merchants and Bureaucrats in Elizabethan London." *Guildhall Miscellany* 4, no. 3 (October 1972):149–60.

Fuller, Thomas. *Church History of Britain*. Edited by Rev. J. S. Brewer. 6 vols. Oxford: At the University Press, 1845.

_____. *The History of the Worthies of England*. Edited by P. Austin Nuttall. 3 vols. London: Tegg, 1840.

Gater, Sir George, and E. P. Wheeler, eds. *The Strand*. Survey of London, vol. 18. London: London County Council, 1937.

Gibbons, Brian. *Jacobean City Comedy*. Cambridge: Harvard University Press, 1968.

Godfrey, Walter H., and William McB. Marcham, eds. *Tottenham Court Road and Vicinity*. Survey of London, vol. 21. London: London County Council, 1949.

Greater London Council. *No. 17 Fleet Street*. London: Greater London Council, 1967.

Greaves, Isabel. "The Parish of St. Clement Danes: Churchwardens' Accounts, xxi–xxii Elizabeth." *Transactions of the London and Middlesex Archaeological Society* n.s. 2 (1911–13):367–82.

Harbage, Alfred. *Annals of English Drama*. Rev. by Samuel Schoenbaum. London: Methuen, 1964.

Harben, Henry. *A Dictionary of London*. London: Jenkins, 1918.

Hatton, Edward. *A New View of London*. 2 vols. London: R. Chiswell, 1708.

Herbert, William. *The Twelve Great Livery Companies of London*. 2 vols. London: Herbert, 1836–37.

Hosley, Richard. "A Reconstruction of the Second Blackfriars." In *The Elizabethan Theatre—1*, edited by David Galloway. Waterloo, Ontario: Macmillan of Canada, 1969.

Hunt, Stanley R. "Bucklersbury and the Merchant-Venturers." *Pharmaceutical Journal*, December 24, 1966, pp. 660–62.

Ingram, William. "'Neere the Play Howse': The Swan Theatre and Community Blight." *Renaissance Drama* n.s. 4 (1971):53–68.

Johnson, David. *Southwark and the City*. London: Oxford University Press, 1969.

Kaplan, Joel H. "Dramatic and Moral Energy in Bartholomew Fair," *Renaissance Drama* n.s. 3 (1970):137–56.

Kennedy, James. *The Manor and Parish Church of Hampstead and Its Vicars*. London: Mayle, 1906.

Kent, William. *An Encyclopaedia of London*. 3d ed., rev. by Godfrey Thompson. London: Dent, 1970.

Kingsford, C. L. "Historical Notes on Mediaeval London Houses." *London Topographical Record* 10 (1916):44–144.

_____. "London Topographical Gleanings." *London Topographical Record* 13 (1923):33–54.

Kittridge, G. L. "King James I and *The Devil Is an Ass*." *Modern Philology* 9 (1911):195–209.

Knights, L. C. *Drama and Society in the Age of Jonson*. 1937. Reprint. New York: Norton, 1968.

Knoll, R. E. *Ben Jonson's Plays: An Introduction*. Lincoln: University of Nebraska Press, 1964.

Levin, Lawrence. "Clement Justice in *Every Man in His Humour*," *Studies in English Literature* 12 (1972):291–307.

Lewis, Samuel. *A Topographical Dictionary of England*. 3 vols. London: Lewis, 1835.

Lovell, Percy W., and William McB. Marcham, eds. *Old St. Pancras and Kentish Town*. Survey of London, vol. 19, London: London County Council, 1938.

McCulloch, Rev. Joseph. *The Pictorial History of St. Mary le Bow: The Church of Bow Bells*. London: Pitkin, 1964.

McDerby, Margaret. *Official Guide to the Metropolitan Borough of Finsbury*. London: Pyramid Press, 1963.

Mackenzie, Gordon. *Marylebone: Great City North of Oxford Street*. London: Macmillan, 1972.

McMillin, Scott. "Johnson's Early Entertainments: New Information from Hatfield House." *Renaissance Drama* n.s. 1 (1968):153–66.

Maitland, William. *The History and Survey of London from Its Foundation to the Present Time*. 2d ed. 2 vols. London: Osborne, 1756.

Maxwell, Anna. *Hampstead: Its Historic Houses, Its Literary and Artistic Associations*. London: Clarke, 1912.

Merrifield, Ralph. *Roman London*. New York: Praeger, 1969.

Miles, Theodore. "Place-Realism in a Group of Caroline Plays." *RES* 18 (1942): 428–40.

Miller, Frederick. *St. Pancras Past and Present*. London: Heywood, 1874.

Mingard, Walter. *The Story of Islington and Finsbury*. London: Laurie, 1915.

Mitchell, Rosamund J., and Mary D. R. Leys. *History of London Life*. London: Longmans, 1958.

Morley, Henry. *Memoirs of Bartholomew Fair*. London: Chatto & Windus, 1880.

Norman, Philip. *London Signs and Inscriptions*. London: Elliot Stock, 1893.

Norrie, Ian, and Mavis, eds. *The Book of Hampstead*. London: High Hill Books, 1960.

Norrie, Ian, ed. *The Heathside Book of Hampstead and Highgate*. London: High Hill Books, 1962.

Ormsby, Hilda. *London on the Thames*. London: Sifton, 1924.

Palmer, Samuel. *St. Pancras: Being Antiquarian, Topographical, and Biographical Memoranda Relating to the Extensive Metropolitan Parish, St. Pancras, Middlesex*. London: Palmer, 1870.

Park, John J. *The Topography and Natural History of Hampstead*. London: White, 1814.

Partridge, E. B. "*Epicoene.*" In *Ben Jonson: Twentieth-Century Views*, edited by Jonas Barish. Englewood Cliffs, N.J.: Prentice-Hall, 1963.

Pearce, E. H. *Annals of Christ's Hospital*. London: Methuen, 1901.

Perkinson, Richard H. "Topographical Comedy in the Seventeenth Century," *ELH* 3 (1936):270–90.

Pinks, W. J. *History of Clerkenwell*. London: Pickburn, 1865.

Preston, J. *The Story of Hampstead*. London: Staples Press, 1948.

Priestley, Harold. *London: The Years of Change*. New York: Barnes and Noble, 1966.

Roberts, Sir Howard, and Walter H. Godfrey, eds. *Bankside*. Survey of London, vol. 22. London: London County Council, 1950.

Robins, W. J. *Paddington Past and Present*. London: Robins, 1853.

Rogers, Kenneth. *The Mermaid and Mitre Taverns in Old London*. London: Homeland Association, 1928.

——————. *Old Cheapside and Poultry*. London: Homeland Association, 1931.

——————. "On Some Issuers of Seventeenth-Century London Tokens, Whose Names Were Not Known to Bayne and Williamson." *Numismatic Chronicle* 5th ser. 8 (1928):61–97.

——————. *Signs and Taverns round about Old London Bridge, Including Gracechurch Street, Fenchurch Street, and Leadenhall Street*. London: Homeland Association, 1937.

Rowan, D. F. "The Cockpit in Court." In *The Elizabethan Theatre—1*, edited by David Galloway. Waterloo, Ontario: Macmillan of Canada, 1969.

Rubenstein, Stanley. *Historians of London*. London: Peter Owen, 1968.

Sheppard, F. H. W., ed. *Spitalfields and Mile End New Town*. Survey of London, vol. 27. London: Athlone Press for the London County Council, 1957.

Smith, Thomas. *A Topographical and Historical Account of the Parish of St. Marylebone*. London: Smith, 1833.

Steele, Mary Susan. *Plays and Masques at Court*. New Haven: Yale University Press, 1926.

Stone, Lawrence. *The Crisis of the Aristocracy 1558–1626*. Oxford: Clarendon Press, 1965.

————. "Inigo Jones and the New Exchange." *Archaeological Journal* 114 (1957):106–21.

Sugden, Edward. *A Topographical Dictionary to the Works of Shakespeare and His Fellow Dramatists*. Manchester: Manchester University Press, 1925.

Tannenbaum, Samuel A. *Ben Jonson: A Concise Bibliography*. New York: Tannenbaum, 1938.

————, and Dorothy R. Tannenbaum. *Supplement to a Concise Bibliography of Ben Jonson*. New York: Tannenbaum, 1947.

Trent, Christopher. *Greater London: Its Growth and Development through Two Thousand Years*. London: Phoenix House, 1965.

Wagner, Leopold. *London Inns and Taverns*. London: George Allen & Unwin, 1924.

Walcott, Mackenzie. *Westminster: Memorials of the City, St. Peter's College, The Parish Churches, Palaces, Streets, and Worthies*. London: Masters, 1849.

Wheatley, Henry B., and Peter Cunningham. *London Past and Present*. 3 vols. London: John Murray, 1891.

Wheeler, C. F. *Classical Mythology in the Plays, Masques, and Poems of Ben Jonson*. Princeton, N.J.: Princeton University Press, 1938.

Wilson, F. P. *The Plague in Shakespeare's London*. Oxford: Clarendon Press, 1927.

Wright, Louis B. *Middle-Class Culture in Elizabethan England*. 1935. Reprint. Chapel Hill: University of North Carolina Press, 1958.

Wroth, Warwick. *The London Pleasure Gardens of the Eighteenth Century*. London: Macmillan, 1896.

MAPS AND GAZETTEERS

Burrow's Pointer Guide Map of the City of London. London: Burrow, 1970.

"London: Map No. 1" (Esso Petroleum Company). Printed by Geo. Philip, 1975.

"Map of London and Environs." In *The Blue Guide to London*, edited by Stuart Rossiter. London: Ward, Lock, 1965.

"Plan of London. Scale: Three and Three-Quarter Inches to the Mile." Edinburgh: John Bartholomew & Son, 1970.

The Reference Atlas of Greater London. 13th ed. Edinburgh: John Bartholomew & Son, 1968.

Survey Gazetteer of the British Isles. Edinburgh: John Bartholomew & Son, 1932.

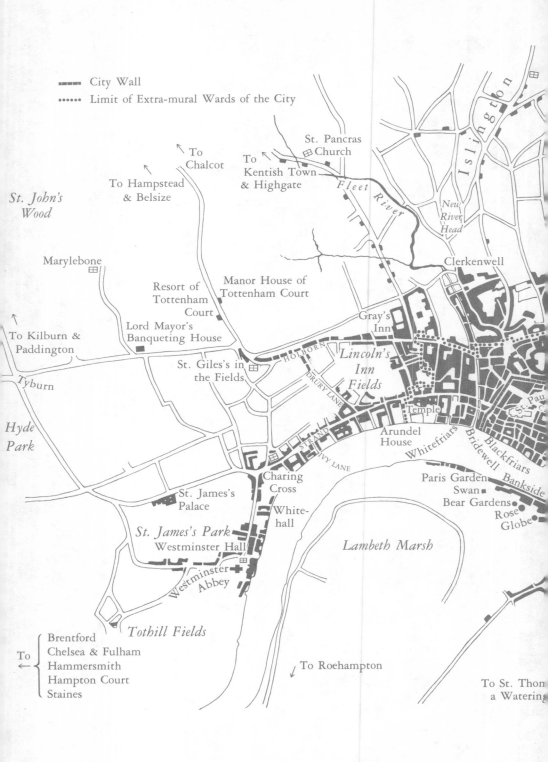

City Wall

Limit of Extra-mural Wards of the City

St. John's
Wood

Marylebone

To Kilburn &
Paddington

Tyburn

Hyde
Park

To
Chalcot

To Hampstead
& Belsize

To
Kentish Town
& Highgate

St. Pancras
Church

Fleet River

Islington

New
River
Head

Clerkenwell

Resort of
Tottenham
Court

Manor House of
Tottenham Court

Gray's
Inn

Lord Mayor's
Banqueting House

St. Giles's in
the Fields

HOLBORN

DRURY LANE

Lincoln's
Inn
Fields

St. Paul's

Temple

STRAND

Arundel
House

IVY LANE

Whitefriars

Bridewell

Blackfriars

Bankside

Charing
Cross

St. James's
Palace

White-
hall

Paris Garden
Swan
Bear Gardens
Rose
Globe

St. James's Park

Westminster Hall

Lambeth Marsh

Westminster
Abbey

Tothill Fields

To ← { Brentford
Chelsea & Fulham
Hammersmith
Hampton Court
Staines

To Roehampton

To St. Thon
a Watering